CULTU

A Survival Guide to Customs and Etiquette

SINGAPORE

Marión Bravo-Bhasin

Marshall Cavendish
Editions

Photo Credits:
alt.TYPE/Reuters: 253, 267; Ramlah Anwar: 76; Richard Lee: 36–37, 218,
232, 275; Elsie Loh: 199; Patricia Ng: 5, 27, 33, 35, 38, 71, 103, 105, 116,
130, 147, 149, 150, 151, 167, 174, 188, 194, 206 (both), 211, 234, 236,
269, 276 (both), 303, 369; Photolibrary.com: 14, 19, 21, 41, 46, 128, 143,
158–159, 164, 165, 185, 198, 209, 215, 243, 293; Tatjana Schantz-Johnsson:
vii, 3, 163, 213, 214, 224, 241, 245, 248, 249. ▪ Cover photo: R Ian Lloyd.

All illustrations by TRIGG

Copyright © 2006 Marshall Cavendish International (Asia) Private Limited

Published by Marshall Cavendish Editions
An imprint of Marshall Cavendish International
1 New Industrial Road, Singapore 536196

All rights reserved

No part of this publication may be reproduced, stored in a retrieval system
or transmitted, in any form or by any means, electronic, mechanical,
photocopying, recording or otherwise, without the prior permission of
the copyright owner. Request for permission should be addressed to the
Publisher, Marshall Cavendish International (Asia) Private Limited, 1 New
Industrial Road, Singapore 536196. Tel: (65) 6213 9300, fax: (65) 6285 4871.
E-mail: te@sg.marshallcavendish.com

The publisher makes no representation or warranties with respect to the
contents of this book, and specifically disclaims any implied warranties or
merchantability or fitness for any particular purpose, and shall in no events
be liable for any loss of profit or any other commercial damage, including but
not limited to special, incidental, consequential, or other damages.

Other Marshall Cavendish Offices:
Marshall Cavendish Ltd. 119 Wardour Street, London W1F 0UW, UK ▪ Marshall
Cavendish Corporation. 99 White Plains Road, Tarrytown NY 10591-9001, USA ▪
Marshall Cavendish International (Thailand) Co Ltd. 253 Asoke, 12th Flr, Sukhumvit
21 Road, Klongtoey Nua, Wattana, Bangkok 10110, Thailand ▪ Marshall Cavendish
(Malaysia) Sdn Bhd, Times Subang, Lot 46, Subang Hi-Tech Industrial Park,
Batu Tiga, 40000 Shah Alam, Selangor Darul Ehsan, Malaysia

Marshall Cavendish is a trademark of Times Publishing Limited

National Library Board Singapore Cataloguing in Publication Data
Bravo-Bhasin, Marión, 1964-
CultureShock! : Singapore / Marión Bravo-Bhasin. – Singapore : Marshall
Cavendish Editions, c2006.
p. cm. – (CultureShock!)
Includes bibliographical references and index.
ISBN : 981-261-131-2
1. Etiquette – Singapore. 2. Singapore – Social life and customs. I. Title.
II. Series: CultureShock!
DS609.9
959.57 -- dc22   SLS2006024900

Printed in Singapore by Times Graphics Pte Ltd

ABOUT THE SERIES

Culture shock is a state of disorientation that can come over anyone who has been thrust into unknown surroundings, away from one's comfort zone. *CultureShock!* is a series of trusted and reputed guides which has, for decades, been helping expatriates and long-term visitors to cushion the impact of culture shock whenever they move to a new country.

Written by people who have lived in the country and experienced culture shock themselves, the authors share all the information necessary for anyone to cope with these feelings of disorientation more effectively. The guides are written in a style that is easy to read and covers a range of topics that will arm readers with enough advice, hints and tips to make their lives as normal as possible again.

Each book is structured in the same manner. It begins with the first impressions that visitors will have of that city or country. To understand a culture, one must first understand the people—where they came from, who they are, the values and traditions they live by, as well as their customs and etiquette. This is covered in the first half of the book.

Then on with the practical aspects—how to settle in with the greatest of ease. Authors walk readers through topics such as how to find accommodation, get the utilities and telecommunications up and running, enrol the children in school and keep in the pink of health. But that's not all. Once the essentials are out of the way, venture out and try the food, enjoy more of the culture and travel to other areas. Then be immersed in the language of the country before discovering more about the business side of things.

To round off, snippets of basic information are offered before readers are 'tested' on customs and etiquette of the country. Useful words and phrases, a comprehensive resource guide and list of books for further research are also included for easy reference.

CONTENTS

Introduction vi

Acknoweldgements x

Dedication xi

Map of Singapore xii

Chapter 1
First Impressions   1

Likely First Impressions   8

Chapter 2
The Land and Its History   12

Geography   13

Climate   15

History   16

Singapore Today   26

Government System   27

Chapter 3
The People of Singapore   29

Background and History   31

The Singapore Identity   51

Chapter 4
Socialising and Fitting In   56

Singapore Society and Culture   58

Singapore Etiquette   62

National Service   65

Socialising   65

Chapter 5
Settling In   84

Formalities   85

Moving In and Out   96

Accommodation   100

Utilities   111

Telecommunications and Media   113

Furnishings and Appliances   119

What to Bring From Home   120

Domestic Help   122

Children   125

Financial Matters   131

Health   136

Transportation   142

Shopping   155

Safety and Security   166

Chapter 6
Food Glorious Food   170

A Taste of Local Food   172

Eating, Singapore Style   180

Eating Places   182

Taxes, Tipping and Other Charges   192

All Manner of Signs   193

Drinks   195

Shopping for Food   196

Entertaining   201

Chapter 7
Enjoying Singapore   204

Clubs and Groups   205

Places to Visit, Things to Do   207

Sporting Activities   218

After Dark Entertainment   223

Traveller's Tales   225

The Cultural Side   227

A Year of Celebrations   236

Annual Events   270

Chapter 10
The Different Tongues 273

Malay	277
Chinese	279
Tamil	283
Singlish	285
Communication Overall	289
Non-verbal Communication	289

Chapter 9
Work and Business 291

Are You Allowed to Work?	292
Setting Up a Business	295
Working Life	300
Working with the Locals	303

Doing Business	306
Women in the Workforce	312

Chapter 10
Singapore at a Glance 313

Famous People	316
Acronyms	332
Culture Quiz	337
Do's and Don'ts	346
Glossary	349
Resource Guide	358
Further Reading	376
About the Author	384
Index	385

INTRODUCTION

From my first impression of Singapore back in 1991—when I spent only a few hours in transit but managed to leave the airport, have a meal in the East Coast, spend the night in an HDB (Housing Development Board) complex, and delight in Changi Airport's efficiency—I knew it was a pleasant place to live. Today, after moving to Singapore in August 1999, I realise my first impression was not misleading. I had experienced some of the best things the country has to offer: lush greenery, modern roads and architecture, excellent food and the world-class airport—all only at surface level of course, but enough to leave a positive impression. That is what is so appealing about this country, the good is out there to see, to experience and to appreciate everyday. You do not have to spend too much time in Singapore to realise how smoothly everything functions and that there is an underlying efficiency behind it all. It's 'comfort zone living' par excellence!

Maybe Singapore is going to be your home or perhaps you are simply curious to learn more about this culturally diverse island. Whatever your circumstances, this book aims to help take away the sting and shock of moving to and settling in Singapore. By reading this book, speaking to people who have or are living in Singapore and, most importantly, by willingly going along for the ride with open eyes and mind, you will be well prepared to enjoy and make the best of your stay.

Quite frankly, if I may generalise, I must say the 'culture shock' of arriving and living in Singapore is not really that shocking to many people. If you are from the East, there are enough elements of the East here to make you feel comfortable. The same if you are from the West. It's this unique mix and identity that makes Singapore what it is. But culture shock comes in many waves and disguises. Living away from family and friends plus trying to set up a life in a different land is not without its difficulties. This should not be undermined. In fact, I find that the distance from your loved ones is the hardest part of adapting to a new country. It leaves one torn between the two with no easy solution but to make the best of where one has chosen to be and to surround oneself with new friends who, in the best case scenario,

An overview of the Suntec and Marina area, looking out to sea.

essentially become one's family. It's the best survival tip I can offer.

To better deal and be prepared with a move overseas, let's look a little deeper into what culture shock is. If culture is defined as the 'total of inherited ideas, beliefs, values and knowledge which constitute the shared bases of social action' by Collins English Dictionary then 'culture shock' is best defined as the physical and emotional 'discomfort' of having to adapt to and learn a completely new set of ideas, beliefs, values and knowledge. In essence, one's culture determines the way one acts, the manner in which we relate to others and the way we think and interpret events happening around us. So experiencing a new culture and a little culture shock gives one the rare opportunity to see everything in life in a new and different light, from the language, to using a telephone, to paying for groceries etc.

The fascinating aspect of culture shock is that it is inescapable when first arriving in a foreign country, no matter how long you have lived overseas. It may not be such a shock and it may not be prolonged, but adapting to new customs, beliefs and rules takes some time. The symptoms of culture shock (homesickness, withdrawal, anger, irritability, family and marital stress, physical ailments etc.) can appear at different times and at different levels for it's a process with five stages. Each stage can be ongoing or even appear only at certain times. Of course, some people do not really suffer from culture shock but rather, breeze through the stages while others may seem to find great difficulty in getting over the language barrier, for instance. We all come equipped with different personalities, experiences and backgrounds that will help determine how well we cope; but coping and accepting, in the end, the new culture can be a life shaping experience.

CULTURE SHOCK

Here, in a nutshell, are the five stages of culture shock and some of the feelings you are likely to encounter.

- Stage One: The Honeymoon
  Everything is new and exciting. The best thing to do is learn to observe with curiosity and interest; learn to focus on the similarities and how we are really very much alike.
- Stage Two: Initial Confrontation
  Difficult times and crises in daily life begin to occur as the focus shifts from the similarities to the differences, which are suddenly everywhere! Communication may be a problem and feelings of dissatisfaction start to creep in. You may even feel discontent, impatient, angry, sad and generally a little incompetent as you try your best to cope.
- Stage Three: Gradual Adjustment
  You begin to gain some insight and understanding of the new culture, and a feeling of pleasure and sense of humour may be experienced. The environment is more familiar and

a feeling of wanting-to-belong begins to take over. You start to evaluate and compare the old ways and the new ways, and may encounter some confusion over your own identity as a result.

- Stage Four: Adaptation
A greater integration into the new culture occurs and you start to get solid feelings of belonging and ease. There is increased enjoyment in new customs and ways of doing and saying things. It becomes clear that the new culture has good and bad things to offer. You then start to realise that there will be things you will miss when you return home!

- Stage Five: Re-entry Shock
Moving back to one's country of origin has new consequences and you may find that things are no longer the same (because of course, you are no longer the same).

The above list is what you have to look forward to but like I said earlier, just reading this book and arriving with an open mind, wide-open eyes and a closely guarded mouth, you will be well on your way to adapting to your new country. And if there is one final thing to say, it is that I find expatriates and Singaporeans overall, content. It's wonderful and contagious to be surrounded with happy people. Certainly, it's not that life is perfect or ideal but rather, it's that people really seem to appreciate and realise all the good Singapore has to offer. I wish you the best and I hope that you will be able to say the same after your stay.

ACKNOWLEDGEMENTS

As working on this project had tight time constraints, it almost seems too unfair to list everyone that helped me in so many ways, since they probably didn't even realise they assisted in any way and I relied heavily on my personal seven years experience, conversations and friendships. Everything and everyone was fair game! But then again, not listing anyone is not fair either, since I couldn't have done it on my own, so here goes my best attempt at thanking everyone who contributed: foremost is Patricia, my editor for all her many hours and contributions to the entire project, and all the others at Marshall Cavendish who assisted in compiling information, proofreading and fact-hecking. Special thank you to Tanty, Sha, Mas, Rohaniah for their insight and valuable input with regards to Malay customs and etiquette; thank you very much to Mr P Kesavan for his kindness and helpfulness with the Tamil glossary; to Barbara, Amelia, Tina, Tatjana, Helle, Christine, Linda, Judy, Lucy, Jennifer, Savi, Yuko, Caterina, Cecilia, Rana, Zahra, Carolina M, Eugenia, Carmen Gloria, Carolina O, Zahira, Cathy, Edward, Alan, Robert, Inci, Angela and Maria, thanks for your insights and for answering all my questions. And finally a special thank you to Sanjay for your comments, suggestions and enthusiastic support in everything.

For Sanjay, Alejandro and Gabriel
My boys in love and travel

MAP OF SINGAPORE

MALAYSIA

JOHOR STRAITS

SINGAPORE

SINGAPORE STRAIT

The Republic of Singapore is made up one main island and 63 smaller islands and islets. Pulau Tekong, one of the largest of these smaller islands, which lies to the north-east of the main one is not shown.

FIRST IMPRESSIONS

CHAPTER 1

'If you reject the food, ignore the customs, fear the religion
and avoid the people, you might better stay home.'
—James A Michener

WHETHER YOU ARE A TOURIST ON A SHORT VISIT or planning to make Singapore your new home, the opening quote is probably the best overall advice one could receive, surely. It aims directly at what a visitor in a foreign land should strive for—openness, non-judgement and a big sense of discovery. For in the end, it's through your own personal discovery that experiences will become real and treasured. So with your final goal in mind, probably the most important step in getting there is to gain some knowledge beforehand and to begin your journey with some understanding of the many layers that make up Singapore.

So, let's talk about Singapore. If there is one point to begin with, it must be that this teeny, tiny country in the South China Sea can certainly conjure up a lot of talk, press and publicity! For some place so small, it could have easily been forgotten and overlooked. Not Singapore. This island state works relentlessly at promoting itself and conversely, the world cannot seem to ignore or to be impressed by this little Asian dynamo.

I believe it's pretty accurate to say that few countries immediately conjure such divergent responses. There is definitely the group of people who have a lot of admiration for this small, unique island nation. Admiration for what it has achieved in such a short period of time, at such an astounding speed of constant change; admiration for its leaders with vision and action; and admiration for the comfortable, safe

A bird's eye view of central Singapore (foreground) with the Central Business Disctrict (more commonly known as CBD, background), the area where much of the business activity of the country is centred.

environment it has created for all its residents. On the other hand, there are those who will immediately go on about all the ridiculous laws, rules, regulations and controls the government has placed on its citizens, the human right laws it has violated, the exorbitant car prices, censorship, chewing gum laws, etc. In response to the second group, it's all true; the government is strict and has implemented some unpopular policies but what is admirable is that it is also re-evaluating and changing many of these laws—the 'iron fist' is loosening its grip.

A 2005 *Time* magazine article that featured an interview with the country's first prime minister and elder statesman, Lee Kuan Yew, insightfully builds on the vast influence that Singapore's success has had on Asia and other far-reaching countries to pinpoint the future challenge for Singapore—can it 'marry continued economic prosperity to a more open, tolerant, creative and yes, messy society—and hence create a new miracle, from which other nations, bigger, more powerful and more potentially frightening than Singapore, could one day learn anew'? Only the future will tell.

Singapore is definitely a perfect example of a country's reputation far preceding the reality of life on this island. It may seem like a dictatorship to some, but a benevolent one at that. I may have to agree with the comment that living in Singapore means giving up a bit of the 'excitement' of life, especially if you have lived in a large buzzing metropolis like New York City, Paris or Shanghai, but one certainly gains, in its place, comfort and safety—no small issues to ignore in today's world. Even then, it's all relative; maybe you have just arrived from a remote town in New Zealand and Singapore seems like a buzzing metropolis! So before I say too much, the bottom line is that living here is truly a great experience.

New Found Respect

For me, the prime example of how the government works —with speed, ruthlessness, and authority but always for the good of the people—was the SARS outbreak in early 2003. Singapore being a major hub for air travel in the region was in the firing line of the epidemic. I know of many families who left for extended stays in their home countries, scared and frightened for their life. I stayed put with mine, knowing that we were being taken care of, everything imaginable and unimaginable was being done by the government to control the deadly virus but more importantly, to assuage the public's fears. Borders were closely monitored, suspected SARS carriers were identified and reported in the daily newspapers, schools were closed, temperature scanners set up at the airport and other entry points and to ensure no breaking of the home quarantine orders, electronic picture cameras were installed in the patients' homes. Where else in the world would all of that have been executable and even possibly effective? We may have been in the middle of the epidemic but I felt completely safe. Singapore earned new respect in my eyes.

So if there is one thing to say to someone who is reading this book and contemplating on moving here or just arrived in this country, it would be relax, the quality of life you have to look forward to will be hard to match in most places. Singapore is 'Asia for beginners', but even for the advanced, it's a breath of fresh air. It's an efficient, non-corrupt business environment with English as the working language. It's skyscrapers, modern high-rises alongside restored ethnic neighbourhoods and lush, landscaped greenery. It's a microcosm of Western innovation and efficiency with

Singapore is a modern country with a built-up infrastructure and lush tropical greenery.

Eastern values, traditions and face. It's a complex place that is evolving and changing right before everyone's eyes. It tries hard at everything it does. Call it what you will—the garden city, an amusement park island, the air-conditioned island, the nanny state, the little red dot—but for those of us lucky to call it home, it's a great place to be.

Aside from its friendly people, which in the end we all know is what makes every country worthwhile and special, you may have started to conclude by now three major points that really have made Singapore all that it has become—size, location and policymakers. The small land size has literally set the stage for everything else. The main island is only about 640 sq km (247 sq miles), and the reason Singapore is so controllable, manageable... and vulnerable. It has been said that because of its small size, it doesn't take much to rock the boat; Singapore is like a canoe, not a steamship afloat on the ocean. Harmony within its society, unity among its people and peace with its neighbours are at the centre of keeping the little boat from capsizing. It's all about keeping the status quo.

Secondly, there is location. Separated from Malaysia by only a short causeway, the island's coveted geographical position has been pivotal in establishing Singapore's success. With the opening of the Suez Canal in 1869, Singapore was perfectly poised to become the major port between the west and east. Call it destiny, fate or luck, but the island's future was forever changed. Additionally, its location at just a few degrees from the equator has brought it heat, rain, humidity and air-conditioning. While some people absolutely love the weather, the days-on-end of sunshine, others yearn for a chance to wear boots and pullovers plus a little snow at Christmas time. You can't please everyone! But in the end, it has made Singapore the only industrialised nation along the equator.

Lastly, there are the policymakers. When it comes to describing Singapore, you cannot escape the topic of the government. Its astute leaders, from the patriarch and first prime minister Lee Kuan Yew who moulded the island-state into his vision of Asia, to the current prime minister Lee

Hsien Loong (and eldest son of Lee Kuan Yew), its leaders have run the country like a profitable business and have managed to maintain their status as the most non-corrupt, efficient government in Asia. Like policymakers around the world, they certainly are also the reason for the 'bad press' that people who have never visited or lived in Singapore judge the country by; but for those who reside here, they are also the reason why it is so liveable.

All these complexities and dichotomies are Singapore. The longer one resides here, the more one realises and understands what makes this country so unique. Only when one has learned to peel away the layers and to find the heart inside does one really appreciate the place, any place, really.

And there is one more interesting aspect to living in Singapore and experiencing 'culture shock', it's not only the multicultural Singaporeans you will acquire in your life, but also the variety of cultures that you will encounter—and probably be afflicted with a little shock from all of them! I'm not just speaking of the three dominant Singaporean cultures (Chinese, Malay and Indian) but also of all the tightly-knit expatriate cultures you will certainly encounter either at school, clubs or through socialising, and then there is also the live-in domestic helper (most likely from the Philippines, Indonesia or Sri Lanka) who will probably introduce you to an entire new set of cultural behaviour and communication. Singapore will definitely present you with a fascinating mix, giving you valuable insights into many, many cultures and hopefully, you will gain a greater understanding and tolerance for all the different cultures. It's truly a multi-rich crucible of an island in more ways than one.

LIKELY FIRST IMPRESSIONS
Lush, Tropical and Green
For such a small urban city with no rural or country landscapes in sight, Singapore has done an admirable job at creating a stunning garden city. It has taken a lot of planning, execution and maintenance, but Singapore is truly a city within a garden.

Hot and Humid On The Outside...
There is no other way to say it, Singapore feels like a sauna! Being only a few degrees from the equator, the heat is

year-round and non-stop. And not to mention the short and sudden tropical showers that also occur all year round. There is no 'cool' season, although the locals may certainly not agree. The good news is that you will eventually get used to the humidity and the perpetual sunshine can do a lot for one's mental health!

...Freezing Cold On The Inside

Although you may be sweating and sweltering while crossing the street, be prepared for an arctic blast upon entering any building. Lee Kuan Yew once called air-conditioning the greatest invention of the 20th century, and for Singapore, where it has helped transform the tropical fishing village into a modern, high-rise developed nation, it is no small factor. Air-conditioning is key to Singapore's success story but it's almost an issue of overkill. Recent newspaper headlines have brought to the forefront the common sub-zero indoor temperatures and its effects on costs, productivity and health. We can only hope that someone in charge of the dial is listening. Meanwhile, be prepared with a cardigan, shawl or extra thick shirt.

Cosmopolitan and Fast Paced

Singaporeans didn't make it this far in their short 40-year history without a lot of hard work and innovation. What other country in the world can claim to have moved its status from Third World to First World, or developed nation status in one lifetime? Things are happening here, and they happen quickly. More housing needed—done. Better MRT (Mass Rapid Transit, the underground and overland train system) access for more people—working on it. Need more tourists—Integrated Resorts underway!

Fast and Abrupt Way of Speaking

Yes, English is one of the official languages and yes, they are probably speaking English to you although it may not seem that way! The confluence of the ethnic population has created a local patois with a very different tone, structure and cadence that has affected the way the locals speak English;

more precisely, Singlish, as it is known locally. This will take some getting used to but be assured, you will be able to spot a Singaporean anywhere in the world and it will probably bring a smile to your face and an instant reminder of your time in this unique country.

Multicultural
The Chinese, Malays and Indians who make up this nation have created a unique and harmonious home. The food, religion and traditions of these people can be found and seen around the island and are truly the core of what makes Singapore so colourful.

Unique Scents and Aromas
Durians, shrimp paste, fried garlic, jasmine and tuberose garlands, medicinal herbs and other dried goods—just walking down the neighbourhoods is a feast for the senses. The unique aromas and scents from the Chinese medical halls, food courts (eating places), Malay hawker stands, Little

India, plus the food and Asian ingredients all produce either memories or reactions you will long remember, for better or worse.

Location, Location, Location

Singapore is small. As mentioned before, there is one main island and many small islets. Individually, each island is small; together, they are still small! So not surprisingly, a common ailment of expatriates is 'island fever' and the need for a change of environment, change of weather, new faces... just the need for a change. And there are numerous, beautiful, fascinating places to visit and explore within a few hours from Singapore. With its small, efficient and award-winning airport, leaving and arriving back home in Singapore is a joy. Just the fact that one can take full advantage of Asia's sights from Singapore is a major advantage to living here and one that should be fully exploited.

THE LAND AND ITS HISTORY

CHAPTER 2

'There was a time when people said
That Singapore won't make it, but we did...
We built a nation, strong and free,
Reaching out together, in peace and harmony...'
—lyrics from national song, 'We are Singapore'

GEOGRAPHY

Situated about 137 km (85 miles) north of the equator, Singapore is strategically located off the southern tip of the Malay Peninsula and separated from the hinterland by the Johor Straits. Nestled between Malaysia and Indonesia, it is the focal point for South-east Asian sea routes and this has played an important part in its history and development. Singapore, as a whole, consists not only of the main island but also 63 smaller islets which are scattered nearby. And as mentioned in the previous chapter, this doesn't really add up to much—the combined area of this small country, including the islets, is a mere 682.7 sq km (263.6 sq miles), just slightly more than four times the size of Washington DC. And this area is a result of land reclamation, the country being only 581.5 sq km (224.5 sq miles) before 1960. This, however, has not daunted the nation's efforts to use its geographical position to its advantage, allowing it to be a gateway to the region.

The main city lies in the southern part of the main island, but the country's small size and rapid expansion over the years has caused boundaries between town and country to be blurred. Hence, Singapore is often known as a city-state. About 50 per cent of the island is now either residential, commercial or industrial with many of the natural rainforests cleared long ago to make way for urban development. The land is generally very flat with its highest point only 163 m

A section of the Singapore River in front of Boat Quay.

(534.8 ft)—Bukit Timah Hill—above sea level. Sungei Seletar (*sungei* being the Malay word for 'river'), spanning 15 km (9.3 miles), is the longest river in the country although the Singapore River, only 3 km (1.9 miles) long, is the most well-known, being the site of many events and a number of the island's nightspots such as Boat Quay.

As the 'River' Runs

Singapore has a number of rivers—although 'river' might not be an appropriate term considering that most of them are so small and so short. A local recounted how she discovered the truth behind the Singapore River.

'I'd always been told that the source of a river was on higher ground and that the force of gravity leads it to flow downwards and wind its way to some outlet. As I stood on the bank of the Singapore River along Havelock Road, it occurred to me that the country's most famous river must have its beginnings in Bukit Timah Hill, or thereabouts, since that was the highest point on the island. So when I got home I did some research and found out that the length of the river (3 km) was from its mouth to Kim Seng Road, just further up from where I was standing earlier. A check with the maps confirmed that beyond that, the river was known as the Alexandra Canal. And no, it didn't flow down from any high point. It then suddenly dawned on me: the Singapore River was actually an inlet! I was surprised and disappointed all at the same time. But I supposed it was to be expected since the country's so small. After all, there are lakes in the world that are larger than our island!'

CLIMATE

If you're someone coming from a country with changing seasons, one of the biggest challenges you will face on arrival is the climate. It's likely to take you a good few months before you will feel 'comfortable' again. And just when you thought you'd acclimatised, the weather changes yet again. No, Singapore doesn't have four seasons—although some might disagree with that assessment—but it does experience modifications in its weather patterns that makes you feel like things aren't always the same.

Being situated in the equatorial monsoon region of South-east Asia, the city-state has a tropical climate all year round. Humidity is your constant companion as the country receives year-long precipitation, helping to keep temperatures relatively low, averaging 25°C (77°F) in January and 27°C (81°F) in June. The hottest time of the year is in July, coinciding with the south-west monsoon, which normally blows through Singapore from June to September. This monsoon period is the time for the least rainfall and the highest temperatures due to the relatively lighter winds that blow across the island. This is probably not the best time to arrive in Singapore as the humidity and heat can be overwhelming. Even those who have lived here for many years need to know where the nearest swimming pool is! The converse is true at the end of the year, when the north-east monsoon runs from December to March, and the country receives copious amounts of rain, heavy winds and even though the temperature may still be 26°C. the winds make it feel cooler.

Some locals smile and say that the time of the north-east monsoon is the country's winter, while that of the south-west monsoon is summer, with spring and autumn falling in between those two periods. To some extent that is quite true. Temperatures aside, you will see many of the local flowers coming into full bloom in April and May while many trees tend to shed their leaves in October and November. But climatic patterns have shifted slightly over the last five years or so, thought to be the result of global warming. While the flora patterns haven't changed, many Singaporeans have commented on freak weather such as heavy thunderstorms and cold winds during June and July, and very hot and humid weather in December. Perhaps all this is a matter of perception, as the country becomes more industrialised and more Singaporeans spend a good part of their time in air-conditioned rooms.

Thunderstorms are frequent in the afternoon and early evenings and sometimes you can even set your watch by it! An average of 250 mm (10 inches) of rain falls during these months and for many it is a welcome break from the extensive heat of the south-west monsoon.

HISTORY
Pre-Colonisation

A lack of comprehensive written records has resulted in little being known about the island before the 19th century. Most of this comes mainly from travellers' tales, court transcripts and the oral accounts that have been passed down through the generations. The island not being known by the same name to different people has caused further confusion. In the 3rd century, Chinese traders make reference to 'an island at the end of the peninsula'—Pu-luo-chung—while Mongol court transcripts from the 1320s describe a harbour on an island in this area as Dragon's Tooth Strait or Long Yamen. In the 13th century, Marco Polo mentions an island called Chiammasie while the Chinese traveller, Wang Ta-Yuan, writes about a place called Tan-Ma-Hsi in 1330.

Piecing together what they could, historians have built a picture of what they think life was like on the island between the 11th and 14th centuries. Many believe the main island was used as an outpost for the Sumatran Empire of Sri Vijaya, which capitalised on its strategic location as a thriving seaport for trade in the region. It is thought that ownership of the island then passed to the Javanese kingdom of Majapahit. Under this rule, the island was attacked many times by neighbouring kingdoms wanting to exploit its advantage as a seaport and boost their own kingdom's trade in the region.

Javanese inscriptions dating to the end of the 14th century suggest that at that time, it was called Temasek, meaning 'sea town'. This name appears in the *Nagarakretama*, a Javanese record written in 1365, and again in another Javanese record from the 15th century, the *Pararaton*. However, at some point, the island was given the name 'Singapura' (Sanskrit for 'lion city'). This name could have been coined by Rajendra, the ruler of the southern Indian Cola Kingdom but some believe it was bestowed by Buddhist monks in the 14th century who believed the lion was symbolic. According to the Malay Annals or *Sejarah Melayu*—a historical literary work in Malay that recounts the events of the Malay Peninsula over a period of 600 years—the island was named by Sang Nila Utama, a king who ruled for 48 years from 1299–1347.

Sang Nila Utama

One legend of how the island came to be named Singapura involves the Sumatran prince, Sang Nila Utama. The story has many versions but the most popular states that while hunting in one of the Riau islands, he climbed a huge rock and looked out across the waters, catching a glimpse of a distant island with pristine white beaches. Taken by its charm, Sang Nila Utama set sail with his followers but the sea turned rough, and it was only after throwing his gold crown into the water that the weather calmed. When they landed on the island, a majestic beast with a black head, furry mane, red body and whitish neck appeared. As the prince raised his bow and arrow, the animal merely stared at him with golden eyes, let out a ferocious roar and leapt gracefully into the dense of the jungle. Sang Nila Utama was mesmerised by the beast and asked what it was. A wise man among them claimed that it was a lion. Believing the beast to be a fortuitous omen, the prince decided then to stay on the island and rule as king. He named it Singapura, *singa* meaning 'lion' and *pura* meaning 'city'.

Sometime at the end of the 14th century, after much warring between kingdoms, the island of Singapura fell into decay. Attention had turned to Malacca (Melaka) which then became the most important port in the region and Singapura was disregarded. For the next 400 years, the island became home to a handful of Malay fishing villages called *kampungs* and pirates operated the Straits of Malacca.

British Colonial Days

By the mid to late 18th century, the various colonial powers—namely the Portuguese, Dutch and British—had extended their reaches into South-east Asia. Through the British East India Company, the British had already set up a trading post in Penang (1786) and Malacca (1795). Sir Thomas Stamford Raffles (1781–1826), an agent of the company and posted to Penang in 1805, was well aware of the political undercurrents and the growth of Dutch influence in this region. He realised the importance of the trade route through the Straits of Malacca and felt the need to secure a port of call, south of the Straits, for British ships passing through this area, either from the homeland or India, and heading towards China, their newest trading partner. On 29 January 1819, while out surveying for a possible island in the Riau peninsula, Raffles landed in Singapore. Upon his arrival, he discovered a swamp-covered island, home to a handful of Chinese planters, aborigines and Malays. Experience, however, had taught him that the positioning of any location would be its the real advantage and he knew immediately that this island was just what the company needed. Within a week, he had signed a formal treaty with the Sultan of Johor (then the ruler of Singapore) and the Temenggong (his representative on the island). Both were to receive a total annual payment of 8,000 Spanish dollars (the currency of choice at the time) from the British in exchange for the exclusive right to set up a trading post and settlement on the island. For his foresight, Raffles is often hailed as the founder of Singapore.

Soon after, Raffles set sail for other ports at the bidding of the British East India Company, leaving Colonel William Farquhar (1774–1839) as Resident to look into the development of Singapore. Farquhar, a man of experience having been Resident of Malacca for 15 years, set about getting the settlement in order. Forests were cleared for more housing to be built but this resulted in a number of threats from rats, insects, tigers and crocodiles so Farquhar had to implement measures to deal with this. When skulls from the victims of pirates washed up on the beach, he made sure that these were cleared regularly so as not to discourage sailors from docking at the island. Despite his best efforts, his hands were sometimes tied as Raffles and the Company imposed restrictions on what he could do. One limitation he faced was the inability to tax trade as Singapore was touted as a tax-free port. In order to raise money for expenditure on public projects e.g. setting up a police force, Farquhar took extreme measures and legalised the sale of opium and gambling.

A statue in honour of the man who founded Singapore, Sir Thomas Stamford Raffles. The statue in this picture was erected along the Singapore River and was supposed to mark the spot where Raffles first landed. To make way for urban development, it has since been removed and a replica now stands outside the Victoria Memorial and Concert Halls.

Raffles sailed into port infrequently and on his trip back in 1822, he was disappointed at some of the policies that Farquhar had put into place so decided to take matters into his own hands. He carved out different physical areas for the major ethnic groups (Malays, Chinese, Indians and Eurasians) and each group was to appoint a *kapitan* who would act as the liaison with the British and keep their respective communities in order. He replaced the older wooden houses with those made from brick and tiles and ensured that proper streets were laid down within the commercial district. He then initiated the building of government buildings in the Fort Canning area. Gambling dens were closed, slavery was abolished, landholdings were registered, a botanical garden was set up, and funds were raised for the establishment of an institution of learning for civil servants and local teachers. He appointed magistrates (chosen from the local British community) who would help in administering the law.

Having disapproved of the way Farquhar had handled some of Singapore's problems, Raffles eventually asked for the Resident's resignation, which was given reluctantly. His replacement, John Crawfurd (1783–1868), arrived in May 1923 and three weeks later, Raffles left Singapore for the last time.

By 1823, Singapore had far exceeded the expectations of the British and surpassed Penang as a primary port of call for ships plying this route. The Anglo-Dutch Treaty of 1824 designated the spheres of influence in this region, and Malaya and Singapore went to the British. The island was later ceded over to them by the Sultan of Johor. By 1825, the port's trade in South-east Asia surpassed that of Malacca and Penang combined. Singapore's reputation as a free-trade port attracted traders and merchants from the Middle East, Europe and America. In 1826, Singapore, Penang and Malacca combined to become the Straits Settlements. Trade at all three ports flourished and in 1832, Singapore was made the administrative centre for the three areas. As the British East India Company lost the monopoly of trade to China, their interests in their Malayan outposts waned and in 1867, the Straits Settlement was made a Crown Colony under the direct control of the British Government.

During this time, however, Singapore became prosperous and its growing wealth attracted many Chinese, Indians and Malays who arrived in search of work. The country's population began to soar, reaching about 80,000 in 1860. Singapore's power as a trading hub was further enhanced with the invention of steamships, and the opening of the Suez Canal in 1869. In the 20th century, as the West demanded ever-increasing amounts of tin to satisfy the packaging industry and rubber for the automotive industry, Singapore's prime location made it one of the greatest ports in the world. This eventually led to the building of almost 5 km (3 miles) worth of wharves along Tanjong Pagar in 1921. At the same

The wharves along Tanjong Pagar still exist today.

time, a naval base (and later an air base) was also constructed as the British felt the need to build up their defences in Malaya, especially after World War I.

The Japanese Occupation

The outbreak of World War II led to a bleak period in Singapore's otherwise glorious history. The British had always considered the island impregnable but in the early hours of 8 December 1941, Singapore came under attack from Japanese bombers. At the same time, the Japanese Imperial Army began to advance towards the small island, moving in from Malaya. In February 1942, they crossed the Johor Straits and began to move through the island, engaging in combat with British troops who fought as best they could to protect the land. This, however, was in vain and on 15 February 1942, Singapore fell to the Japanese.

For the next three and a half years, life on the small island was extremely harsh, more so than it had ever been under the British. Ironic, as the Japanese had claimed they wanted to liberalise their South-east Asian counterparts from the clutches of their colonial masters. While under Japanese rule, Singapore was renamed Syonan-to ('Light of the South Island') and during this time, the people of Singapore lived in fear of their lives especially from the Japanese secret military police, the Kempeitei, who were known to incarcerate, torture and kill for the weakest of reasons. The Sook Ching massacre, where tens of thousands of ethnic Chinese were systematically exterminated, is just one example of the atrocities carried out by the Japanese.

Hear It For Yourself

You can listen to some first-hand accounts of what life was like under the Japanese at:

http://www.knowledgenet.com.sg/singapore/
index.asp?title = OH/OH.html&hdr = BI

Ration cards were handed out for basic necessities but the quantities allowed were reduced as the war dragged on. The issuance of banana money (so named because each note had the banana tree printed on) by the Japanese allowed them to control the economy and this resulted in an increase in black market operations. Over time, banana money became over-inflated as more was simply printed when the need arose. As basic resources became scarcer, many more lives were lost to malnutrition and disease.

The Japanese finally surrendered to the Allies on 14 August 1945 but it would be about another month before the British would take over the reins. In the interim, the island was in a total state of disarray with much of the infrastructure destroyed and people looting and killing.

The Journey to Independence

When British forces took over in September 1945, Singapore was placed under British military administration. Following the dissolution of the Straits Settlements in 1946, Singapore became a Crown Colony while the Malay peninsula (including Penang and Malacca) became the Malayan Union. (The Union would later become the Federation of Malaya in 1948.) This was mainly because the British thought that the island's predominantly ethnic Chinese population would pose a problem if they wanted to institute common citizenship for the union. This worked in Singapore's favour and the island made progress constitutionally. The first elections, albeit only for six members of the Legislative Council, were held in March 1948. In June of the same year, a state of emergency was declared after communist elements attempted to take over both Malaya and Singapore; this was to last for 12 years. Yet in that time, recommendations were made and steps were taken to take Singapore towards self-government. In 1955, elections for a number of ministerial and Legislative Assembly seats were carried out and a coalition government was formed with David Marshall as its first Chief Minister. A year later, he resigned after talks with London, to allow the island to be totally self-governing internally, broke down. His deputy, Lim Yew Hock, took over the position and Marshall's campaign for control, finally negotiating new terms for Singapore's constitution which was formally signed with London on

28 May 1958. Elections were held in 1959 for all 51 seats in the Legislative Assembly. The People's Action Party (PAP)—who had won four seats in the 1955 elections—won 43 seats this time around. On 3 June that year, a new constitution was proclaimed and two days later, the Government of the State of Singapore was sworn in with Lee Kuan Yew as its first prime minister.

A Turbulent Time

The 1950s were a turbulent time for Singapore, even as the island—proclaimed a city by the British in 1951—made headway to get back on its feet after the war and work towards independence.

One of the worst incidents during this decade was the riots sparked off by the Maria Hertogh custody case. Violence broke out on 11 December 1950 when Muslims were enraged at the Supreme Court's rejection of an appeal to overturn a decision that awarded custody of 13-year-old Maria Hertogh to her Dutch Catholic biological parents, despite her being raised as a Muslim by a lady she called 'her mother', Aminah binte Mohamed. The chaos lasted three days and ended with 173 injured and 18 killed.

In late April 1955, strikes by workers of the Hock Lee Amalgamated Bus Service (mainly members from the Singapore Bus Workers' Union) and Chinese students later escalated into the Hock Lee bus riots on 12 May, later to be known as 'Black Thursday'. Even as police tried to disperse the 2,000-strong crowd of strikers and students with tear gas and water cannons, they were pelted with stones. Buses with passengers were not spared. A woman, who was in her mid-20s at the time and pregnant with her first child, recounts the fear she and her colleagues went through when the bus they were on—contracted by her company to pick up employees and send them to work—was stoned by rioters. It made no difference that there was a Malay policeman on board to help. They finally made it through but the unrest continued till the next morning. By that time, there were four people dead and 31 injured.

In 1956, students from the Singapore Chinese Middle School Students Union—which had been dissolved by Chief Minister Lim Yew Hock—staged a sit-in at two schools for a period of two weeks, holding demonstrations and meetings. In October, an ultimatum was issued for the premises to be vacated and the students retaliated by rioting. This lasted five days by which time, 100 people were injured and 13 were killed. About 900 people were later arrested in connection with this and they were detained until 1959.

In May 1961, the Malayan prime minister Tunku Abdul Rahman proposed a merger between the Federation of

Malaya, Singapore, Sarawak, North Borneo and Brunei, with a central government for the alliance responsible for internal security, defence and foreign affairs. A referendum held on 1 September 1962 on this matter showed that the people of Singapore supported this merger overwhelmingly and on 16 September 1963, Malaysia was formed. Brunei was the only one who declined to join the merger. This union, however, didn't last long. Two years later, on 9 August 1965, Singapore separated from Malaysia and declared its independence.

Pro-Communists

In a bid to cut ties with British colonial powers and win total independence for Singapore, the PAP (as the main political party in government) entered in an uneasy alliance with pro-communist elements in Singapore. However, things came to a head in 1961, and the pro-communists broke away to form their own party, the Barisan Sosialis ('Socialist Front').

Early Independence

Since its independence, Singapore has embarked on a massive yet intensive industrialisation plan. Industrial parks were expanded or set up and Acts (employment and industrial relations) were passed in 1968 to ensure that there was harmony in the workforce.

Public housing was an important issue and the Housing and Development Board (HDB), set up in 1960, saw to it that housing estates and new towns were established and flats were sold at a low price. Home ownership was encouraged and Singaporeans were allowed to use money from the Central Provident Fund (CPF)—a compulsory savings scheme for all working Singaporeans—to pay for these.

Milestones

As a sovereign, independent and democratic nation, Singapore was admitted into the United Nations as its 117th member on 21 September 1965, and into the Commonwealth of Nations on 15 October 1965. On 22 December of the same year, it was made a republic with Yusof bin Ishak installed as its first president. In 1967, Singapore was one of the founding members of ASEAN (Association of South East Asian Nations).

The country's infrastructure was also looked into. Roads were constructed and telecommunications were implemented. Port and harbour facilities were modernised.

The Economic Development Board (EDB), set up in 1961, was re-organised in 1968 to meet the needs of a growing economy. In 1970, the Monetary Authority of Singapore (MAS) was established to formulate and implement policies. In the same year, the Development Bank of Singapore (DBS) was founded. as was the Jurong Town Corporation. In 1972, the Post Office Savings Bank (POSB)—a banking entity that had been in existence since 1877—was made into a statutory board and it offered interest-free savings accounts. This was a bid to entice Singaporeans to save on their own account.

Education became a priority as well and policies were modified. English was chosen as official language to facilitate communication with other nations in the world as well as forge a common bond among all Singaporeans, regardless of their ethnic backgrounds.

Singapore knew that eventually it would have to be responsible for its own defence and in 1966, it set up the Singapore Armed Forces Training Institute (SAFTI). Compulsory national service was introduced the following year. As Singapore entered the 1970s, an air defence command and a maritime command had already been put into place. By the time the British forces pulled out of the country in October 1971, the little nation was capable of looking after itself.

SINGAPORE TODAY

The Singapore of the 21st century is a far cry from the little fishing village and pirate town of the 1800s or even fledgling nation of the 1960s. Today, the country still has few natural resources but it has capitalised on its strategic location and, by implementing a free trade zone, continues to act as a world centre for commerce and industry. It is now considered one of the busiest ports in the world, with up to 700 vessels in its waters at any one time.

However, the country does not rely solely on its status as an entrepôt but has instead developed and evolved into a financial and banking centre, particularly in South-east Asia. It has also developed a manufacturing sector, particularly in electronics, as well as oil refining and distribution bases.

Singapore has become a choice destination for tourists in part to the efforts of the Singapore Tourism Board (STB) who has visitors' centres like these in Singapore and certain cities around the world. Much of the country's exotic appeal has been captured in the Singapore Girl, Singapore Airlines' trademark flight attendant, who also helps bring in more visitors.

This has been possible due to its political and economic stability, developed infrastructure and communications network. In addition, the Singapore Tourism Board (STB) has succeeded in making Singapore an attractive destination for many travellers. In the space of ten years (1996–2005), visitor arrivals has increased by more than 22 per cent, with 8.9 million tourists coming into Singapore in 2005. This number is set to improve in future with more international activities being planned and the opening of two Integrated Resorts (IRs) by 2009.

GOVERNMENT SYSTEM

Singapore is a republic with a parliamentary democracy. Voting is compulsory for every registered adult citizen over the age of 21.

The unicameral parliament currently allows for 84 elected and nine nominated members, of which at least three of these seats must be candidates from a non-governing party. Since 1959, the PAP has held majority seats and at times has been the only party to be elected into power. In the country's latest 2005 elections, the PAP won 82 seats with one seat each going to the Worker's Party and the Singapore Democratic

Alliance. Of the nine nominated members (known as Non-Constituency Member of Parliaments or NCMPs), eight will be leading Singaporeans who have made some significant contribution to the community. The remaining seat will be offered to a candidate from the opposition party who scored the highest percentage of votes in the election. (In 2006, this has been offered and accepted by a member of the Worker's Party.) Parliamentary seats are normally held for a five-year term.

Political authority rests primarily with the prime minister and the cabinet. The prime minister is chosen from the majority ruling party and he or she, in turn, will appoint cabinet ministers.

The Man Who Made Singapore

Without a doubt, the man who made the most impact on Singapore's development since its post-war years is Lee Kuan Yew. A world-renowned figure, Lee is the man who has helmed not just the republic but also the PAP. He was Singapore's first prime minister and held the office for 31 years since 1959. Lee has been instrumental in implementing various policies to ensure that the economy and country has grown, and that the people have a better life. He stepped down in 1990 to make way for Goh Chok Tong. In the 14 years when Goh was prime minister, Lee was appointed Senior Minister. When Lee's son, Lee Hsien Loong, took over the role of prime minister from Goh in August 2004, Lee Kuan Yew was appointed Minister Mentor and Goh Chok Tong, Senior Minister. Now in his 80s, Lee Kuan Yew's mind is as sharp as ever and he still is a force to be reckoned with.

The President is head of the state and, since the 1991 constitutional changes, is elected by the people. The changes have also expanded the president's powers, giving him or her more say over internal security matters, government budgets and legislative appointments. It is the president who appoints the NCMPs, based on nominations from a select committee.

The judiciary is based on English common law and power is held by the Supreme Court, consisting of the High Court and the Court of Appeal. Supreme Court judges, consisting of the chief justice and seven other judges, are appointed by the president.

THE PEOPLE OF SINGAPORE

CHAPTER 3

' 'Multi-everything' makes us Singaporean:
multi-lingual, multi-racial, multi-religious, multi-cultural,
multi-tasking, not to forget our multi-storey car parks.'
—Otsuka Keiko, student published in the book,
Things That Make Us Singaporean

ASK ANY LOCAL OR FOREIGN PERSON living in Singapore to describe the country in just a few words and 'multicultural' will surely be on almost everyone's list. The people are a mix of four main ethnic groups and each of their heritage and values are deeply ingrained into the country's past and present. The nation was built on immigrants from neighbouring countries and the government has always insisted and strived for harmony among its citizens. The leaders had the foresight to see that with such a small country, if its people were divided, the country would be weak; consequently, racial harmony is one of Singapore's major building blocks. And more admirable is the fact that the different racial groups are encouraged to maintain their own customs and traditions so as to not create one melting pot—more of a mixing pot—where everyone is distinct, identifiable and still part of the whole. Locally, they'd say the society is *rojak*, referring to the Malay salad of mixed fruit and vegetables which has come to mean mixture and variety. Justifiably so; it's a great source of national pride to showcase Singaporean racial diversity and harmony.

Even as a foreigner, one will quickly find one's place in society. With one out of four people in Singapore being a foreigner, one is hardly a 'novelty'. Yes, you do immediately fall into the popular 'expat' and '*ang moh*' (the Hokkien word for 'red hair' and the term used to refer to Caucasians) category and all the stereotypes associated with it; and yes, it can get very annoying when you are immediately classified into any category. I still struggle with the fact that one has to be labelled something, but that is the Singaporean way—everything has to have a name and purpose. There are expat publications, expat services, expat holidays, expat everything; it's truly an 'ethnic group' of its own, but hey, it probably wasn't the locals who named and started the targeted publications, services or holiday!

In Singapore, this type of categorisation is just part of their nature and is not usually used in a derogatory manner. Here, probably more than anywhere else in Asia, a foreigner can integrate into the society. It may take time and some perseverance but the most important element is present—the fact that the people are used to mixing and living with different religions, cultures and backgrounds. Being that the population has disposable income, a good majority of Singaporeans travel overseas quite a bit and have probably studied and visited many foreign lands, maybe even yours.

Celebrating Harmonious Living

Racial harmony is so important to Singapore's culture is that a special day, 21 July, has been designated to celebrate this concept. This date was chosen because it was on this day in 1964 when Singapore saw race riots. Racial Harmony Day is commemorated at schools and serves to teach students what social division cost the country in the past and encourages them to reflect on and celebrate the success the nation has had since that time.

There is much that can be said about Singapore's diverse cultures, more than there is space in this book. The following is a brief look at the background and history of multiculturalism in Singapore, followed by a more extensive look into each of the four major ethnic groups. This, however, is not exhaustive but will give you enough to get by until you start to discover things on your own.

BACKGROUND AND HISTORY

As mentioned in the previous chapter, Singapore was set up as a trading post by the British back in 1819. With hopes of a better life for their families, many people started arriving from China, India and Indonesia, to work and live side by side with the Malays who were already inhabitants. When

Raffles separated the various ethnic groups, that is how the distinct neighbourhoods of Chinatown, Little India and Arab Street were formed.

However, when Singapore became an independent nation, its government had the vision to see that a small country could not prosper if there was any tension as well as physical and emotional distance among its inhabitants. Unity was vital and consequently, solidarity and social cohesion became the basis for a multicultural government policy. Because of their unique history, even Singapore's four ethnic races assume a lot more racial diversity than is suggested by just the word 'Chinese', 'Malay', 'Indian' and 'Eurasian'. Additionally, it should be noted that, as it often happens with immigrant groups who establish themselves in a foreign land, the community hangs on to its language, religion and traditions and creates a 'sub-group' of their original culture. For instance, most Indians have been here two, three or even four generations, so it comes as no surprise that they are not representative of the Indian people from the subcontinent; neither are the Chinese representative of the mainland Chinese. They are all, above everything else, Singaporean, and they will proudly tell you so.

The Chinese

The numbers say it all, at 76.8 per cent of the population, the Chinese are the majority and therefore, the dominant influence in Singapore. Originally from the coastal south-eastern part of mainland China, the Chinese are also richly diverse in dialects and cultures. The five original Chinese ethnic groups, which still remain today, are the Hokkiens (from the southern Fujian Province), Teochews (from Shantou in the eastern Guangdong Province), Cantonese (from the central Guangdong Province), Hakkas (from central China) and the Hainanese (from the island of Hainan in the southern part of China). Many Chinese also came from Malacca and Penang and other parts of the Malay archipelago.

In the early days, the Chinese were among the first to arrive to make their fortune, in spite of the fact that most were not very skilled workers. Most were labourers and

The ethnic Chinese of today are descended from various provinces in China and this determines their dialect group. Intermarriage between the people from differing dialect groups means that many are 'mixed' and know at least a smattering of different dialects.

craftspeople that specialised in certain trades. They settled in the separate districts of Chinatown (to avoid quarrels) along the Singapore River. Historical records can be found where Raffles has demarcated certain areas of what is now Chinatown by provinces: Hokkiens in Telok Ayer and Amoy Street, Teochews closer to the Singapore River and Cantonese in the Kreta Ayer Area. It's interesting to note how the various ethnic backgrounds seemed to drift towards specific trades. The Hokkiens excelled in trade and general agriculture, which explains their success in the rubber trading and banking industries. The Teochews were also good traders and agriculturalists. The Cantonese and Hakkas were seen as good house workers since they were excellent at carpentry, brick making and the domestic arts of baking, barbering, tailoring and shoemaking. And the Hainanese were known for their catering and personal services, with their culinary skills.

Characteristics and Values
The Chinese are known as hard-working, family oriented, thrifty, superstitious and traditional. Although many Singaporeans, born and bred in this country, may feel

no strong ties to their motherland, many still hold fast to the work ethic brought over by their forefathers. Despite modernisation and Westernisation, there has been a strong effort to retain traditional values.

The Chinese people have a strong sense of mutuality, of being connected through affection, obligation and responsibility to specific other people such as their parents (filial piety), siblings, family at large, community, nation. The individual is never the building block, like is common in the West. It is this incredibly strong bilateral relationship in the Chinese person's life that gives meaning to 'saving face', (*for more on this, see* Chapter Four: Socialising and Fitting In, *page 58*) or never doing anything that would embarrass or shame yourself for it would also shame your family.

The Golden Rule

'Do unto others what you would want them to do to you.'
—Confucius

The Chinese people are strong believers in Confucianism, which is more a code of conduct; or philosophy on how to live life rather than a religion. A better understanding of Confucianism offers great insight into the Singaporean mentality and how the Confucianist value system has also played a major role in guiding the government. For example, Confucius advocated a paternalistic government in which the sovereign is benevolent and honourable and the subjects are respectful and obedient. That is clearly visible in Singaporean Chinese.

Having said that, it must be noted that many Chinese are Buddhists or Taoists. While many will claim that these are 'religions', many others will tell you that both of these are a way of life as the teachings contain precepts on how to live in order to attain a heavenly goal. There also seems to be an increasing number of Chinese who are believing in Christianity. It is important to remember that even though a Chinese is a Christian, that does not mean that he or she is not a Chinese. There are still many traditions that are ethnically based and many Chinese Christians will follow these customs e.g. celebrating Chinese New Year and uphold Christian beliefs at the same time.

Yet, despite their religious inclinations, many Chinese still cling to, or at least have a basic understanding, of ancient

Some Chinese have altars just outside their front doors to pray to the God of Heaven (above) and the God of Earth.

The Yueh Hai Ching Temple (Temple of the Calm Sea) is the oldest Taoist temple in Singapore and holds particular significance to the Teochews who used to be a seafaring people. This was the place they would visit before and after a journey to pray and give thanks for protection. Today, the temple is a national monument partly because of its unique architecture: it has two shrines, each with its own entrance, one dedicated to Xuan Tian Shang Di (Heavenly Emperor) and the other to Ma Zu (Mother of Heavenly Sages). The prayer incense coils pictured above contain slips of paper on which people would write their wishes. The coils are then lit and the smell of incense is supposed to calm the gods, at the same time alert them that there was a wish to be granted.

The Chinese zodiac is similar to the Western one in that it is also made up of 12 signs. All of them are animals (even one mythical one) and your sign is determined by the year you are born in.

beliefs such as Chinese astrology and geomancy. Everyone knows there are 12 signs in the Chinese zodiac, many (even those who are Christians) are extra careful during the seventh lunar month (the month of the Hungry Ghosts), and just as many are aware of what *feng shui* is and how it affects one's good or bad fortune. This is a legacy from their forefathers and is likely to be passed down through the generations no matter how Westernised they become.

Traditions

Chinese people usually have two 'given' names and a 'family' name which is placed first. For example, if a man is called Goh Cheng Jun, his family name is 'Goh' and his actual name is 'Cheng Jun'. Thus he will probably be called Mr Goh in formal circumstances and Cheng Jun or just Jun by family and friends. Similarly a woman will take on her father's family name at birth and may or may not relinquish it when she gets married. In the olden days, women were not considered part of their birth family once they marry so were known primarily by the husband's family name. As Singaporeans become more Westernised, Chinese women can now choose how they want to be known. For example if Goh (in our example above) married Lim Mei Lin, his wife may choose to change her name to Mrs Goh Mei Lin or retain it as Mdm Lim Mei Lin. Many opt to use the title 'Ms' so as to remain ambiguous. Another trend that is slowly catching on is double-barrelled surnames so Mei Lin may also choose to call herself Lim-Goh Mei Lin. Normally, it is their own surname which comes first, followed by their husbands, but in some cases, the order gets mixed up. Perhaps this has something to do with the way the name sounds when put together.

Today, it is common for many Singaporeans to take on a Western name. In some cases, this name has been given to the child from birth, especially so if the parents are Christians. There are a good number, though, who pick their own Western names when they grow up and sometimes there's no telling what you might get. Like one local celebrity who took the name Ix supposedly because he liked the number nine and this is nine in Roman numerals.

A person can have both a Western and a Chinese name. For example, our fictional couple above may decide to name their eldest son Adam Goh Teck Seng and their second son Benjamin Goh Teck Meng. Yes, some families have one character in their Chinese names that is carried among all the sons and another among the daughters. (In this example, 'Teck' is the Chinese character that is shared by all the sons.) This custom, however, is slowly dying out.

Singaporean Chinese wear Western-style clothing every day. The traditional Chinese ladies' dress, the *cheongsam*, is still worn but primarily only for special occasions such as weddings or Chinese New Year.

The Malays

The Malays are the second largest ethnic group at 13.9 per cent and Singapore's original inhabitants. They were once the majority but soon were overtaken by the Chinese. 'Malay' is a general term which has come to encompass a variety of people from the neighbouring region.

First President

The first President of Singapore was a Malay, Yusof Ishak (1910–1970) who was in office from 1965–1970. Today, his picture appears on the two, five, ten, 50 and 100 dollar currency notes.

The majority of Malays come from the Malay Peninsula but also various Indonesian ethnic groups from Sumatra, the Riau Islands, Java and Sulawesi have all been assimilated into the Malay population. United by their common Islamic faith that plays a dominant role in their lives, the Malays are a warm and hospitable people who have left their indelible mark in making Singapore what it is today. From the food, to the street names, language, national anthem and more, the rich cultural background and Malay influence is evident everywhere on the island.

Although they were the original inhabitants of the island, the Malays did not have an easy start. The colonial powers had their preconceived ideas and beliefs, and regarded the Malays as simple peasants. This, however, did not stop them from exploiting the latter's loyalty and deference. The Malays made excellent policemen, army soldiers and unskilled workers in the public sector. It is interesting to note that even today, military commands are still declared in Malay.

But the Malays have made huge strides in this competitive society. While some have felt marginalised by the dominant Chinese culture and policies, others have strived to rise above their position and many have demonstrated their resilience and talents throughout Singapore's history. They have made great contributions to the arts and literature, as well as the media, among other areas. In the 20th and 21st centuries, an increasing number of Malays are making their mark in business and politics and among these are many prominent and influential women.

Characteristics and Values

In Singapore, almost every Malay is Muslim, as are a number of Indians and a small minority of Chinese. They are quite moderate in their beliefs and tolerant of other faiths. Additionally, from the time they are young, great value is placed on courtesy, humility and social etiquette. The Malays also have the greatest sense of community and charity giving among the different races. However, to better understand Malay values and culture, it is important to have a basic understanding of Islam.

Masjid Sultan or Sultan Mosque is a national monument and lies in the heart of the Malay enclave of Kampong Glam. The original mosque was built in 1826, with money donated from the British East India Company but its current architecture only came about in 1924 when it was redesigned and reconstructed.

Most Malays are members of the Sunni sect of Islam. The Sunni Muslims have six pillars of faith (Rukun Iman), the five pillars of Islam (Rukun Islam) and the spiritual pillar (Ihsan). The five pillars of Islam which influence the daily lives of every Muslim are:

- *shahadah* (profession of faith)
  Affirming their belief that there is no God but Allah and that Prophet Muhammad was His Messenger.
- *salat* (prayer)
  Ritual prayers are conducted five times daily to ensure that Allah is paramount in the devotee's mind.
- *zakat* (tithe)
  This is a form of institutionalised charity. There are two types of *zakat*—*zakat fitrah* and *zakat harta*. The former is an annual levy for each individual Muslim, and this is payable in the month of Ramadan. *Zakat harta* is the levy of 2.5 per cent on one's personal wealth and assets, subject to a minimum called *nisab*. It is payable yearly and the time varies for individuals and business entities.
- *sawm* (fast)
  The fast of Ramadan serves to refocus the mind on spiritual rather than material concerns and fosters empathy with the less fortunate.
- *haj* (pilgrimage)
  At least once in their lifetime, every adult Muslim should endeavour to make a pilgrimage to the holy city of Mecca in Saudi Arabia.

These five pillars are at the core of daily life for Muslims and their influence permeates all celebrations, holidays and life's milestones. Friday is the day for community prayers in the mosque. There are no images in their place of worship; rather the mosques are decorated with carved geometrical designs and plant motifs as well as Arabic calligraphy, an important part of Islamic art. In the mosque, prayers are held under the direction of a religious leader, the *imam*. Men and women worshippers are not permitted to mix.

Despite modernisation and many Western influences, Malays young and old still hold many superstitions and taboos, most commonly attributed to their long history of animism and religious transformation. Wind or *angin* is seen as a powerful source and one will hear Malays (and Asians in general) speak of 'wind' with reference to physical illness (an imbalance in one's *angin*) or the 'wind' a woman has in her body after giving birth.

Muslims also have strict rules with regards to their diet and what they are allowed to eat. The most commonly known rules are that they do not eat pork or pork derivatives (the pig is seen as an unclean animal) and they do not drink alcohol. The food they eat should be *halal*, or that the meat they eat must be slaughtered by a Muslim according to proper Islamic rites. This even applies to the food utensils used in preparation and consumption must not have come into contact with non-*halal* food. They are also not allowed to eat amphibious animals (e.g. frogs, snakes, and crocodiles), carnivorous animals or birds (e.g. tigers, bears, eagles, hawks) and creepy-crawlies (e.g. insects, lizards). Also, with regards to animals, Muslims will not pet or touch a dog. They belief a dog's saliva is unclean and any part of the body or clothing that comes into contact with the dog's saliva has to be washed. For this reason, if you invite a Malay guest to your home, remember to keep the dog in a separate room in order to make your guest at ease.

It is common practice for Malay names to be influenced by both Islam and the Arabic language. This is because Malay parents hope that their child will live up to those names that have connotations of heroism, dignity or good attributes.

Malay family names do not last more than one generation and this is as simple as adding the father's name to the end of the child's name. In other words, Iskander Fariis may be called Iskander or Mr Iskander and not Mr Fariis as that is his father's name. His son, Abir, will be known as Abir Iskander or Abir bin Iskander. *Bin*, or *binte*, means 'son of' or 'daughter of' respectively. This may be included in the name but today, more often than not, it is dropped. Additionally, the title Haji for men and Hajjah for women (both written as 'Hj') is used before the names to indicate that he or she has made the Muslim pilgrimage to the holy city of Mecca.

Singapore Girl

The traditional Malay *sarong kebaya*, has become synonymous with Singapore and is recognised the world over mainly through the efforts of Singapore Airlines (SIA) and its advertising and branding of the Singapore Girl. The batik print, designed by Pierre Balmain, is the uniform of the female flight attendants for the country's flagship airlines. Much to the dismay of SIA, the uniform is now sold in every size mainly by stalls catering to the tourists. It has, to some extent, become the unofficial national costume, and the print is found on everything from umbrellas to handbags. Now, there is even a Singapore Girl Barbie doll!

With regards to clothing, it is most common to see younger, modern Malay women and men in completely Western attire. Wearing modest, conservative attire is an individual choice for Muslims in Singapore. Nonetheless, it is also very common to see many Malay women still wearing the traditional *baju kurung*, a long-sleeved tunic worn over an ankle-length skirt, known as a *sarong*. The head scarf, known as *tudung*, normally covers the head, ears, neck and bosom. The *tudung* can be worn with traditional Malay dress or appropriate Western attire (i.e. for women, it must be long-sleeved, cover the chest and be ankle-length). Another common accessory is the *selendang* (shawl), which is often draped loosely over the head or neck.

For Malay men, the traditional costume is known as the *baju kurung Melayu Telok Belanga*, which consists of a loose, long-sleeved shirt (*baju*), worn over a *kain sarong* (wrap-around skirt) or a *seluar* (trousers) of the same material and colour. On formal occasions, the ensemble of shirt and trousers is completed with the addition of a *kain samping*, a short *sarong* reaching to the knees, usually made of a rich, woven material. The formal velvet cap is called a *songkok* and the common white skullcap is the *songkok Haji*.

The Indians

Forming the smallest of the three national ethnic groups at 7.9 per cent, the Indians were also originally immigrant workers who arrived in Singapore to make money and provide for their families back home. In fact, many Indians were on board the same ship as Sir Stamford Raffles, as soldiers, known as *sepoys*, in the British Army. Indian women and complete Indian families were rare before World War II. Over time, the Indian men brought their families and settled down permanently. Tamils from South India make up about 60 per cent of the entire Singaporean Indian population with the balance a mix of Malayalis, Sikhs, Gujaratis, Punjabis and others from the subcontinent who shared neither language nor religion. The Indian community in Singapore is a tight-knit group, still practising and maintaining many of the traditions and customs from the motherland.

By the mid 1800s, the Indian population grew to about 10 per cent of the total population, with the overwhelming majority of the Indian immigrants being labourers (called *coolies*) from South India and convicts who excelled in construction work—such as clearing the jungle, building bridges and roads—and more skilled work like brick making, carpentry and blacksmithing. During this time of growth and expansion for Singapore, their work was much sought after and has endured the test of time through such contributions as the Sri Mariamman Temple on South Bridge Road, the Istana (the President's official residence) and Saint Andrew's Cathedral. After completing their prison sentence, many of

The Sri Mariamman Temple in South Bridge Road is a testament to the skill of the Indian convicts who were sent here in the mid-1800s. Today, it plays a major role in a number of key Hindu festivals.

the convicts chose to stay in Singapore and continue their work as labourers or to set up small businesses.

One of the trades that the Indian Muslim immigrants in the 19th century were known for was moneychanging. Even today, Indian moneychangers can still be found along Serangoon Road, Orchard Road and in the banking district. And another type of banking service, moneylending, was provided by the South Indians who were known as Chettiars. They lent money to people who wanted to set up their businesses since there were few banks in Singapore at that time. In fact, the early Chettiars even built a temple for themselves which was commonly known as Chettiar's Temple. The temple was run by Annamalai Chettiar who organised a grand celebration of the Hindu festival of Thaipusam, which was attended by the British and other important leaders of the time. Today, the Chettiar's Temple in Tank Road is still the centre of activity for the annual Thaipusam procession.

Other Indian trades and skills have left their mark in current day Singapore. The North Indians reared cows, buffaloes and goats for milk. Their cattle sheds were built in the Serangoon Road area which was abundant with water and grass (in the heart of Little India today). Two roads, Buffalo Road and Kerbau Road (kerbau is the Malay word for 'buffalo'), serve as reminders of the cattle sheds that once stood in the area. Additionally, the construction of the Rochor Canal brought irrigation to this area and in turn attracted the Indian laundrymen (called dhobis) who set up their businesses along what is now Bras Basah Road and Serangoon Road. Today's Dhoby Ghaut interchange along the MRT lines marks the spot (not exactly, but close to it) where much of the laundry business took place and pays homage to the lost trade. Incidentally, Dhoby Ghaut means 'washing place'.

Like the Malays, the local Indian population has its issues with class stratification. Although a fairly large group occupies the middle and higher sectors of Singaporean society, the community is disproportionately represented at the bottom of the social ladder. With recent waves of emigration by well-qualified Indian Singaporeans to

English-speaking developed countries, the imbalance seems to have been enhanced. From the 1990s onwards, Singapore has attracted a fairly large group of highly skilled, well-educated professional and business people, with expatriate Indians constituting a large part of that group. It remains to be seen whether these will choose to stay on in the long term and become Permanent Residents (PRs) or even citizens. There is also the sub-group of Indian 'foreign workers' who come on short-term work permits as unskilled or semi-skilled workers. There tends to be little to no interaction between this group and the expat or local Indian communities.

Hinduism

A Hindu believes that living things have souls that are reborn after death, and that people's conduct in the present will have a direct effect on what becomes of them in the future. It is a religion that one cannot convert to; one must be born a Hindu. The temple is their place of worship and plays an important part in every stage of life. Most Hindus will visit the temple at least once a week, and the temple is a focal point during festivities. Hindu temples are always dedicated to one of the Hindu trinity—the gods of creation, preservation, and destruction—who can be worshipped through any one of a number of attendant deities. Singaporean Hindus, being a minority, are a devout group and even maintain some religious customs that have almost died out in India.

Names

Names in India vary a lot depending on the state or region where the family is originally from. For example, Tamil Singaporeans do not have family names. They place the initial of their father's name before their own e.g. R Subramanian where Subramanian is the man's actual name and R is the first initial of his father's name, Ravichandran. It is also common for many South Indians to shorten their names as they can typically be very long.

Among the older generation, you may come across names that have the letters 's/o' and 'd/o'. This stands for 'son of' and 'daughter of' respectively and is used between a given name and the person's father's name e.g. Sunita d/o Kumar. These days the 's/o' and 'd/o' is dropped although the name pattern remains.

The North Indians tend to use the more Western method of given name plus family name. And the Sikhs all use the surname Singh (for males) and Kaur (females) to denote themselves as Sikhs. When an Indian woman marries, she will cease to use her father's name. Instead, she will very often use her personal name with her husband's name.

The Indian population has a strong belief in family and loyalty to the nation that is shared by the other ethnic groups. At the core of Tamilian values are hospitality and alms, or charity giving. Ancient Tamil legends tell of a king who gave his chariot to a jasmine plant; the moral here is that even if you don't have anything, give the best to others.

Religion

Slightly more than half of the Singaporean Indian population is Tamil Hindu. The remainder is mainly either Christian or Muslim, with a minority of Sikhs, Jains, Zoroastrians and Buddhists.

The Eurasians

Today in Singapore, the term 'Eurasian' is most often used to refer to anyone with mixed European and Asian heritage. But this wasn't always the case. The first Eurasian communities were formed and shaped in the 15th century, lead by Vasco da Gama, and other early European explorers from Portugal, Spain, Netherlands, England and France. Intermarriage with the local women occurred and over time a unique and distinctly European and Asian subculture began to thrive. Eurasians have contributed a great deal to the development of Singapore; one prime example is Dr Benjamin Henry Sheares (1907–1981), who was not only the second president of Singapore, but a renowned obstetrician and the first Chancellor of the National University of Singapore (NUS).

Being that most of the fathers were European men, most Eurasian names are European and give some clue as to where the European ancestor came from, e.g. Cardoza (Portuguese), de Souza (Portuguese), Jansen (Dutch), van Culenburg (Dutch) and Clarke (English). These days, you will see a number of Eurasian-looking Singaporeans with Asian surnames, a testament to the changing trend.

Values and Traditions

Because of their European heritage, many Eurasians are Christians and tend to follow Christian traditions such as baptism for births, church ceremonies for weddings and a wake for funerals.

Not surprisingly, Eurasian dishes are a mix of Portuguese, Dutch, British, Indian, Chinese and Malay food. It is rich food with spicy, strong flavours.

The Peranakans

Also known as the Straits Chinese or Straits-born Chinese, these people pride themselves on their unique culture which has evolved and developed over four centuries.

The word *peranakan* is actually a Malay word that means 'local born' and today is used to denote the descendants of unions between the Chinese men who have settled in the Malay archipelago since the 17th century and the non-Muslim women in this region. Needless to say, these women were not of the same race as Chinese women were not allowed to leave the mainland until the 19th century. The result has been a unique Peranakan culture,

Peranakan men are known as Babas, the young ladies as Nonyas and older Peranakan women are called Bibiks.

different from that of mainland China and yet contaning many Chinese, Malay and colonial elements. It is also no coincidence that the three major centres for Peranakans are in Malacca, Penang and Singapore, the three areas that used to be the Straits Settlement.

The Peranakans even have a language of their own called Baba Malay, which is a mixture of Malay and the Chinese dialect, Hokkien. They were also among the first groups of people in the area to begin learning English and to pick up Western customs which led to strong relationships with the European colonists. As a result, many started steamship companies while others worked in banks and trading houses.

In Singapore, the Peranakan people have dwindled in numbers and it has only been in the last decade or so that there has been a revival of sorts. Part of the problem stemmed from the fact that many more Peranakans were marrying the local Chinese and Singapore's demographics has them categorised as 'Chinese' and not distinctly as Peranakans. An increasing number of Peranakans are also becoming more Westernised and many of the old customs are fading away. Among these are the traditional methods of preparing a number of uniquely Peranakan dishes. While the recipes still exist, many modern Nonyas resort to more convenient methods of preparing food instead of the old ways of preparing everything from scratch. To the Peranakans of old, cooking was a labour of love and taking the time to prepare each stage made all the difference to the taste.

Nonetheless, their colourful ceramics, beadwork and silverware still live on in the region. The East Coast neighbourhood of Katong in Singapore was, and still is. known as the prime Peranakan neighbourhood. Another area that used to house many Peranakans is Emerald Hill, just off Orchard Road. In these two areas you will get to see the typically Peranakan architecture of ornate, tiled shophouses that today play host to offices, restaurants and shops, many of which sell the elaborately worked Peranakan clothing and accessories.

THE SINGAPORE IDENTITY

I guess this depends on who you ask, a Singaporean or an expatriate. Singaporeans are extremely patriotic and proud. All you have to do to notice this patriotism is be in Singapore during July, the month leading up to its National Day on 9 August, when the whole country seems to be in hyper-active mode just practising and making preparations for this big day. Red and white flags hang from just about every HDB flat window. Fighter planes zoom overhead, displaying their military prowess in preparation for the big National Day

Parade (NDP). Singaporeans queue up for hours on end to obtain tickets for the special NDP celebration and show that is simultaneously broadcast on television and radio. The parade is also amazing to watch because the entire audience wears red shirts and waves the red and white Singapore flag. Television snippets, poems, books, contests—any platform to express national pride is fully exploited and relished by all. My personal favourite is the huge Singapore flag flying proudly and displayed for all to see by two small helicopters. It is quite a sight to behold.

What Makes Them Singaporean?

Quotes from the book, *Things That Make Us Singaporean* published by the Executive Committee of the 2003 National Day Parade (NDP).

'Multi-racial, Singlish speaking,
Always for the better seeking.
Studying hard for a degree,
Pay for one and get one free.
Hawker centres and smelly durians,
Those things make us Singaporeans.'
—Vanessa Manap, student, 12

'360 degrees of greenery.'
—Sherry Tan Wanxin, student, 16

'Truthfully, it is our passport
Seriously, it is our taste for delectable food
Generally, 'The Great Singapore Sale'
Honestly, the 'mama' shops
Frankly, it is the PAP winning all the elections.'
—Lay Chee Kian, student, 14

'Singaporeans when travelling have certain traits:
We insist on chillies wherever and whatever we eat.
We go to the most remote corners of the world in search of the perfect meal. We try to calculate the monetary value of everything we see, be it properties, cars or paintings.'
—Richard Eu, CEO

To celebrate racial diversity and to be the best at whatever you can be—it is these qualities so evident on National Day that have also uniquely shaped the Singaporean mindset.

That constant battle to find the proper balance between a cosmopolitan Singapore and the traditional values of the diverse Singaporean people is an issue that has preoccupied the local leaders since the 1990s. Singapore has been famous for its public discussions of social identity, ethnicity, and the proper relation of Singaporeans to worldwide popular culture. Even today, the public debate continues with topics such as Singlish or mother-tongue languages. The country is truly an experiment in the making—can a society remain in touch with its Asian roots but assimilate cosmopolitan and Westernised influences while maintaining a competitive edge in a worldwide arena? If only they had a crystal ball...

But, if we have to resort to stereotypes, however, it would be hard to argue that Singaporeans are not obsessed with food, bargaining and shopping. In fact, the Singaporean cuisine is a great source of national pride and one topic where you will have plenty of feedback and opinions. Everyone has their favourite neighbourhood haunts and hawker stalls, as well as a firm opinion on what makes for a delicious plate of chicken rice and where the best *char kway teow* (a type of fried noodle) can be found. It is no joke when people say that eating is a national pastime.

Shopping is the other national obsession. Just one look around Orchard Road and you can instantly see that it is a favourite hobby, to the extent that they have made a national event out of it. The Great Singapore Sale which runs in the months of June and July is heavily promoted locally and in the region. Tourists and locals will queue, crowd and sift through endless piles of bargains in the numerous shopping malls. Discounts can be substantial during this much-anticipated event and every outlet has some promotion to offer.

Finding the best deal is in the Singaporean blood. A bargain, discount, special price, any little price break will be requested, insisted on and appreciated. But be prepared to not receive such a substantial discount (from a Western point of view) in your transactions at the local market or neighbourhood shop; usually just a dollar or two. Accept the banter as the game and any price break you may receive as a reward.

If you ask Singaporeans to describe themselves as a nation, one word that will probably come up most often would be *kiasu*. Literally translated, this is Hokkien for 'afraid to lose' and typifies the Singaporean trait of hating to lose out and wanting the best. Sometimes this is shortened to 'KS' (ah, the love of acronyms and short forms—another Singaporean trait!) and can also be used to mean *kiasi* (literally, 'afraid to die'), a variation of *kiasu* but meaning much the same thing. If there is a free gift somewhere, the masses are there. All you can eat buffet? You can expect that the Singaporeans have probably starved themselves in advance. It definitely seems like a very fine line between being *kiasu* and being *yeow gwee* or having 'greedy guts'. But I guess that all depends on personal motivation after all! Singaporeans don't want to miss out and they love any kind of offer, discount or savings—of any amount. It always amuses and surprises me that when a petrol station has a few cents discount per litre, you will see a queue around the block trying to get into the action. Is it worth the wait? For me, definitely not. For a Singaporean, getting in on the action is half the fun!

And then there are those drivers who will go to any lengths to stop their Mercedes Benzs or BMWs on the highway just before the time is about to switch over, all in order to avoid paying the ERP (Electronic Road Pricing) toll charge of S$ 1. Rows of cars will be parked on the entrance ramps at 9:29 am, waiting for the ERP to be swtiched off at 9:30 am. *Kiasuism*?

It won't be long after you arrive that you will hear that Singaporeans aim to attain the 4Cs in life. These 4Cs have nothing to do with diamonds; rather they are Cash, Car, Credit card and Condo. Some people would even add a fifth C— Country club membership. And don't forget my favourite, the list of five personal goals: one spouse, two children, a three-bedroom flat, four wheels (car) and a five-figure salary. How straightforward is that? It's hard to not notice that both lists seem to be quite materialistic and money oriented, but let's not forget—Singapore has the second highest living standard in Asia (after Japan) and Singaporeans are accustomed to things that are new, pristine and of good quality.

To counterbalance this outwardly, flashy, expensive exterior, it is true to say that Singaporeans (this goes for all the races) are extremely family- and child-oriented. Children are received almost everywhere with sweets, smiles, cheek-pinching and much attention. A family's life will revolve around the children's school schedule, extra-curricular activities and well-being. Weekends are family time, ranging in everything from outdoor activities or strolling through the shopping malls at 10:00 pm with the children in tow. For a foreigner, this may seem unnecessary and almost unfair to the child who should probably be in bed asleep. However, for a working Singaporean parent, this is family time, squeezed into whatever hours they can manage with their children.

For all their materialism, Singaporeans are also a giving lot as can be seen from the amounts raised everytime a call for donations goes out. And this need not be in money alone. During the 2004–2005 Asian tsunami disaster, Singaporeans came out in full force to help with money, other donations and their personal time and effort. So many people turned up to help at the various collection centres that just as many were turned away for lack of space. No, Singaporeans will definitely not shy away from helping others in need.

SOCIALISING AND FITTING IN

CHAPTER 4

'Do not be concerned about others not appreciating you.
Be concerned about your not appreciating others.'
—Confucius

IT'S ALWAYS A TRICKY THING TO TRY TO EXPLAIN, define and make sense of 'how to fit in' to another culture. Primarily because this depends so much on the individual, his or her experiences, cultural background, tolerance, education, interests, etc. Additionally, 'fitting in' can mean so many different things to so many people—we all have our own threshold. It's human nature to stick to what is familiar and comfortable and Singapore certainly offers endless opportunities to remain in your own little world. But what is the purpose of moving around the world, uprooting yourself and your family to another country if you are not prepared to see, hear, taste and experience what the new culture has to offer? After all, you are not a tourist but someone who actually has the rare chance to participate and to gain first-hand knowledge of another culture and another way of life. Do it at your own pace, on your own time and at your own comfort level, but I urge you to go below the cultural iceberg and really try to experience and understand what makes the local people who they are. You will gain invaluable insight, appreciation and friendships.

Of course, this may all be 'easier said than done' but I find that 'the three Es' will lead you through it—experiment, expand and explore.

- Experiment with the local food—attend the Chinese New Year celebrations, dine at the hawker centres, shop at the wet markets. (More on all this a little later on.)

- Expand your mind by discovering the different religious beliefs, etiquette, traditions and social customs; you may not agree with them but it's their way and it's the right way here.
- Explore the neighbourhoods, the island and the surrounding countries.

Singapore is an open society and people are friendly. If you speak some English, most of the barriers will be down. As the opening quote says, put the focus on others, try to walk in their shoes and understand why they behave and act the way they do; you will only gain from the experience.

SINGAPORE SOCIETY AND CULTURE

To better understand Singaporean culture and behaviour, it is best to break it down into the commonly studied cultural dimensions of a society.

Group Dependence

The concept of group, harmony and mutual security are more important than that of the individual. This is definitely in tune with the Asian way, and being of Chinese, Malay and Indian ethnic backgrounds, this is a trait that is common in all of the Singaporean races.

The cornerstone of this group concept is the family, which is the centre of the social structure and emphasises loyalty, unity and respect. Family generally includes extended family and, in some cases, close friends who are treated as family members. Respect for the elderly and viewing the family as the central pillar of support for the individual is integral to Singapore society.

Face and Respect

This is more the influence of the Chinese culture but one that is key to understanding the Singaporean people.

Face, in the Asian context, has nothing to do with physical appearance and everything to do with personal dignity, not just of the individual but of the social group that means most to that person. As a result, you may find the concept of face coming into play with regards to one's family, school, company and even the nation.

Face is a prized commodity that can be given, lost, taken away or earned. It is inherent in personal qualities such as a solid reputation, good character and being held in esteem by one's peers. It is very much tied up with respect as the more you respect a person, the more likely you will 'give them face'. And this respect need not come about purely because of an individual's character. It could be the respect given because of the hierarchical social structure (*see the next section*). Singaporeans are very sensitive to retaining face in all aspects of their lives and this is what makes them strive for harmonious relationships.

Hierarchy

Despite claiming to be an egalitarian society, strong hierarchical relationships can be observed in the relationship between parents and children, teachers and students, and employers and employees. Seniority and rank are highly respected in Singaporean society and this ties in very closely with the important cultural value of group dependence as well as of face. For the Chinese, this has much to do with Confucianism which emphasises having respect for age and status. For the other races, this is an aspect of their culture that has been handed down through the generations.

Elders are introduced first, are given preferential seating, are given the choicest food and overall, put on a pedestal. The elderly are treated with the utmost respect and courtesy, whether or not you know them personally. One should always address an elder person by their title, surname or as 'Auntie' or 'Uncle'. Mind you, calling someone 'auntie' or 'uncle' doesn't make you related to them but is simply a respectful way of acknowledging someone who is older. This came about because of old Chinese customs where a person would call someone more senior by a term of respect.

Seniority is status. For example, it is interesting to note that Minister Mentor Lee Kuan Yew has a higher protocol rank than the current prime minister.

Those in positions of authority are usually given a measure of respect, even though they may be much younger than other people. While it is quite natural for students to revere their teachers, you will find, by the same token, that some older folks speak in awe-tinged tones about their parliamentary ministers, a result of the respect given because of the latter's position. This is just part of the Singaporean's upbringing. However, this trend seems to be changing as many among the younger generation are becoming more independent in their thinking, perhaps due to the influence of the Internet and television. They may not be outrightly anarchistic; they consider themselves more discerning about who they want to give respect to. All good and well except when it crosses the line to become disrespectful or a threat to the harmonius society everyone else wants to live in. Take for example the law passed in 1996 that compels children to assume the financial responsibility for their elderly parents, should the need arise. This is indicative of not only the high status of the elderly, but also of the challenges facing a small country where the subsequent generations are becoming more individualistic.

In the workplace, employees are deferential to those in more senior positions which might explain why you may not hear grouses or constructive feedback even during face-to-face encounters and the junior staff is encouraged to speak up. Not only is there a fear of repercussion, there is also the mentality that senior management, being at the top of the hierarchy, should know what they are doing.

Monochronic Time Culture

Monochronic time cultures value punctuality and time management. Meetings start on time. Trains and buses run on time. Schedules are important and valued. People are expected to be punctual for meetings, concerts and appointments. Soon after the new arts centre, The Esplanade, opened in 2002, it made headlines because the concert doors were closed promptly at show time and latecomers were expected to wait until the first break before anyone would be allowed in for seating. Discussions ensued but it was final—the doors are shut at show time and now everyone knows and that is the way it will be.

On the other hand, you may encounter that Singaporeans can be very late for informal or casual social situations. Can that be a throwback to the old Chinese village culture of being late to weddings so as to not appear greedy? Perhaps it is the more laid-back attitude of the Malay *kampung*. Or is it just a result of their modern day lives and hectic schedules? Who really knows. It is, however, common courtesy to notify your host or friends of your tardiness and try not to be more than 15 minutes late for appointments.

High Context Culture

A high context culture is one where less verbal interchange is necessary to convey the message—people can be indirect in what they are saying and still convey the meaning. Conversely, in a low context culture, people can be very direct with their words and leave little to the 'unspoken word' to convey the message. It is thereby quite easy to see how someone from a high context culture (such as Asians in general) can be very taken aback with the 'rudeness' and 'forwardness' of the low context communicator (Americans and Europeans in general). This is why foreigners living in Asian countries must learn through their experience with Asians that a 'yes' may be a 'no', and that it is more important to look for non-verbal cues such as the tone of voice, facial expression, vague phrases and avoidance of eye contact.

The above traits may seem daunting to some, but in reality, it doesn't take too much getting used to. The Singaporean people are very accepting, and used to dealing with foreigners. As in life, if you are humble, respectful and friendly, you will always be fine.

Singapore is an interesting place because socially and work-wise, the culture is different. Socially, do not be surprised with indirect communication when it comes to declining requests, making criticisms or even giving personal feedback. It has everything to do with the 'saving face' syndrome. But then, in a work situation, Singaporeans can be much more direct, using objective English and stating facts and figures to support the argument. (*See* Chapter Nine: Work and Business *for more information on business etiquette and working in Singapore.*)

SINGAPORE ETIQUETTE

Despite the many different races and religions, there are three basic etiquette rules that will carry you through most of your daily interactions:

- Use your right hand only for social interaction, eating and exchanging gifts. For the Muslim and Indian community, the left hand is used only for bathroom chores and is considered 'dirty'. All gestures, especially pointing (and, above all, in temples and mosques) should always be made with your right hand and with your knuckle rather than your finger, to be more polite.

- Remove your shoes before entering places of worship (except at churches and synagogues) and all private residences. The collection of shoes near the door will most obviously be an instant reminder and since one is usually in sandals because of the heat, it is not a tedious task to do.

- Give and receive money, credit cards and business cards with two hands. This is a Chinese custom that is done to symbolise how 'precious and valuable' the item you are giving or receiving is. For the Hindus, this is also an important practice, although for different reasons. Hindus believe that one's life force or *prana* is passed along through the hands to the gift. The receiver will also receive with two hands. This is especially important when presenting offerings to a deity.

Overall, Singaporeans are very conservative so use good sense with regards to personal space, language, tone and manners. If you're unsure of what the local etiquette is, it makes good sense to ask a Singaporean friend or colleague what is appropriate. However, if you make a genuine mistake, you'll find people are generally accepting and forgiving based on your lack of familiarity with local practices.

Other General Etiquette and Cultural Tips

- Greetings will follow a strict protocol most often based on both the ethnic origin and age of the person.
- The younger generation or those who are exposed to the West may adopt the concept of shaking hands with everyone, but that is not the case with older or more reserved Singaporeans.
- Ethnic Chinese shake hands. The grasp is rather light but the handshake itself may be more prolonged.
- In general, men and women may shake hands, although the woman must extend her hand first. Introductions are always done in order of age or status.
- Between men, ethnic Malays shake hands and the women use the *salaam* gesture, in which they touch hands and then bring the hand to the chest. Children usually kiss the hands of elders when meeting or when saying goodbye.
- Muslims are not permitted to have physical contact with each other, including shaking hands unless they are related by blood or marriage. It is better to refrain from shaking hands with a Muslim of the opposite sex unless he or she offers his or her hand first. The younger generation of Muslims may be more open to shaking hands but it's best to take the cue from them.
- Ethnic Indians shake hands with members of the same sex.
- When being introduced to someone of the opposite sex, nodding the head and smiling is usually sufficient.
- As with the other groups, the elderly or the person with the most status is introduced first.
- The head is considered sacred by many religions so do not touch.
- Most Singaporeans speak softly so do not scream or raise your voice, if at all possible. Loud talk is a sign of poor manners.
- A smile or laughter may be used to cover anxiety or embarrassment rather than to express amusement.

(Continued on the next page)

Other General Etiquette and Cultural Tips

(Continued from previous page)

- Feet are believed to be unclean, therefore, never move, kick or touch anything with your feet as this is considered rude. When seated, be careful not to cross your legs in such a way that the sole of your shoe is pointed at someone.
- Pointing with the finger is considered bad manners, but using the thumb is acceptable. Or tucking in your thumb and pointing with four fingers is acceptable.
- Beckon with your whole hand, palm down in a swooping motion. Never with palm up and wagging fingers.
- Pounding a clenched fist into an open hand is seen as obscene.
- Gifts are not opened in front of the giver (for all ethnic groups), unless requested by the giver.
- Chinese like things in even numbers, for example, giving two mandarin oranges as a token when you go visiting during the Lunar New Year.
- Some numbers are considered lucky or unlucky because in Chinese, they sound similar to other Chinese words e.g. two (*yi* = easy), six (*lok* = wealth) and eight (*patt* = prosper) are lucky while four (*sei* = death) is very unlucky.
- Taboo gifts for the Chinese are clocks (*song zhong* = sending you to your grave), handkerchiefs (associated with tearful partings) and umbrellas (associated with mishaps).
- For the Chinese, red is an auspicious colour, as are other bright colours such as orange, while black is frowned upon by the older generation, especially during festive occasions. Muslims favour green while Indians like brilliant hues like yellow and purple.
- Muslims do not eat pork or drink alcohol and the meat should be from a *halal* food supplier.
- Hindus do not eat beef and some are strict vegetarians, as are some Buddhists.

To sum up the general etiquette and socialising rules, sage advice would be to engage in food (although do not criticise or joke about their food), travel, sightseeing, family, history or business for general conversation. Pay compliments on appearance, family and accomplishments. Avoid discussing local politics, religion, race or sex. And unless you're just feeling a little mischievous or are among friends, stay away from trying to use too much humour. It never seems to 'translate' too well. But then having said that when they do 'get it', humour can certainly provide one of those great 'cultural delights and exchanges'. Proceed at your own risk! This is good advice for taxi rides and sales people.

NATIONAL SERVICE

One could say that this is the Singaporean passage to manhood. Since 1967, all male citizens aged 18 or older are expected to serve at least two years of full-time national service. They start with three to six months of Basic Military Training (BMT) before being posted to various units within the armed forces. Some will also join the police or the civil defence force. Afterwards, they become reservists, who form 80 per cent of the army. As a reservist, one may be called on at any time, so maintaining one's skills is vital during compulsory in-camp training each year. Every now and again, you will see small print flashing across the top of your television screen on weekends with words such as 'Flying Hippo', 'Lady Bug', 'Electric Eel' and 'Hermit Crab'. This is the open mobilisation exercise, the government's call for the reservists.

SOCIALISING

As in every culture, the three major passages of life—births, weddings and funerals—are steeped in tradition and customs. Entire books have been published on the fascinating and ancient customs of the Chinese, Malay and Indian people. In today's modern society, ethnic practices vary a lot depending on the family's tradition and the influence by elders. Young people of all ethnicities are breaking away from many of the elaborate rituals and celebrations that may seem expensive and impractical in this day and age. Nonetheless, a celebratory feast and symbolic ceremony is still the norm for life's major milestones.

What I've listed below is a practical guide to the ways and beliefs that you will probably encounter in Singapore today. As in every other aspect of life, traditions are being 'tweaked' and adapted to accommodate life's fast pace. Schedules, money constraints, distances and mixed marriages have all lead to new 'customs' and a blend of East and West. It's the classic case of that inevitable dilemma between 'tradition' and 'progress' but with such culturally rich backgrounds, there is still a lot to draw from, learn from and carry forward.

Chinese Customs
Pregnancy

With the Chinese being such a superstitious people, it is not surprising that there are so many customs and beliefs surrounding a pregnant mother and her unborn child. These are primarily meant to protect both mother and child from bad influences that may result in pregnancy and birth problems. Many of these beliefs have to do with the environment and behaviour of the expectant mother. For instance, working with glue or other adhesives may cause birthing complications and hammering nails is thought to cause deformity in the foetus. Restraint in daily life is also expected from the mother—no foul language or the baby may be cursed as a result. Others revolve around what she can or can't eat e.g. drink more soya bean milk to have a fair baby and refrain from coffee or your baby will be very dark. Despite all these restrictions and demands, a pregnant women is still expected and encouraged to continue working, as it is believed to ease labour and delivery.

As you can imagine, most of these beliefs are primarily those of the older generation and in today's modern society, fewer women are as strict about following these customs. However, it is still fascinating to me how many taboos as well as do's and don'ts still exist when it comes to food and 'superstitions' surrounding pregnancy. The younger generation may not be traditional in many ways, but when it comes to a mother's influence and the expectations of carrying a new life, it is better to err on the side of caution and stick to the traditions. After all, it can't hurt!

After childbirth, one tradition that still seems common practice for many modern Singaporean women is some form of 'confinement'. An old Chinese saying is 'confinement well done, your trouble thereafter are none'. Although in today's modern life the practicality of adhering to a strict, traditional confinement period is almost impossible, many Singaporean moms will do whatever they can to take care of themselves within given time, cost and help constraints.

Naming a Child

As mentioned in the previous chapter, the Chinese normally have three parts to their name, provided they don't have a Western name. When it comes to naming a child, parents (or grandparents in some cases) will choose a name that encompasses traits they want the child to have. Some more traditional families go so far as to get a name chosen for the child. This would depend greatly on the elements (fire, water, metal, earth and wood) that are present at the exact time and date of birth. The chosen name, when written in Chinese characters, is supposed to make up for the elements which the child lacks thus giving him or her a better life.

The traditional confinement period is 40 days but can vary from six to eight weeks. If possible, one's own mother helps out in the care, but 'confinement nurses' have become a business unto itself. Excellent help can be hired to make your food and to help care for the infant. The mother's diet, exercise and routine is closely watched so as to ensure a smooth recovery and to avoid further health problems later in life. During this period, the new mother takes special care to keep herself warm, reduce the air in the stomach and take tonics.

Gifts

An appropriate gift for the mother is either a food hamper or other rejuvenating and 'energy' providing nourishment. Flowers are not usually given as they are typically given to sick people or at funerals; although in reality, many young mothers and more Westernised Chinese will certainly not be offended by flowers. Gifts for the baby such as toys, clothes or a small piece of jewellery are also well received. Gold and jade are popular choices for the Chinese as they are considered lucky, as are pink, gold, red and orange colours for clothing and wrapping. Cash gifts should be in even amounts and an even number of bills for good luck.

The big no-no is to use a stork picture or emblem on anything to be given to the woman for the ancient belief is that they symbolise a woman's death. In many countries, the US in particular, the stork is a symbol for childbirth.

Birthdays

In the olden days, back in mainland China, conditions were often so harsh that many babies didn't make it past their first month. Those who did were likely to survive for a while and thus the one-month mark became a cause for celebration. Also, in ancient times, the baby was not supposed to leave the house during the mother's one-month confinement period so, in a sense, this was the child's coming out party.

This tradition carries on in Singapore today. Normally, if the child is a first-born, parents are likely to host a red-egg party. This could be a small gathering at their home with some catered food, or a slightly larger party at a restaurant. It is never good to go empty-handed so guests bring gifts, usually red envelopes with money for baby boys and expensive jewellery or clothes for baby girls. In return, the parents hand out red-dyed eggs, which symbolise happiness and the renewal of life.

Some parents dispense with the party and give out cakes and red eggs to relatives and close friends. Usually, an odd number of eggs will be given if it is a boy and an even number if it is a girl.

For school age children, I find it is most often one of two extremes. Either the child's birthday is not a major celebration (usually just a family affair) or it is a big celebration with many children, lots of food and entertainment. Gifts are never opened during the party; they are set aside and opened in private so as to not show greed. Even for children.

You may also find that some Asians, on their young child's birthday, will give their child's friends and acquaintances a small gift, even if there was no birthday party. It is not necessary to reciprocate with a gift, rather acknowledge and express your good wishes for the child and his or her family.

Previously, the ancient Chinese only celebrated their first month and then when they turned 60. Nowadays, people celebrate their birthdays annually and this celebration could just be a dinner at a fancy restaurant. Some of the older folks also commemorate certain landmark birthdays such as 61, 71 and 81 with a huge celebration with relatives and friends. On one's birthday, it is common to eat specially prepared dishes like longevity noodles, which represent long life. As a present, most people tend to give money these days but some may choose to give something that promotes good health such as an expensive tonic.

Weddings

In Chinese culture, like in most Asian cultures, a wedding is not just a love pairing between two people but the beginning of a relationship between two families as well. The extent of parental involvement and the degree of observance of traditional customs and superstitions varies a lot in today's society but two important elements of Chinese culture are still quite visible when it comes to marriage, and even more so when the marriage is that of the eldest son—the need to avoid embarrassment (saving face) and to conspicuously display wealth and prosperity. Failure to provide a lavish wedding could lower the status of the family, bring shame upon them and encourage criticism from relatives.

Today, a Singaporean Chinese bride will most probably wear a white wedding gown (although some might also wear the Chinese *kwa*), have her hair and make-up done by professionals, have an elaborate tiered wedding cake, hire and decorate a Mercedes Benz or other fancy car to take her to the banquet and pose for professional photographers in various picturesque settings around town. The groom wears a Western-style tuxedo or suit. Yet, despite these Western influences, many couples still participate in the traditional tea ceremony. In ancient times, it was the tea ceremony that formalised the marriage as this was the first time both groom and bride would be formally introduced to the members of each other's family and be accepted by them. To some extent, this hold true today. The tea ceremony is usually held at the groom's house first and still plays an important role in initiating the couple into the family and establishing their position within it. The ceremony is attended only by family members, but this also means the extended family so aunts, uncles and cousins are all present. Tea is served in order of age and 'rank' within the family so it begins with great-grandparents (if any are still around) and moves onto to grandparents, parents then uncles and aunts in order of rank (i.e. the oldest to the youngest). Then comes the cousins or immediate siblings, depending on who is the most senior according to the previous generation. It all sounds really complicated but there is usually someone there who has all this mapped out and will indicate who should go next.

As a sign of respect, the newly-weds will kneel to serve their relatives tea. (In some families, kneeling is not required when serving tea to those of the same generation.) After each one has been served, the couple is given a *hong bao* (red packet) which can contain money or jewellery. Also the immediate younger siblings of the groom will serve the happy couple tea and receive a *hong bao* from them. The couple then pays a visit to the bride's home to perform the tea ceremony there.

In the evening, there is usually a banquet for extended family, friends and work acquaintances. Many of these lavish banquets are held in hotels and ballrooms to accommodate the large numbers. The newly-weds will go around from table to table and have a drink and toast with their guests, often exclaiming 'Y-A-M-S-E-N-G!' (something akin to 'bottoms up!'). Although there may be live music, dancing is usually not done at Chinese weddings. The eating and drinking are the entertainment.

In recent years, a variation of the traditional Chinese wedding banquet is the wedding buffet. A buffet not only presents a cost savings but also allows for more time for additional entertainment such as karaoke or performers after the meal. At a wedding banquet, guests typically leave soon after the meal as a symbol that they are satisfied. All the festivities occur during the meal with the banquet. The buffet, on the other hand, requires guests to stay on for the entertainment. It is customary to give money (an even number) in auspicious red *hong bao* packets.

Funerals

'Be filial to your elders when they are alive and mourn their passing when they die' is a Confucian teaching on filial piety. And a decent funeral is considered one of the most important acts of filial piety to one's parents and elders. The funeral wake usually lasts anything from three to seven days so that many friends and relatives may attend the wake. This is usually held at home, in the void deck of an HDB complex (the large, empty space below on the ground level of all blocks), or in funeral parlours. The immediate family will normally be dressed in

The wake area usually contains a number of tables and chairs for the many visitors the bereaved hope will come. The more traditional Chinese will have huge lanterns hanging from the ceiling near the corner to tell people who has passed away. This will normally tell you the name, whether the deceased is a male or female and his or her 'age'—the real age plus an additional three years, one each for earth, heaven and man.

If space is available, families will erect tents in the open space for the funeral. Most, however, opt to use the void deck (pictured above), the open area at the bottom of HDB blocks. The void deck is also the venue of other festivities such as Muslim weddings.

funeral clothes, usually in black, brown or blue tones. The colour, as well as the piece of cloth pinned to their upper arm will indicate their relationship to the deceased.

Visitors are welcomed throughout the day but most will turn up in the evening to pay their last respects and offer sympathy. As a sign of respect, the visitor should stand at the foot of the coffin and bow three times towards it while a family member kneels and burns incense paper quietly beside the coffin. One does not kneel to bow at the coffin unless one is a close friend. Joss paper and prayer money (to provide the deceased with sufficient income in the afterlife) are burned continuously throughout the wake.

Even though Chinese funerals are essentially quite similar, the various rituals such as burning of joss sticks etc. would depend on what religion the person was. As more Chinese are now becoming Christians, some funeral rites have become more Western so instead of joss paper, you may get candles.

You will be offered refreshments which sometimes takes the form of a full meal. Polite conversation and a kind comment on how peaceful the deceased looks is a thoughtful gesture. Visitors should dress in sombre colours such as white or solid darks. Red, pink and gold should be avoided as they are considered happy colours. You should not shake hands with the deceased's family members or say good bye to them. The Chinese believe it is good luck to have many people at a funeral. The bereaved family distributes red threads to all visitors to wish them a safe journey home as this is meant to ward off any bad luck associated with death. Discard the threads once you arrive home. Usually this is placed on the gate, door or window and allowed to blow away naturally. At some wakes, red folded packets containing a coin are also given. Traditionally, the coin is used to buy a sweet, also meant to dissociate you from the dead and to ward off any bad luck. These days, sweets are placed on a table for visitors and you are advised to take one or two before you leave.

In order to help cover the expense of a funeral, it is common practice to give a gift of money to the family, usually placed in an envelope. The envelope should be white or brown and given to the person in charge of gifts or to one of the bereaved. For deaths, money is usually given in odd amounts (and odd number of bills) to symbolise the separation of the loved one. It is not uncommon for wealthier families to request a donation to a charitable organisation in lieu of receiving money. Flowers and wreaths are appropriate to send to a funeral. Some will also send a blanket with condolence messages and this is usually hung up at the wake.

Prayers are often said at funeral wakes but the major ones may not take place every night. The type of prayers would depend on which religion the person believes in. For Buddhists and Taoists, a priest is usually engaged to chant prayers if not on all nights (especially if is it is a short wake) then on the night before the actual funeral. Christians normally have church groups come over for prayers as well, sometimes with a religious leader present.

On the day of the funeral, the deceased's immediate family will follow the hearse for a short way before getting onto the bus or van that will transport them to the crematorium or cemetary. You are welcome to join them but it is advisable to hang back and quietly follow what others are doing. At all times, be respectful.

> If you happen to have a funeral in the immediate neighbourhood you live in, try to find out discreetly the time the coffin will be leaving for the crematorium or cemetary. This is because the Chinese believe that you should not be 'coming in' when the coffin is 'going out' and if this occurs at the same time, there is a 'clash'. Whether you believe in this or not, just err on the side of caution.

Another ritual that is common to Chinese funerals is the burning of paper 'property' such as a house, a car, a mobile phone and money. In this manner, the deceased will receive the items in the netherworld and will not be in need of the basic items to survive. This is normally done about a week after the funeral but many families now choose to do this even before the body is cremated or buried.

Most Chinese families will go into mourning for a period of time—anything from one month to one year, depending on what the individual families prefer. During this time, the family members will use more sombre colours in their everyday wear and pin a small square piece of cloth to their sleeve as a sign of respect.

Malay Customs
Pregnancy and Births

Through trade which started way back in 100 BC, Hinduism spread to Malaya and left an influence on the Malayan culture which still exists today in arts, language and rituals. Many of these ancient practices are evident in the customs associated with pregnancy. One of these is the ritual of *lenggang perut* (literally, 'swinging the stomach'), which takes place when the woman is seven or eight months pregnant. She is first bathed in flowers (meant to ward off bad spirits and negative energy) before lying down on seven sarongs (each about 7 ft long), placed one on top of another. The midwife will then take both ends of the sarong and gently swings the cloth, with the woman on it, once or twice before pulling the sarong from under her. This swinging motion is repeated six more times. With the final sarong, the midwife wraps the mother's abdomen to help position the baby for his or her entry into this world.

Commonly associated with any good and happy news in a person's life such as being pregnant, having the baby or celebrating a birthday is the leaf-wrapped, yellow glutinous rice packages known as *nasi kunyit*. Like a Malay friend says, "Many times if a woman doesn't want to announce that she is pregnant but is happy about the occasion, she may just pass these little rice parcels out to family, friends and collegues. Nothing needs to be said directly but others can 'knowingly' share and delight in her happiness."

Most women in Singapore would have heard of this practice but it is a ritual that is slowly fading out. However, there are small pockets of ladies, especially at the request of an older matriarch, who will still take part in this ritual, especially if they are having their first child. Those who don't sometimes opt to have a *doa selamat*, a small gathering of family members where they feast and say prayers for the health of the mother and the safe delivery of the child.

After childbirth, many modern Malay women, like their Chinese counterparts, will abide by whatever degree possible to the confinement diet and routine. A special diet to help eliminate 'wind' in the body, having post-natal massages which include having the abdominal area wrapped tightly in cloth to help the body return to its normal state and restricting the amount of activity for the new mother is all common practice and believed to aid in her smooth recovery and healthy future.

When the child is born, Malay tradition dictates that after the baby's first bath, the father must whisper into the infant's ear, *azan* (call for payers) in the right ear and *iqamat* (the recitation before the start of prayers) into the left ear. This is to protect the child and declare that the baby is a Muslim. Something sweet, such as honey, is then rubbed onto the roof of the mouth of the newborn to ensure that all the words he or she speaks will be 'sweet'. A ritual shaving of the child's hair, or at least cutting a few strands, is done a week or a month later depending on convenience, after which a feast is held for family and friends. As a rite of passage, Malay boys are still circumcised at or before puberty (normally when they are five or six years old) though circumcision is now quite commonly done while the child is still a baby.

Another ancient practice in the Prophet's tradition is the Aqiqah. In ancient *kampung* days, this meant having a feast seven days after the birth of the child. Two goats or sheep were sacrificed for a boy. For a girl, just one animal is sacrificed. Today, the sacrifice may be done in Singapore but some families arrange for money to be sent to their families or friends in Malaysia or Indonesia so that an Aqiqah can still be held in honour of their child. It is considered good luck and abides by the Malay belief of alms giving. However, this rite is not compulsory and only those who are financially able will arrange for it.

Weddings

Malay weddings are resplendent with music, bright colours and much festivity. The celebration normally lasts for two days. The first day is the private family ceremony and the second a large public one.

It is common practice that the couple does not live together until after the *bersanding* (sitting on a decorated dais as 'king

This Malay bridal couple pose on the *pelamin* (raised platform) during the *bersanding* ceremony. The bride is usually elaborately made up (notice the henna on her hands) and may have a few changes of costumes.

and queen'). The ceremony begins with a group of percussion musicians, *kumpulan hadrah*, who announce the arrival of the groom at the bride's home. Accompanied by *bunga manggar* (thin bamboo sticks with colourful and shiny paper strips to resemble a mango blossom) carriers, friends and relatives, the groom leads the procession. There will be a charade and game of 'bribing' the bride's relatives before they will allow him to see the bride. An entire room of an apartment or the void deck will be completely and elaborately decorated and done up so the *pelamin* or raised platform where the 'king and queen' will sit can be easily seen by the guests. Petals and rice, both fertility symbols are sprinkled on them by family and friends.

Everyone then takes part in a *kenduri*, or celebratory feast. It is considered polite to arrive on time, to dress modestly and to stay long enough to eat, chat and greet the parents and wedding party. A Malay wedding is usually a more casual affair than Western-style weddings and the Malay people are so hospitable that even bringing along a companion or guests is not considered inappropriate. When you arrive, greet the couple's parents with a *salaam* and do the same with the newly-weds. The appropriate gift is money in a card or envelope and the amount depends on your relationship with the recipient. An acquaintance is not expected to give money but a small household gift is usually well received. As part of the wedding buffet, *nasi minyak*—rice cooked with ghee, milk or yoghurt, onions and garlic—is commonly served but now it is also common for guests to have a choice of white rice, as people have become more health conscious. Also, guests traditionally receive wrapped and decorated eggs as a symbol of fertility although cakes, chocolates or other small gifts are also commonly given today.

While the highlight of the wedding is the *bersanding* ceremony, the *akad nikah* or marriage solemnisation by a religious official (*kadi*) is what joins the couple as man and wife and makes the marriage valid. The other practices, including the *bersanding*, are secondary to the *akad nikah* which can be performed before the day of *bersanding* to allow the couple some breathing space on this very hectic day.

Funerals

Islamic religious beliefs do not allow for cremation as Muslims believe the body should remain intact and not be changed or harmed in any way. Although death is seen as the separation of body and soul so that the soul may move onto the next stage of existence, it is still treated as a sad and solemn occasion. Wailing, prolonged weeping or screaming are forbidden though crying is allowed.

Muslims are buried as quickly as possible after death, usually within 24 hours. The body is cleaned by close relatives of the same gender as the deceased, sometimes with the help of a Muslim undertaker who is familiar with the proper procedures and necessary prayers. The body is then wrapped in three to five pieces of unsewn white cloth from head to toe and positioned so that the head faces Mecca. Camphor, powdered sandalwood and perfume are applied to the body since the body is not embalmed. During the burial, the body is not placed in a coffin; rather it is placed on its right side

directly on the earth. The shroud covering the head is slightly loosened so the deceased's cheek touches the earth while facing the direction of Mecca.

Relatives of the deceased inform others, attend the funeral and the burial itself. It is appropriate to wear white or other sombre colours to a Muslim funeral. Non-Muslims can attend the funeral of Muslims, and can visit the house even after the burial to offer condolences. The most important thing to remember is that a Muslim funeral is always a simple and subdued event. One pays respect by standing quietly, bowing the head and making a silent prayer. Flowers can be sent to the home, although wreaths are not customary. Depending on the relationship, money can be given to the family. It should be given in a white envelope and presented to the chief mourners. The amount depends again on the relationship; about S$ 10–20 is average. Sometimes the family might organise prayers and the recitation of the Qur'an to pray for blessings for the deceased but this is not compulsory.

After the funeral, the family will gather on the third, seventh, 40th and 100th day after for the *kenduri arwah* (prayers for the soul of the deceased). Thereafter, prayers will be offered on each death anniversary.

Indian Customs

Since the 19th century when immigrants began coming to Singapore, the largest Indian group has been the Tamils from South India. Others included the Tamils and Sinhalese from Sri Lanka, the Punjabis and Sikhs from North India, the Bengalis from Bengal and the Pakistanis. Rich in culture traditions and customs, the Singaporean Indians have continued with their ancient rituals, especially with regard to births, weddings and funerals.

The small Indian community (7.9 per cent) is difficult to generalise or categorise due to its vast regional and religious mix. The majority of Singaporean Indians are Hindus (55.4 per cent) with the other larger groups being Muslims at 25.6 per cent and Christians at 12.1 per cent. The Indian Muslims tend to follow very similar customs as the Malay Muslims and the Christians those of the Christian faith. The following traditions and rituals will focus on the Hindu faith.

Hinduism

Like the Islamic religion, Hinduism is more than just a religion but also a philosophy and way of life. Strictly speaking, Hindus believe in a supreme power that has no form, colour or name. All representations of God symbolically represent one central power—Brahma. Brahman is the creator, Vishnu (Krishna) is the one who preserves the world through his many incarnations and Shiva is the god who will destroy the world that will eventually be rebuilt by Brahma. These three gods are the Hindu Holy Trinity. All the 330 million Indian gods are merely different aspects of Brahma.

One chief Hindu belief is that of reincarnation. Hinduism teaches that everyone has a soul (*atma*) which, based on its conduct, is connected to the greater being Brahma, and this soul enters the body at birth and leaves at death. The cycle of birth, life, death and rebirth is known as *samsara*. This cycle continues uninterrupted until the soul reaches a state of enlightment called *moksha*. Consequently, every Hindu is encouraged to think good thoughts and do good acts and devotions from the time of birth so that his or her soul may attain *moksha*. Conversely, the more sins one commits, the more one's soul will seek a lowly physical being such as a cockroach. *Karma*, or the accumulated sum of one's good and bad deeds, decides the kind of birth cycles one is going to have in the next life—one is paying for one's past deeds and establishing what one will be in one's next or future incarnation.

Pregnancy and Births

Even before the baby is born, rituals are performed to help ensure a healthy baby and mother. Charms may be worn to help ward off the evil eye. In the third month of pregnancy, the Punsavana (foetus protection) ceremony may be performed to make sure the baby grows up strong. Then the Simantonnyana may be performed during the seventh month. This is like a baby shower, and prayers, blessings and gifts are presented to the mother-to be.

After birth, a priest traditionally selects the first letter of the baby's name and on the 28th day (a lunar month), the child's head is shaved to give thanks and remove impurities. It is also common practice for baby girls to have their ears pierced at this time. In Singapore, one has two weeks to register a birth and child's name, so the more traditional families may wait 28 days before calling their child by his or her registered name. It is only polite to bring a gift for the child and this could be gold or silver jewellery, a cup or rattle for the baby. Clothes or toys are also appropriate.

Weddings

Indian weddings have gained worldwide attention with recent movies such as *Monsoon Wedding* and *Bride and Prejudice*. And having had an Indian wedding myself, I must add that what you have seen and heard is probably right. Weddings in the Indian culture are between the two families and much importance is placed on the sacredness of matrimonial life. The younger generation may have their disagreements with their more traditional parents and relatives; however, a traditional Indian wedding is probably something most children wouldn't deny their parents. For one thing, they are too much fun!

Traditionally, arranged marriages, marrying quite young, dowries and extended family living were all the norm. Today, due to modern ways, many of these customs are not practised in Singapore. The emphasis is more on true love between the newly-weds.

The actual wedding ceremonies vary a lot depending on the family's religion and ethnic origins; however, they all seem to have similar overall symbolic Indian rituals. The bride is made beautiful and calmed of any nervousness by bathing her feet in milk, having a bath in special cooling oils, cleansing her skin with ground pulses, and having her hands and feet painted with elaborate henna designs.

Then there is usually some kind of fertility ceremony to ensure offspring and a healthy life for the couple. This may involve planting a tree and various other types of rituals involving spices, sugar, seedlings or cereals.

For the marriage ceremony or *vivaha*, the bridegroom arrives in a procession accompanied by music and dance. The father usually gives his daughter's hand in marriage to the bridegroom, called Kanyadan, symbolically renouncing rights over his daughter. The wedding party (bride, groom, immediate family and the priest) is all seated around a holy fire. The fire represents Agni, the God of Fire, the mightiest power in the cosmos. Offerings are made to the fire while the ceremony is being conducted. Next, the mark of marriage is tied around the bride's neck by the groom. The chain with a gold pendant is known either as the *mangalsutra* in the north or the *thali* in the south. The gold pendant is tied to a yellow rope, dyed yellow using saffron or turmeric and the groom knots the rope three times (to represent mind, spirit and body). The tying of the *thali* is done at a predetermined auspicious time, and loud, fast music is played so as to muffle any inauspicious sounds at that critical moment. After the tying of the *thali*, all guests convey their good wishes by sprinkling yellow rice and/or flower petals on the couple.

Gifts of money (always in odd numbers e.g. S$ 51, S$ 101 or S$ 251) or jewellery can be given at this time.

Attire for an Indian wedding will be traditional and colourful so if you are invited to attend a wedding, bright festive colours and conservative clothing (nothing too short or revealing) are appropriate.

Funerals

For Hindus, the funeral ceremony is usually held at home, with a *pundit* (Hindu scholar) and the eldest son of the family performing the funeral rites of his parents. The body of the departed is given a bath and dressed in fresh clothes. Some sandalwood paste is applied to the corpse and decorated with flowers and garlands. Purificatory chants and rituals will be performed and the body is placed facing either north or south. Friends and relatives gather to see the deceased and to pay homage. Hindus cremate the body, although children are buried rather than cremated. Usually, the body is cremated on the same day at a crematorium and the ashes immersed in a holy river or the sea.

At a Hindu funeral, after the prayers and rituals, the widow or widower will stand to one side so visitors and family can pay their respects to her or him and then to the body. When paying respect to the body, bow your head and say a silent prayer. After paying your respects, visitors are free to leave.

It is customary to send flowers or flower wreaths to the family. Gifts and money are not given. Wear sombre colours such as white, black, grey; avoid bright cheerful colours and prints.

Other Hindu Rituals

- Domestic worship
  The home is the place where most Hindus conduct their worship and religious rituals. All Hindu homes will have a special place or room reserved for worship. The most important and auspicious times for these rituals are dawn and dusk. After a bath, there is personal worship of the gods at the family altar, lighting of a lamp and offering

foodstuffs and flowers before the images and idols of the gods.

- Temple worship
Hindu temples are dedicated to a deity or several deities who are believed to preside over the temple. Rituals at temples fall into one of three categories: those performed daily (*nitya*); those performed on specific occasions (*naimittika*) and those performed voluntarily (*kamya*). Hindus visit temples to worship the temple deity or to worship another deities of their choosing by means of these three types of rituals.

Non-Hindus are allowed to enter and visit a temple; however there are a few etiquette tips to keep in mind.

- Always remove your shoes. Footwear is considered impure.
- Menstruating women should not enter a temple.
- Indians step over the threshold, never on it.
- Worshippers will always bathe before entering a temple. Upon arrival, they will again wash their feet, face and eyes. As a visitor, you should wash your feet as a sign of respect. There are sinks in the courtyard for this purpose.
- Do not touch any statues or pictures inside the temple.
- Do not speak in a loud voice.
- The small shrines or Sanctum Sanctorums are small rooms with a screen or gate at the entrance. The screen is removed before daily worship and only priests are allowed to enter these shrines.
- Show respect by dressing modestly. Cover your legs and remove hats.
- Ask before taking any photographs.
- If you sit, never stretch your legs out in front of a shrine, altar and temple, or even toward another person. This is considered disrespectful.

'I cannot deny it. My urban working-class upbringing has left me totally unprepared for the trials and tribulations of living in a tropical Asian country and it is wonderful. Every incident in Singapore is a brand new experience that I am wholly unequipped for. And the best part is, I know another one will come along tomorrow.'
—Neil Humphreys, *Notes From an Even Smaller Island*

As THE AUTHOR, NEIL HUMPHREYS SAYS IN THE OPENING QUOTE, it is the pure joy of experiencing something new, refreshing, unexpected that makes living in Singapore such a unique experience. But in order to start enjoying the little 'delights' of everyday life, you must first settle in well. Your first encounters and dealings with the local system and people can greatly influence your future expectations. Hopefully, some helpful background will ease the learning process and assist you in establishing your new home, the sooner the better.

Singaporeans want you to feel at home. Recognising that people are Singapore's greatest resource in maintaining its economic strength and success, the country is very open to receiving foreign professionals, entrepreneurs, skilled workers, graduates and anyone who can contribute to the country's social and economic success. Singapore's open immigration policy makes it possible for businesses to bring in employees in less than two weeks.

FORMALITIES

Singapore offers four different types of visas to enter the country:

- General visit visas
- Employment pass/dependant's pass
- Student pass
- Work permit

General Visit Visas

Typically provided to tourists, families and friends, these visas allow visitors to stay for durations ranging from a few days to a few months. There are three sub-categories of general visit visas:

- Social Visit Pass

  You will need a Social Visit Pass for short stays in Singapore, to attend job interviews and business negotiations. You may not, however, work in the country. The pass has an initial validity period of between two and four weeks and it may be subsequently renewed for up to three months.
- Long-term Social Visit Pass
- Dependant's Pass

Visa Required

Visitors from the following countries will require a visa to enter Singapore

- Assessment Level I countries

  Commonwealth of Independent States (Armenia, Azerbaijan, Belarus, Georgia, Kazakhstan, Kyrgyzstan, Moldova, Russia, Tajikistan, Turkmenistan, Ukraine, Uzbekistan), India, Myanmar, People's Republic of China and holders of Hong Kong Document of Identity and Macao Special Administrative Region (MSAR) Travel Permit.
- Assessment Level II Countries

  Afghanistan, Algeria, Bangladesh, Egypt, Iran, Iraq, Jordan, Lebanon, Libya, Pakistan, Saudi Arabia, Somalia, Sudan, Syria, Tunisia, Yemen, and holders of Palestinian Authority Passport, Temporary Passport issued by the United Arab Emirates (UAE) and Refugee Travel Document issued by Middle East countries.

Employment Passes

In order to work in Singapore, you need an Employment Pass (EP). To apply, you need a local sponsor, most likely your employer, who will probably be applying for the EP for you. The two types of EPs issued to foreigners depend on the qualifications of the applicant.

- P Pass

  Foreigners are eligible to apply for a P Pass if they hold acceptable tertiary, professional, technical qualifications and are seeking professional, administrative, executive or managerial jobs. They can also be entrepreneurs or investors. Successful applicants who earn a basic monthly salary of more than S$ 7,000 will be issued a P1 Pass. while those who earn between S$ 3,501–7, 000 will be issued a P2 Pass.

- Q1 Pass

  This is issued to foreigners whose basic monthly salary is more than S$ 2,500 and who possess degrees, professional qualifications or specialist skills.

An EP holder may apply for Dependant's Passes for his wife and unmarried children under 21 years old. Application of Dependant's Pass (i.e. Form 12) should be made with the EP application to avoid delay in processing.

Application Procedures

A local sponsor (i.e. a Singapore-registered corporation), normally the applicant's employer, is required for the EP application. The normal processing time is about two to three weeks upon receipt of application form by the department, depending on whether this is done electronically or in person. If the application is successful, the fee for an EP is S$ 30 per year. Should the applicant be from a country where a visa is required to enter Singapore, he or she can apply for a Multiple Journey Visa which is S$ 20 per issue.

You will need to produce the following document when filing an application:

- Two copies of the duly completed Form 8 per applicant. The forms must be signed by both the applicant and an authorised officer from the sponsoring corporation. The forms should also be endorsed with the corporation's stamp or seal.
- One copy of the applicant's travel documents especially the page showing the person's particulars.
- One recent photograph (passport size and taken within the last three months) of the applicant.

- One copy each of all the applicant's qualification papers and past employment testimonials (e.g. college degrees, certification, awards, etc.).
- Those setting up professional practices here must furnish one copy of the sponsorship letter from a well-established local corporation stating its responsibility for the maintenance and repatriation of each applicant. Otherwise, a banker's guarantee of S$ 3,000 per applicant is required.
- If the applicant is a regional representative, there must be one copy of the letter from the International Enterprise (IE) Singapore giving approval for the setting up of the Representative Office, and a letter from the Representative Office's headquarters stating the purpose of the application, the duration of the applicant's assignment, and an undertaking of the maintenance and repatriation of the applicant.
- Applicants for nursing, medical, teaching and legal positions must submit a certificate of registration or relevant with the respective professional bodies or accreditation agencies:
  - Nursing   Singapore Nursing Board
  - Doctor   Singapore Medical Council/Traditional Chinese Medicine Practitioners Board
  - Teacher   Singapore Ministry of Education
  - Lawyer   Singapore Attorney General's Chambers
  - Dentist   Singapore Dental Council
- Companies/businesses registered with the Accounting and Corporate Regulatory Authority (ACRA) must produce the business profile/instant information from ACRA.
- Companies/businesses not registered with ACRA must produce registration papers from their respective professional bodies.

The fee for the issue of Dependant Pass is S$ 30 per year and those who wish to apply for this must submit the following:

- Two copies of duly completed Form 12 (one original and one photocopy or both original) and signed by the applicant. Children travelling on their own passports must submit separate Form 12s each. Parents can sign on behalf of their children if the latter are below 12 years old.

- A copy of the official marriage certificate.
- A copy each of the official birth certificates of children showing both the parents' names and the child's name.
- Court papers on the custody of the children (if applicable).
- Two recent photographs (passport size and taken within the last three months) of the applicant. Photographs are not required for children below 12 years old.

Work Passes

Since 1 July 2004, the S Pass has replaced the Q2 pass and is considered a work pass, not an EP or work permit. This was introduced to help employers fill the gap between the two. This pass is for foreigners with a minimum income of S$ 1,800. Applicants for this pass will be assessed based on a points system. The areas taken into consideration include salary, educational qualifications, work experience, skills and job type. Employers must pay a monthly levy of S$ 50 per S Pass holder and each company has a 5 per cent cap on the number of S Pass holders it can hire, depending on the number of local workers and work permit holders it already has.

S Pass applications can be done in person or online and will take between two to three weeks to process. Companies applying for the new S Pass holders or renewing Q2 Pass for holders must have accounts with the Central Provident Fund (CPF) Board. This is to facilitate the monitoring of the S Pass quota in the company as well as the collection of levy. Companies should attach their CPF contribution statements for the last three months.

Cancellation

Once foreign employees cease employment with the company, their pass is considered cancelled and all physical passes (EP, Dependent's and S) must be surrendered within seven days from the date they stop working for the company. It should be noted that it is an offence if this is not complied with. Once the pass is cancelled, a social visit pass is issued to allow foreigners to stay in the country for two weeks. If there is a change of employment (i.e. change of designation, duties or employer) a new application is required.

The following documents are required for the offical cancellation of passes:

- Letter from the employer stating the reasons for the cancellation of the pass.
- The pass holder's valid travel document and the Disembarkment/Embarkation Card (Green Card) or S Pass Card/Notification letter for the worker to report to Work Pass Services Centre.
- Immigration White Card (IMM27).

Work Permits

Foreigners who intend to work in Singapore and who are earning a basic monthly salary of S$ 1,800 or below are required to apply for a Work Permit with the Ministry of Manpower (MOM). All prospective employers must apply for a Work Permit before employing a foreigner. Application forms are available at the Work Permit Department at 18 Havelock Road [tel: (65) 6438-5122] or online at:

http://www.mom.gov.sg

A non-Malaysian worker must not be in Singapore before In-Principle Approval (IPA) is granted and a security bond is submitted to the department by the employer. The security bond is S$ 5,000 per worker which may be in the form of a banker's guarantee, insurance guarantee, cheque or cash. This bond requires employers to repatriate the foreign workers after their work permits are cancelled. Failure to do so will result in the deposit being forfeited. This rule also applies to domestic helpers from Philippines, Sri Lanka and Indonesia.

EntrePass

This is an employment pass for foreigners who wish to start new businesses or companies in Singapore, and requires that they be actively involved in the operation of this company or business. However, if a foreigner is a shareholder or partner in a Singapore-registered enterprise but is not previously active in the operation of this enterprise, he or she may also apply for an EntrePass should he or she decide to be actively involved in the operation of this enterprise.

The EntrePass has an initial duration of two years. It allows you to leave and re-enter Singapore for either business or leisure throughout its validity period. Applicants may also apply to bring their immediate family to live in Singapore during the duration of the EntrePass.

The documents needed for an EntprePass application are as follows:

- EntrePass Application form.
- Comprehensive business plan. This is particularly important for first-time applicants as your success in obtaining an EntrePass is dependent on the credibility of the proposed plan.
- Information on relevant skills, work experience, and track record of your previous business ventures.
- A recent passport-sized photograph of the applicant taken within the last three months.
- Statutory health declaration.
- All EntrePass applications must be sponsored by a Singapore registered company or state that a banker's guarantee of S$ 3,000 will be furnished if the application is approved. The banker's guarantee has to be furnished when the successful applicant collects the pass. The same requirement applies to each application to bring in a family member.
- You may apply for Dependant's Passes for your spouse and children below 21 years old. It is advisable to submit the Dependant's Pass applications together with that for the EntrePass.
- For married applicants, please submit a copy each of the official marriage certificate if the spouse is a Singapore Citizen, Singapore Permanent Resident or an EP holder.

Application forms and details of the application can be found from the MOM, Employment Pass Department or you can visit the MOM website listed on the previous page.

Student Passes

If you intend to study in Singapore for a long period of time or pursue full-time studies in Singapore, you will need to apply for a Student's Pass. This is usually done after you have been accepted by an institution of learning. You can apply for a Student's Pass if the institution is one of the following:

- Registered with the Ministry of Education (MOE).
- Not registered with the MOE but has obtained permission from the commissioner, Immigration and Checkpoints Authority (ICA) to accept foreign students.
- Licensed by the Ministry of Community Development, Youth and Sports (MCYS) to operate as a childcare centre.

There are some exceptions. You may not need to apply for Student's Pass if you are a:

- Dependant's Pass holder studying in an educational institution registered by the MOE or a childcare centre licensed by MCYS.
- Immigration Exemption Order holder.

In addition to this, you need not apply for a Student's Pass if you are in Singapore on a short-term Social Vist Pass and wish to attend a short course that can be completed either within 30 days or during the validity of your pass. It must, however, satisfy two other criteria:

- The course must be a complete and stand-alone module of its own. Courses with multiple modules are excluded from this Student's Pass exemption scheme.
- The course must not involve hands-on practical occupational training and/or industrial attachments where students have to interact with walk-in customers or which are conducted at premises that are also places of business, e.g. hair and beauty salons.

Foreign students who wish to seek admission to any MOE-registered educational institutions are to approach the school of choice directly. Admission is subject to availability of vacancies in that school.

Students who are offered admission to Institutes of Higher Learning (IHLs) in Singapore can apply for their Student Pass online via the Student's Pass Online Application System (SOLAR system). These IHLs refer to local polytechnics and universities, as well as foreign universities with offshore campuses in Singapore. They include:

- National University of Singapore
- Nanyang Technological University
- Singapore Management University
- INSEAD (Singapore)
- University of Chicago Graduate School of Business (Singapore)
- Ngee Ann Polytechnic
- Nanyang Polytechnic
- Singapore Polytechnic
- Temasek Polytechnic
- Republic Polytechnic.

Foreigners pursuing courses at other educational institutes not mentioned above will have to submit their application through the traditional method until online facilities are extended to other educational institutes. To find out more information and keep track of new developments, check out the ICA visitor's portal at:

http://app.ica.gov.sg/serv_visitor/index.asp

Alternatively, you can call the MOE Customer Service Centre for information. They can be reached at

1 North Buona Vista Drive, MOE Building

Tel: (65) 6872-2220; fax: (65) 6776-4617

Email: contact.MOE@moe.edu.sg

Website: http://www.moe.edu.sg/esp/foreign

Visitor Passes for Various Types of Visitors
Social Visit Pass

A social visit pass enables a foreigner to stay in Singapore for a longer period. The following persons may apply for a social visit pass:

- Business visitor
- Social visitor on short visit
- Social visitor seeking medical treatment
- Social visitor seeking employment in Singapore
- Technopreneur/ entrepreneur scheme
- Female social visitor whose child or grandchild is studying in Singapore on a Student's Pass

- Social visitor seeking permission to deliver a child in Singapore
- Social visitor whose spouse is a Singaporean or Singapore Permanent Resident
- Social visitor (below 21 years old) whose parent is a Singaporean or Singapore Permanent Resident
- Social visitor whose child (above 21 years old) is a Singapore citizen or Singapore Permanent Resident.

For more information, refer to the ICA website at:

http://app.ica.gov.sg/serv_visitor/social_visit/
social_visit_app.asp

Training Visit Pass (TVP)

This is for those who are undergoing training in Singapore and to be eligible, you should either:

- hold an acceptable degree or professional qualification;
- currently be an undergraduate of a university or tertiary institution;
- be able to secure a minimum basic monthly allowance or salary of more than S$ 2,500.

The internship must be of professional, managerial, executive or specialist nature. Applications can be made at the Employment Pass Department and you will need the following documents:

- Company's letter of sponsorship.
- A letter from university or tertiary institution confirming that you are an undergraduate of the university or a copy of the educational certificate if you have graduated.
- Detailed training programme.
- A recent photograph.
- Completed copy of application form.

You may also wish to include a cover letter with the application that states:

- the work attachment
- the name of the company
- the duration of the attachment

For TVPs lasting three months or more, a one-time issuing fee of S$ 40 will be charged per application. This is payable by the employer to the Employment Pass Department. For TVPs shorter than three months, there are no charges.

Professional Visit Pass (PVP)

Foreigners intending to take up a short-term professional assignment in Singapore for the following activities are required to apply for a Professional Visit Pass (PVP).

- To conduct or participate in conferences, seminars, workshops or gatherings of a racial, communal, religious, cause-related or political nature.
- As a journalist or reporter, covering an event or writing a story in Singapore. This applies to accompanying crew members as well.
- As a religious worker who is in Singapore to give a religious or other-related talks.
- As an artiste performing at nightclubs, lounges, pubs or other similar entertainment outlets.

Each pass costs S$ 50 for a period of less than three months or S$ 100 for a three-month period. Those requiring visas will need to pay for an additional S$ 20. Processing will normally take about two to four weeks.

There are categories of foreign professionals who need not apply for a PVP. They are:

- Foreign artistes such as those in cultural troupes and performances.
- Camera crew, film directors, actors, actresses, foreign models and photographers on location shooting.
- Foreigners who are speakers, organisers, workshop leaders, moderators at conferences, seminars, workshops or gatherings that are not of a racial, communal, religious, cause-related or political nature.
- Professional artists who wish to exhibit their works.
- Foreign cultural missions.
- Foreign sportsmen who are engaged by local sports clubhouses or who are here for sports competitions or events.
- Foreign exhibitors in exhibitions or trade fairs.
- Foreign journalists, reporters or accompanying crew members who are supported or sponsored by Singapore

government agencies to cover an event or write a story in Singapore.

Although a PVP is not needed, these professionals are only allowed to stay in Singapore within the validity period of the Social Visit Passes issued to them when they arrive. They are also not exempted from getting approval from the relevant authorities to conduct their performance, exhibitions or other forms of activities. For instance, a foreign artist who wishes to exhibit his artwork in Singapore must apply for a Public Entertainment Licence from the Police. If these foreigners need a longer stay here, the maximum period (including the Social Visit Passes given upon their arrival) is three months. Extensions may be applied for at the Visitor Services Centre of ICA [tel: (65) 6391-6100] at their building in Kallang.

Foreign professionals who are not required to apply for a PVP but require more than three months' stay will have to apply for a work pass from the Employment Pass Department of the MOM. A local sponsor is needed and must be a Singapore-registered organisation. In the case of performing artistes working in nightclubs, lounges, pubs or other similar entertainment outlets, the application must be sponsored by the employer.

MOVING IN AND OUT

Whether this is your first overseas posting or your 15th, relocating anywhere is a stressful and time-consuming job. The best advice is still to be prepared (read everything you can, gain knowledge, speak to people and make lists and more lists), to accept whatever helping hand friends and family have offered (meals, taking care of the children, doing some errands) and hire out whatever services and assistance you can afford, both for your arrival in and departure from Singapore. You simply cannot do it all. You will never have the feeling of having 'accomplished' everything you wanted but certainly you can feel better about having given it all a good effort!

Chances are you are being transferred to Singapore either short-term or long-term and your company will

be assisting with your move. Take full advantage of all the knowledge and information you will receive from the moving company, at both ends (home country and Singapore). Being that Singapore is the world's second largest port (Shanghai is the largest), your container will most probably arrive within five to eight weeks from shipping time (and maybe even sooner) and most likely without any major hassles. Then there is another one to two weeks for unloading, customs and delivery.

If you do not have a designated moving company to work with, look for one with a reputable history of international moves and with sound affiliation to a mover in Singapore. Additionally, the moving company should be willing to handle the dock and customs clearance. Some of the most popular moving companies in Singapore are:

- Allied Pickfords
  Website: http://www.alliedpickfords.com.sg
- Collin's Movers Pte Ltd
  Website: http://www.collinsmovers.com.sg
- Crown Relocations
  Website: http://www.crownrelo.com

- K C Dat
  Website: http://www.asiantigers-kcdat.com
- Raffles Movers
  Website: http://www.rafmover.com
- Santa Fe Relocation Services
  Website: http://www.santaferelo.com
- Unicorn Worldwide
  Website: http://www.unicorn-utg.com

Your moving company should provide you with all the necessary logistical information on a Singapore move but it is true that because of strict Singapore laws, care and attention should be taken with what is included in the shipment. If in doubt, throw it out! Special attention should be noted for items falling into one of following three categories: prohibited, controlled and dutiable. The following is a more detailed list of those categories. You may wish to check with your moving company for a current exhaustive list or refer to the Information for Travellers section of the Singapore Customs website at:

http://www.customs.gov.sg

Prohibited Goods

- Obscene articles, publications, videotapes, discs and software
- Reproduction of copyright publications, videotapes, discs, records and cassettes
- Intoxicating liquors and cigarettes which are marked 'Singapore Duty Not Paid' on the labels, cartons or packets as well as cigarettes with the prefix 'E' printed on the packets
- Chewing gum
- Firecrackers
- Endangered species of wildlife and their by-products
- Chewing tobacco and imitation tobacco products
- Cigarette lighters shaped like pistols or revolvers
- Toy coins and currency
- Controlled drugs and psychotropic substances
- Seditious and treasonable material

Controlled Goods

These items will require special import licences or authorisation from a relevant controlling authority for entry into Singapore.

- Animals, birds and their by-products, including endangered wildlife. Plants with soil.
- Any kind of weapons such as arms and explosives, pistols, revolvers, kris, spears and swords. This also includes items such as bullet-proof clothing and toy guns.
- Pre-recorded cartridges, cassettes, films, tapes, DVDs, laser discs, newspapers, books and magazines will be subject to censorship and this goes much further than just a 'X-rated' listing. You may be charged as much as S$ 75 per item for censors to simply review each one. It is advisable to discard any material which you believe is questionable and that may cause delays or problems.
- Medicines, pharmaceuticals and poisons.
- Telecommunications and radio communication equipment, as well as toy walkie-talkies.

Dutiable Goods

These are subject to a Customs or Excise duty and would depend on which of the following categories your items fall into.

- Intoxicating liquors
- Tobacco products
- Motor vehicles
- Petroleum products

To Bring Or Not To Bring

Depending on whether you are moving for a short-term or if Singapore will be your home for an undetermined amount of time, there are some additional factors to consider.

- Think twice about bringing any electrical appliances other than 220 volts. Converters can be used for small appliances but it is probably more practical in the long run to switch to local electronics which are abundant and not expensive.

- Due to the high humidity (definitely, if you will be living in a home where air-conditioning is not on 24 hours), be forewarned about the climate and its effect on precious photo albums, slides, pianos and leather goods.
- The television formatting here is PAL.
- Video recorders and DVD players should be 'multi-system'.

ACCOMMODATION

Before arriving in Singapore, it seems to be the common misconception that one will be living in a small, cramped HDB (Housing Development Board) flat. This is far from the truth, although they are certainly available if it suits your needs. This small island has a plethora of excellent choices for housing. Take as much time as you can to find something you like for all the right reasons.

Your company will probably set you up with a real estate agent who should know the market's ins and outs and be used to dealing with foreigners and their special needs and requests. If necessary, it is

Due to its small land size, Singapore is the second most densely populated country in the world (Monaco is first) with 6,222 people per square kilometre. To combat its small land size, large vertical apartment blocks and condominiums are the norm with landed property becoming scarcer and increasingly surrounded by high-rise buildings.

recommended you work with a second agent in order to help speed things up and to gain a different perspective. The agent should provide you with a map of Singapore, divided by districts or sectors. This is how the city-state is split up and talked about with regards to real estate. Agents are paid a pro-rated commission, being a percentage of the monthly rental or sale price (depending on whether you are renting or buying).

Your real estate agent is a valuable resource so find one you like. It is common practice for them to hold your hand through the entire process of finding a home and even assist in opening your power supply account and telephone account.

Serviced Apartments

Most people will probably stay in a serviced apartment for a few weeks to a month or more while they look for housing and wait for their possessions to arrive. Or if you know you will be here for a year or less, it may also be a good option. There are over 3,600 serviced apartments in Singapore offering gyms, pools, business centres and maid clean-up service. Most are found in the central area (Orchard Road, Tanglin Road, Holland Road) although there are some in the outskirts.

Temporary accommodation will probably be selected based on its proximity to work, the centre of town (Orchard and River Valley Road area are very convenient) or perhaps a neighbourhood that one would like to better know. It's a good idea to have a checklist with priorities when searching for temporary and permanent housing. If you will be staying in a serviced apartment for longer than six months, it is advisable to bargain with regards to the rent. Rental prices will vary greatly depending on size, location, facilities and services. Some websites to begin your search are:

- Moveandstay (Singapore)
  Website: http://www.moveandstay.com/singapore/
  servicedapartments.asp

- ExpatSingapore
  Website: http://www.expatsingapore.com/startup/
  serviceapt.shtml

Housing Options
HDB Flats

With over 86 per cent of Singaporeans living in HDB towns and more than 90 per cent of them owning their flats, this is definitely the residence of choice for the locals. Seen as a major building block towards nationhood and community spirit, HDB flats are the heart of Singaporean housing. These self-contained housing units have their own wet market or grocery in the area, children's playground, local food centres, local shops, and even Resident Committees and government representation... and of course, the ever important and crucial void deck or empty space at the bottom of the buildings where children play during the day and where Chinese funerals, Malay wedding banquets, Hungry Ghost festivities and other celebrations are held. The flats are classified into three-room, four-room, five-room and executive flats. A typical three-room flat will have two bedrooms, a living room, kitchen and bathroom.

There has been a recent change with the conditions under which a Singaporean is allowed to rent out his or her flat or sublet bedrooms to either a Permanent Resident (PR) or non-citizen with an employment pass, work permit or student permit. An entire flat can only be sublet if the owner has written approval of the HDB. Subletting of bedrooms is only permitted from three-bedroom flats onwards and the landlord does not need approval from HDB.

The classified section in the *The Straits Times* (the local English newspaper) or the *Lianhe Zaobao* (the main Chinese newspaper) is the best place to look for rooms and flats to rent. And of course, you can seek the aid of any registered real estate agent to assist you in your search. The following websites are also helpful for viewing and searching for HDB flats.

- http://www.hdbhousing.com/hdbtowns.htm
- http://www.hdb.gov.sg

Blocks of HDB flats in Queenstown, one of the oldest housing estates in Singapore. Many have been upgraded over time to ensure that housing keeps up with the times.

Scheme for Housing of Foreign Talents (sHiFT)

In 1997, the large local corporation Jurong Town Corporation (JTC) launched the Scheme for Housing of Foreign Talent (sHiFT). A wide range of public housing apartments, houses and dormitory units specially aimed for foreign talents and workers are available for rent at affordable rates. Apartments are unfurnished. For more information and application forms visit their website at:

http://www.jtc.gov.sg

Condominiums

This is the housing choice with the widest spectrum of price ranges, locations and facilities. The decision to live in a condominiums (known locally as condo) will depend very much on your lifestyle and family circumstances. Having lived in a condo my entire time in Singapore, I wouldn't change it for anything. The ease it provides for meeting people, socialising for the children, convenience in maintenance, security if you travel a lot or return to your home country for extended periods of stay, extra facilities (pool, squash courts, tennis courts) is immeasurable. One thing to keep in mind when looking at condos is that balcony space and any entry space outside the front door is included in the overall square metres/rental area. Additionally, balconies facing south are often not very useable because of the high temperatures. East and north facing balconies are nice features in the morning and evening.

The older condos usually have a much larger living area so although they may be in need of some renovations (or you may have to put up with renovations sooner or later), they are worth looking at if you really want some extra space (above 232.2 m or 2,500 ft). Keep in mind that older condos usually do not have many telephone, Internet or television points, but these can be installed at an additional cost.

House-hunting Tip

Singapore uses the metric system so for those who are used to thinking of space in terms of square feet, this might be a little frustrating. One square metre is equal to about 11 square feet so a good rule of thumb for converting square metres to square feet is to add a '0' plus a little more e.g. 50 sq m is about 500 sq ft.

The newer condominiums tend to be built on smaller parcels of land so you might have the apartment blocks situated more closely together. This may be one of your considerations if you prefer more space. Condos normally come with many amenities such as swimming pools and a multi-storey carpark (foreground).

The newer condos tend to be much smaller grounds and the apartment size will also be smaller. However, they are more likely to have telephone, Internet and television points in every bedroom as well as feature highly modern kitchens and bathrooms.

Landed Homes

In Singapore, houses fall under one of three categories: terrace units, semi-detached or detached.

Terrace units are a row of houses that have common walls. The middle ones are known as intermediate terraces and at the end are corner terraces. They are usually one to three floors high with a small private space in the front and back. Some also have a garage. They usually do not have a garden; if it is present, this is normally at one corner.

Semi-detached town houses are defined as a pair of houses that share one common wall. Most are two-storey homes and are popular with families for they usually have a small garden area and may even share a common pool.

Detached homes do not share any wall and are either bungalows with single, double or three storeys. Or they

Swimming Pools

With the year round humidity and sunshine, swimming pools are usually a necessity. Even if the home doesn't have one, if the space is there, above-the-ground pools can be rented and installed at reasonable prices.

are old colonial single or two-storey houses with white walls and black woodwork, often referred to as Black and Whites. These are extremely popular with expatriates for they have much charm and character. The houses try to keep their original structure and do not have central air-conditioning. It is a true tropical living experience for they are often set amidst a large, lush yard with lots of free 'wildlife' (creepy crawlies, lizards, mosquitoes, snakes) as part of the deal. Many have an additional small house for servants and the tenants are responsible for repairs and maintenance.

Renting Black and Whites

Most Black and White colonial houses are rented out by the government and often managed by appointed agents. For a list of available house, you can refer to the Singapore Land Authority website at:

http://www.spio.sla.gov.sg/spio/home.jsp

You can find more listings at the United Premas website at:

http://www.premas.com/acc_rent/index.htm

Alternatively, enquire with your real estate agent on who else you should approach.

Overall Housing Tips
Budget

Work out your budget and living allowance beforehand so you're prepared once you start looking. You should keep within a S$ 500 range so as to not extend yourself too far. One interesting thing here is that property prices fluctuate as a result of the demand by expatriate workers. In 2002, there was a large exodus of expatriates and as a consequence, rents dropped substantially (our rent has dropped almost S$ 1,000 since we moved in seven years ago). Many incentives have been put in place to draw foreign companies back into Singapore, and for now, it seems to be working. Stay

attuned to the market and be sure to ask for an appropriate rent adjustment when the lease is due.

Location

How far is the office? The school? Public transportation? Yes, Singapore is small but it is amazing to notice how quickly one's mentality adapts! Soon you'll be thinking like a local and nothing is that near anymore. For instance, living out in the East Coast, one often hears, "I'm going into town..." a whole 20 minutes away. Lay out on a map where the office, school or club are and try to stay in the vicinity; your life will be made much easier! Consider whether you will have a car. Also, how easy is it to catch a taxi? In the rain? At peak times? Will it be near a bus stop? The MRT station?

Size

Apartments in every size are available and it is advisable to keep looking until something really strikes your fancy. Don't give up too early, there are thousands out there! One bit of advice, opt for the largest space your budget can afford. Storage space is usually not great and with growing families and relatives visiting, one will hardly encounter an 'unused room'. Additionally, it is common practice to list apartments as 'X + 1 rooms', that means X proper bedrooms and one smaller room (usually the maid's quarters) normally found in the back with an entrance through the kitchen. And if the listing says 'X + 1 + 1' that means X bedrooms, one maid's room and one storage or utility room. A study or family room is often listed separately. The other bonus to apartments here is that they usually have more bathrooms than in many countries. En suite bathrooms are not uncommon and are greatly appreciated! Lastly, the vast majority of apartments have a back area where the washing machine, small lavatory and sometimes even a 'second kitchen' or small hob is available so cooking smells will not permeate the house.

Facilities and Amenities

Condominiums come with a host of facilities ranging from swimming pools, squash courts, tennis courts, sauna, gym or fitness area, playground, barbecue decks, mini-market, to even a putting green. Look around and know what you would really utilise and enjoy. With some condos so replete with great resources, additional club membership may not be a priority or even a necessity.

Appliances and Air-conditioning

A few things to keep in mind. Local kitchens may lack some appliances e.g. ovens that are normally part of the kitchen unit in many countries. Consider the size and condition of appliances such as refrigerators, washing machines, dryers and dish washers. Also, air-conditioning is a way of life but if you prefer to not rely on it so much, look for ceiling fans, apartments on a higher floor and windows on several sides for a pleasant crosswind.

Window Guards and Balconies

High-rises are the norm and window guards may not be installed so be sure to request window locks or other safety alternatives before moving in. Balconies are also a concern if you have children. Ask about installing special guards if you are interested in an apartment but are concerned about the safety issues.

Ambiance

Having moved from New York City to Singapore, apartment living was second-nature to me; but I've come to appreciate that this is certainly not the case for most people so here are a few tips. Don't underestimate the importance of the other residents in the condo. This is especially true if you have children. Visit the apartments at around 5:00 pm, prime time for outdoor play, and see how many children you see playing outdoors. Visit on a Saturday morning or late afternoon and observe the pool area. Do you want lots of children, families, expatriates or would you rather have more privacy? And lastly, how important is light and a beautiful view? With so many high-rises, sea or city views and large windows are quite popular, but are you ready to pay the additional costs for your increased electricity bill? The year round sunshine provides little respite from the heat and rooms will become quite warm—time to turn up the air-conditioning! And don't forget that sound travels upwards—especially important if you are near a major road or expressway.

Renting or Buying

Since Singapore is such a regional hub, the city is accustomed to transient residents. You will have plenty of rental choices. And for those who plan to stay longer in Singapore, it is also possible to buy a home. However, foreigners and PRs are restricted to apartments in buildings that are at least six storeys high, or approved condominium units. For all other types of property, you must obtain approval from the Controller of Residential Property (CRP). For flats, shophouses and executive condominiums under the purview of the HDB, eligibility is subject the board's guidelines at that point in time. To buy a flat directly from HDB, you must be a Singapore citizen, and form a family nucleus with either another Singapore citizen or a PR. To buy a flat from the resale market, you must be a Singapore citizen or PR and your application must include at least one listed occupier who is a Singapore PR or citizen.

More Information

Additional information and useful sites for property search are:
- Controller of Residential Property
  Land Dealings (Approval) Unit
  8 Shenton Way, #27-02, Temasek Tower
  Tel: (65) 6323-9829
- http://www.sporeproperty.com
- http://www.condo.com.sg
- http://www.landedhomes.com.sg

Maintenance and Renovations

Be aware of who is responsible for maintenance. Before finalising any agreement, be certain you agree whether it is you, the landlord or your employer who will be responsible for any maintenance, pest control, pool cleaning (if applicable) repairs and air-conditioning servicing.

Renovations are major work, no matter where you live. Of course, if you are renting, approval must be obtained from the landlord (read through your lease carefully) for any changes to the existing structure.

But if you are a owner of landed property and wish to make renovations, there are some things to keep in mind.

- Renovation work may require the approval of the Building and Construction Authority (BCA). There is a good website (http://www.bca.gov.sg/housing/sp/renovating/reno_prvptyguidline.htm) that gives excellent information and guidelines for renovating your home.
- The Renovation and Decoration Advisory Centre (RADAC) was set up as a non-profit voluntary consumer-based watchdog to provide greater controls in the renovation and decoration industry. Their website (http://radac.org.sg) has a listing of accredited renovators and other helpful information.

- Any renovations done to apartments in condominiums must, of course, have board approval. Speak to your management company.
- And, as it is for any renovation project, speak to as many people as possible for advice and recommendations. Most people are sure to have, or to know a friend, relative or acquaintance, that has a story and an opinion.

Moving Into Your New Home

Most likely, either your company will set you up with a moving company or you will have to do it yourself. Nowadays, most moving companies offer a host of services to also help the customers relocate and settle into their new homes e.g. handyman services for helping to set up your new home (they are excellent, efficient and fast), coffee mornings, special tours or talks on local places of interest and customs. This is definitely an added bonus when one arrives in a new country and does not have a list of resources at hand. It may seem strange to rely so heavily on your moving company once your possessions have arrived but here in Singapore, it is your best and first partner in setting up your home. They know the expatriate market and needs extremely well and can certainly provide sound advice and recommendations on where to find things in Singapore.

UTILITIES

If you have used a real estate agent to find an apartment or home, he or she will usually provide you with the paperwork to apply for electricity and water. This is all done through Singapore Power Services (SP Services) even though it is Singapore Power (SP) who supplies electricity and piped gas, and the Public Utilities Board (PUB) who supplies the water. Electricity and gas services are efficient and completely reliable, while tap water is fully treated and potable.

You will receive a detailed statement every month and there are countless ways to pay your monthly bills. You can send a cheque (and an added bonus with regards to utility bills and even credit card bills, they all come with a prepaid envelope for ease of payment) or pay in person either at the SP's customer service centres in Somerset Road or Woodlands, or at the Post Offices. You can also electronically transfer money through the telephone or Internet, SAM (Self-service Automated Machine), the ATMs (Automated Teller Machines) of certain banks such as DBS and OUB, or AXS kiosks. One very convenient option is to pay through GIRO (an automatic deduction of payment from one's bank account). This service offers the benefit of making payments on time and not having to worry about the inconvenience of writing monthly cheques or forgetting to pay. Once your application for GIRO has been approved, your monthly bills will have the date of deduction, usually two weeks away, and always on the same day of the month.

If you have to open a utilities account on your own, you can find out how to do this and the documentation needed at:

http://services.spservices.sg/

Click on 'Frequently Asked Questions' and then find out 'How to Open a Utilities Account'. You can apply in person at the customer services centres, through fax or email, or online at their website. Here is just a brief guideline:

- Business hours are from 8:00 am–6:00 pm on weekdays and 8:00 am–4:00 pm on Saturdays.
- Bring along your passport, cash or local cheque (needed for a deposit ranging from S$ 300–800, depending on the type of housing, whether the account is under company name or a private non-resident), work permit or employment pass and your tenancy agreement or letter from the landlord.
- It will take about three working days for service to start. An express service (installation or termination within 24 hours) is also available for an additional charge.

Some homes may require bottled gas for the stoves. The bottles themselves are produced and managed by the major petroleum companies in Singapore but they normally sub-contract the actual delivery out to small vendors who are located in more convenient places. The best thing to do is check the *Buying Guide* (or

Yellow Pages) under 'Gas—Liquefied Petroleum—Bottled and Bulk'.

TELECOMMUNICATIONS AND MEDIA

Singapore is a completely wired, plugged-in nation. Once again, in typical Singaporean way, service is efficient and reliable. The main governing body of all telecommunications is the Infocomm Development Authority (IDA) of Singapore which looks into all telephony, technological and postal services.

Telephony Services

Currently, there are only three major players in this area, the largest being SingTel (Singapore Telecoms),Starhub and M1 (MobileOne).

First, let's talk about fixed phone lines which are provided by SingTel and Starhub. Applications for a SingTel landline can be made by:

- calling 1609 or 1800-738-1311
- filling out an application form at any post office, SingTel customer service outlet or Teleshop
- applying through the Internet at:
                http://www.singtel.com

For Starhub, call 1633 or 1630 to find out more or arrange for a time when the line will be installed.

When applying for a landline (regardless of provider), ask whether you need to place a deposit with the companies if you are not a citizen or PR, also what documentation they need from you. Also ask about the initial set-up fee. Installation normally takes six to seven working days from the time your application is approved. Another question to ask is whether a physical phone is supplied together with the line or if you have to pay extra should you need one. If you envisage that you will be calling overseas quite a bit or sending many faxes outside the country, you might want to find out about their IDD (International Direct Dialling) rates and sign up for this at the same time.

In March 2002, Singapore moved from a seven-digit local fixed-line system to an eight-digit number

Directories

One interesting side note to the 'telephone system' in Singapore is the method of distribution for telephone directories. Every year you will receive, in the mail, an announcement about your new directories and the locations where they can be collected within a specified period of time. It is up to the individuals to go to the nearest collection point (usually in a large, nearby HDB town) to obtain the directories. They are not delivered to your home, as is the practice in many countries. (You can get them delivered, but for a fee.) The *Buying Guide* (basically the *Yellow Pages*) is, however, delivered annually to private homes. If you cannot collect your directories during the designated dates, then one has to go to the main SingTel office.

by adding the number '6' in front of all existing phone and fax numbers. This change was made to accommodate the growing consumer market and the increase in demand for telephone lines. The transition was quite smooth but you may still on rare occasion find a number that does not begin with '6'—just add it as a prefix and try again.

Once you have a landline installed, you can choose to use another provider's IDD service should they have special rates that you find more suited to your needs. In order to be eligible for the rates, you need to register with the respective provider. Check their individual websites to find out more:

- SingTel
  Website: http://www.singtel.com
- Starhub
  Website: http://www.starhub.com
- M1
  Website: http://www.m1.com.sg

With over 83 per cent of the population owning mobile phones, the ownership of one is no longer just a luxury but has become a necessity, accessory and major status symbol. The same three providers listed above offer a wide range of mobile phone services as well as top of the range mobile phones. You only have to look through *The Straits Times* on Saturday to find pages of advertisements for the the latest phones, all offered with varying types of price plans and promotions. Shop around, call to enquire or visit their outlets to find out more before you make your decision. By the way, mobile phone numbers begin with either '8' or '9' and are also eight digits long.

Internet Services

There are currently three Internet Service Providers (ISPs) in Singapore. As before, shop around before you decide. You can find out more by calling, visiting their websites or a customer service centre.

- Pacific Internet
  Tel: (65) 6336-6622
  Website: http://www.pacific.net.sg
- Singnet (one of SingTel's services)
  Tel: 1610 or (65) 6838-3899
  Website: http://www.singnet.com.sg
- Starhub
  Tel: 1633 or (65) 6820 1633
  Website: http://www.starhub.com

Postal Services

Singapore Post (sometimes called SingPost) operates a network of more than 900 postal outlets, of which more than 60 are full-fledged post offices. The operating hours of these vary, depending on its location but there is generally at least one in the general vicinity (i.e. north, south, east and west) that is open later for those who are not able to get to them during the day. Most post offices offer the full range of services and these include philatelic services, remittance services as well as payment of bills, fines, donations, licences and insurance premiums for certain companies. For the locations and opening hours of these post offices, as well as where the post boxes are, you can call their general line at 1605 or better yet, refer to the SingPost website at:

http://www.singpost.com

If you are not able to get to a post office, there are at least 80 authorised postal agencies and more than 200 stamp vendors scattered across the islands. If that isn't enough, there are almost 200 SAMs (Self-Automated Machines) which allow you to buy stamps (for local and overseas mail) and pay some of your bills. And yes, the website carries a list of where these are located.

SAMs pepper the island. Some, like the ones above, are located next to MRT stations for the convenience of commuters.

Television, Cable and Radio

There are six local television broadcast stations, and of the six, two are in English (5 and Channel News Asia), two are in Mandarin (Channels 8 and U) and one is Malay (Suria). The last, Central, is a real mixture catering to the children (Kids Central), the Indian audience (Vansantham Central) and the more serious and arts inclined. There is also a cable television broadcaster (you can apply through Starhub) providing numerous channel selections. Satellite dishes are illegal so there are no direct satellite channels available. Additionally, there are 15 local radio stations throughout the country and you can find out what they are at the MediaCorp radio website (http://www.mediacorpradio.sg/). Although there is a greater selection and availability today, there are still restrictions on the type of material that can be broadcast, especially with regards to pornography and violence.

In order to own a television or radio in Singapore, one must apply for a television and/or radio licence. The licence is valid for a calendar year and renewable on a yearly basis thereafter. The annual licence fee is S$ 110 for the home and S$ 27 for a Vehicle Radio Licence. The Singapore Broadcasting Authority (SBA) Act requires that individuals purchase a licence for any place where a television or radio receiver is installed, including cars. Failure to obtain a licence can result in a fine of up to S$ 1,000. Licences can be applied for online, at NTUC (National Trades Union Congress) Income Branch offices or the post offices (bring along your passport or identity card). For additional information, visit the Media Development Authority (MDA) website at:

http://www.mda.gov.sg/wms.www/index_flash.aspx

Publications

There is one major daily newspaper in English, *The Straits Times*, and this covers local, regional and world news. (The Sunday edition is called, not surprisingly, *The Sunday Times*.) Business news receives more coverage in *The Business Times* and this is available from Monday to Saturday only. In the mornings, you can also get a free tabloid-style English-language daily, *Today*. The afternoon paper is called *The New*

Paper but this tends to be a little more sensationalistic. The main Chinese-language daily is *Lianhe Zaobao* (its evening edition is called *Lianhe Wanbao*). *Shin Min Daily News* is another Chinese-language evening-time newspaper. The Malay weekday newspaper is *Berita Harian* and its weekend counterpart is *Berita Minggu*. Indians are not left out and they can read the Tamil newspaper, *Tamil Murasu*.

Except for *Today* (which you can pick up at vantage points such as MRT station and bus interchanges), you can subscribe to the daily newspapers and have them delivered to your home. All the major newspapers are published by the same company, Singapore Press Holdings (SPH) and can be contacted at tel: (65) 6388-3838, fax: (65) 6744-4875 or email: circs@sph.com.sg.

The good news is that many of these newspapers are available online as well and you can subscribe to this service, if you prefer. Check out the individal websites at:

- *The Straits Times*
  Website: http://straitstimes.asia1.com.sg/
- *The Business Times*
  Website: http://business-times.asia1.com.sg/
- *The New Paper*
  Website: http://newpaper.asia1.com.sg/
- *Berita Harian*
  Website: http://cyberita.asia1.com.sg/
- *Lianhe Zaobao*
  Website: http://www.zaobao.com/
- *Tamil Murasu*
  Website: http://tamilmurasu.asia1.com.sg/
- *Today Online* (published by MediaCorp Press)
  Website: http://www.todayonline.com/

Incidentally, SPH also puts out a number of local magazines. You can find out more about these at the SPH website (http://www.sph.com.sg/) under 'SPH Magazines'.

You can also get a number of overseas newspapers in Singapore including *International Herald Tribune*, *The Wall Street Journal*, *Asian Wall Street Journal*, *USA Today* and *South China Morning Post*. Besides SPH, other publishing companies produce their own local magazines, plus you get many foreign ones such as *Time*, *The Economist*, *Newsweek*, *Harper's Bazaar*, *Elle*, *Cosmopolitan* and *Vogue*. Check the major bookstores or the larger news stands to find your favourites.

FURNISHINGS AND APPLIANCES

If you have the need for temporary or new appliances, there are several places to start looking. First, if you are looking for used appliances or furniture in good condition, it is not hard to find in Singapore with the number of expat families leaving and looking for a quick sale. Check the notice boards and publications from all the major clubs (*website listed in the box entitled 'Social Clubs' below*), international schools and the 'want/ for sale board' at major grocery outlets such as Tanglin Market Place in Tanglin Mall or Cold Storage Jelita near Holland Village.

If you are looking to buy appliances there are several chains of major, well-priced electronic and appliance stores around the island:

- Best Denki
  Has ten locations around the island.
- Carrefour Hypermart
  The main store is at Suntec City Mall and the second outlet Plaza Singapura. Their website is:
  http://www.carrefour.com.sg/
- Harvey Norman
  The main store is at Millenia Walk and there are over 12 outlets around the island.

Social Clubs

Social clubs provide an excellent means to socialise, to meet people from your country and to enjoy additional facilities and recreational amenities one may not have access to otherwise. International clubs are also very active in maintaining many of their country specific holidays and celebrations. For a thorough listing of the many international and social clubs available, visit:

http://expatchoice.com/relocation_guide/
useful_resources/social_clubs.htm

WHAT TO BRING FROM HOME

I'd almost venture to say that Singapore has everything! And if you don't find it here now, it is just a matter of asking around, persevering and before long, you will certainly chance upon it. This has happened to me innumerable times and it has almost become one of the small joys and games of living in Singapore. But to save you the frustration and hunt that may come with the struggle of trying to find American King Size sheets, here are a few tips:

If you are larger than an American woman's size 10 (Euro 40) and men American 36 (Euro 46), it is advisable that you bring as many clothes as you may need until your next trip abroad. This definitely goes for bras (padded bras are the norm and the selection is very limited for larger than a C-cup), swimwear and lingerie. Larger sizes are available primarily at Marks & Spencers Department Store and Robinson's Department Store but the selection is limited and prices are at a premium.

Anyone with shoe size larger than US 9 or Euro 41 (men US 10, Euro 43) is better off shopping for shoes overseas or

immediately snatching up any shoe you may come across that fits (don't wait for the sale price) since they usually only receive one or two pairs in the larger sizes.

Even though there are hundreds of clothing stores for young children, it is difficult to find nice, plain, solid-coloured T-shirts and unadorned shorts or long pants. Nothing beats the Gap (although the first Gap stores in Singapore will be opening by end of year 2006), Old Navy or Target for inexpensive basics, so stock up.

Certain medication may be difficult to find since it may be under a different brand name or simply unavailable; for example, ibuprofen is not available; the local substitute is Panadol. Bear in mind that there may be some medicines which are bought over the counter back home but which are controlled substances here (they even carry a 'poison' label!) so be careful what you bring in. It's impossible to give a listing but stock up on any necessities before leaving and ask around or see a doctor upon arriving. Also, Japanese pharmacies, usually located near Japanese groceries (Mediya at Liang Court, Isetan basement at Scotts Road or basement of Takashimaya Department Store in Ngee Ann City on Orchard) carry different items from regular pharmacies and many excellent products may be found there.

For appliances, the voltage here is 220 and the plug points may be either two-point prong or three-point. This is the same voltage as Europe and many other countries. However, it is not advisable to use large appliances (stereo, television, vacuum cleaners) with a transformer. Better to leave all your electrical equipment at home and to purchase new appliances here. They are not expensive, easily available and can even be bought in great condition, second-hand, from departing expat families. Singapore is a hub for electronic shopping and you will find the latest equipment from Japan and Korea much earlier than in other parts of the world.

When it comes to bed linen, European sizing is used here so if you are arriving from America, be prepared to stock up before you leave home. Additionally, the linen selection is quite conservative, so if you favour bright, modern prints and colours, it is also a good idea to bring some from abroad.

Alcohol is widely available in Singapore with speciality wine stores popping up at every corner. However, there remains a heavy duty (from S$ 9.50 per litre of wine to S$ 30 per litre on spirits such as whisky and brandy) per bottle, and the widest and cheapest wine selection are from Australia and New Zealand. Upon arrival in Singapore, individuals are permitted 1 litre of spirits and 1 litre of wine or beer—the DFS (Duty Free Shop) at the airport continues to have an excellent selection and some of the lowest prices in town.

DOMESTIC HELP

In Singapore, it is possible and affordable to employ full-time, live-in domestic help. As an employer, you are responsible for your domestic helper, including her health and abidance to the Singapore rules and regulations governing foreign workers. Employment is legally binding and employers are required to post a S$ 5,000 bond in case the domestic helper breaks any Singapore laws or the terms of her work permit.

In addition to the domestic worker's salary (which usually ranges between S$ 200–500 monthly), the employer must pay a monthly levy (that currently stands at S$ 295) to the government. A Foreign Domestic Worker (FDW) can be employed through two methods: the employer brings her in from abroad or finds one through an employment agency. Maid agencies are ubiquitous and quite competitive. Using one takes the red tape out of the process of finding, employing and registering a FDW, although the process is not as complicated or difficult as it may appear, if you choose to proceed on your own. Many maid agencies can be found at Lucky Plaza, Katong Shopping Mall and Peninsula Plaza, to name just a few. The entire process may take two to six weeks, depending on whether the maid is coming directly from a foreign country (and may need to file for a passport) or is transferring from her current employer.

FDWs are regulated and controlled by the government under the MOM. There are over 150,000 FDW from government-approved countries (Malaysia, Philippines,

Indonesia, Thailand, Myanmar, Sri Lanka, India and Bangladesh). This past year, the Singapore government came under intense scrutiny by the Human Rights Watch group because of how Singaporeans treat their maids (with regards to labour conditions, wages, hours of work, days off and physical abuse) and what little legal protection the maids have on their side. There is an undeniable 'ugly side' to the domestic worker issue and this is definitely something that is surprising, upsetting and quite shocking for foreigners to see and to fully understand. Small steps are being taken by the government to help improve the situation such as mandatory orientation for new employers and employees, increased commitment to prosecuting cases of unpaid wages and physical abuse and an accreditation programme for employment agencies. Like the report states, Singapore is definitely ahead of Malaysia in terms of laws and regulations governing and protecting domestic workers but not as far along as Hong Kong (where they are protected under their main labour laws for such issues as days off, maternity leave, public holidays and minimum wage, plus employers must also bear most recruitment and employment fees).

In the end, one is responsible for the worker living in one's home and it is a constant balancing act and learning process for all involved. Although there are eight approved countries, the majority of the domestic workers come from the Philippines, Indonesia and Sri Lanka. Don't be surprised to discover that employment agencies will most often list maids by nationality, religion or language ability rather than years of experience or other more specific work qualifications. For expatriates, maids from the Philippines are a popular choice since they are usually more fluent in English. As a result of their English language abilities, they also command a higher salary and may even incur higher costs when filing through an agency. Below are listed the givens of employing a maid:

- The employer is responsible for all medical expenses (including hospitalisation) of the maid. The employer is also responsible for medical screenings every six months for venereal disease (called VDRL, Venereal

Disease Research Laboratory), pregnancy and HIV. All this usually costs around S$ 50 per medical visit.

- The employer pays for yearly home-leave or the equivalent of an air ticket.

- Days off, extra pay or work, daily routine, use of telephone, toiletries etc. must all be discussed and agreed upon between the employer and maid before signing any contract. It is highly recommended that once discussed and agreed upon, these terms be written down for future reference.

- Single foreign males may not employ a live-in domestic worker for obvious reasons. However, there are agencies that specialise in part-time help. For more information and a place to start looking, refer to:

    http://www.entersingapore.info/country/
    domestic_help/ci_06_set.htm.

- If you have never employed a domestic worker before, it is recommended and even required by MOM to attend a four-hour orientation course before submitting the work permit papers. The International Women's Association also offers classes on employing a maid.

- If you have infants or small children, it is advisable to look for someone with previous child experience and enrolling them and yourself in a CPR and First Aid course. Contact information for localities providing First Aid and safety courses can be found at:

    http://www.entersingapore.info/country/
    Health/Ci_11_set.htm

Essentially, finding good, affordable domestic help is a big plus for many expatriates moving to Singapore, especially those with children. It is, however, not without its inherent difficulties and adjustment. It can be true culture shock for everyone involved, the worker and the family. As the employer, you must always keep in mind that English is certainly not their first language, nor may it be yours. Communication may be slow and with difficulties; religion may play a part in the food that the worker is allowed to eat and in her daily routine, food habits will differ; it may be the first time the worker has lived in a suburban city and find all the modernisation and being away from her family (parents and spouse or children of her own) quite a hardship. But this is her big break and she is most likely supporting a large extended family with the wages she makes in Singapore and sacrificing her own needs for a better future for others. It is a complicated situation that will require a lot of luck, good fortune, patience and tolerance from all parties involved. Like a friend said, "Having one will give you a headache; not having one will give you a backache." The decision is yours but as most will agree, just thinking of how busy, hectic and frantic your life could be trying to juggle work, family and home, the decision is 'maid'.

CHILDREN

Singapore is a great place to raise children—bottom line. I haven't come across one person in my seven years who does not agree with this statement, either foreign or local. The safety factor, the warm weather, the good education and the overall acceptance and love of children in shops, restaurants and most places makes it a friendly, comfortable environment for the family and child. But there are a few downsides, as in everything. Due to the humid, tropical weather and densely populated island, children will probably fall sick more often. It is not uncommon for a child to catch a cold up to seven times a year. And you may also be surprised to see how easily and frequently doctors may prescribe antibiotics. Many children and parents will have to learn to live with runny noses, allergies, asthma and night-time coughing. The good news is that most children outgrow this by the time they are around seven years old. Additionally, many common, highly contagious diseases such as Hand, Foot and Mouth (HFM), chicken pox and microplasm spread quite quickly. It's advisable to take any necessary precautions and to become acquainted with basic illnesses and preventive measures for living in the tropics.

Another area that is slowly changing with regards to children is baby pram/stroller access. Many buildings, buses, MRT stations and sidewalks do not have ramps and special access for strollers. It can be difficult to manoeuvre around. The good news is that this is changing, but it will still take some time.

Since most Singaporean families have both parents working, day care centres are available and regulated by the MCYS. There are about 600 day care centres (called Child Care Centres or CCCs) in Singapore, run by employers, co-operatives, private business, volunteers and for children aged 18 months to six years old. However, there are a limited number of day care centres that will take infants from 2–18 months. For a comprehensive listing search of government registered day care centres search

http://app.mcys.gov.sg/WEB/
faml_nurture_childcarectr.asp

Most of the centres offer kindergarten programmes (or structured pre-school education) for children aged three to six. Singapore has over 200 kindergartens that are registered with the MOE, as well as several international schools with kindergarten programmes that cater specifically for the expatriate community. Locally registered kindergartens are required to teach in English and a second local language.

Day care centres offer full-day, half-day, holiday and emergency programmes. Finding the right centre for your child may take some time, but you should visit as many centres as possible and:

- speak to the teachers;
- observe the classrooms and the equipment that will be used;
- observe student/teacher interaction;
- consider the school's leadership and communication methods with the parents;
- inquire about the teacher's qualifications, background, etc;
- inquire about the food or meals that may be served and the centre's policy on drop-off, pick-up and late pick-up.

For primary and higher education, Singapore also offers excellent international schools that may enable your child to continue with the programme and curriculum of your home country. International schools are also known as Foreign System Schools, so called because they adhere to the education system of their country of origin. These schools are registered with the MOE but they are allowed to follow the educational guidelines of their home country. International schools only grant admission to foreign students and permanent residents, as specified by MOE. Here are some helpful tips for deciding on a school:

- What degree, curriculum does it offer?
  Check the educational year compatibility and holidays/school breaks. If you know you will be here a short time, it will definitely be much easier to join a school that is on the same calendar year. The curriculum varies according to country of origin e.g. Australian school starts the year in January and ends in December while Overseas Family School starts in August and ends in June.
- What are the school hours and most importantly, bus hours?
- Location and transport.
- Is there a wait list and is a deposit required?
- After school sports and activities, does it offer a wide selection (more than just academic and sports), and more specifically those your child shows an interest in?
- Foreign language choice; not only the language but some schools begin offering it at different grade levels.
- Does your child have any special learning needs? Schools differ quite a bit with regards to the amount of extra assistance they offer, although Singapore is still lagging behind in its handling of special needs.
- Class size. The average would be around 18 but some can be as small as ten or as large as 25.
- Facilities available.

Admission criteria vary from school to school. Some only accept students who are of their own nationality and speak the local language, while others have English language proficiency requirements. Some of these schools are listed in the Resource Guide but if you require a full listing of schools, you can download the document from MOE at:

http://www.moe.gov.sg/privatesch/
directory/foreign % 20systems.doc

Fees per year for international schools range from S$ 4,600–14,000 for the lower grades and S$ 8,000–23,000 for the upper grades. The trend today seems to be for employers to not include the 'full expat' package and your child's education is a major negotiating point—especially if you have more than one.

Local School System

Education is of paramount importance to a country like Singapore that has no natural resources. Its people are its primary resource and providing an excellent education to its people is a task the government takes very, very seriously. As an outsider, the education system may seem harsh, demanding and unfair (due to the competitive nature, the demanding high level of achievement, emphasis on exams, and lack of encouragement on creative thinking skills) but Singapore consistently shows excellent results, especially with regards to math and

Local Singaporean children in their school uniforms.

sciences. And like everything else about Singapore, things seem to be loosening up and new emphasis is being placed on a more flexible, diverse and broad-based educational system.

For a better understanding of the local school system that is based on the British system, here is a brief overview. The first ten or so years of schooling are categorised under two phases—six years of primary education and the next four or five years in secondary school.

A child starts studying at Primary One at the age of seven and continues for six years. The child then takes the Primary School Leaving Examinations (PSLE) before moving on to secondary school for another four or five years. At the start of the secondary school level, the students are then 'streamed' according to their PSLE results. Sixty per cent of the students are placed into the Special and Express courses and 35 per cent continue with the Normal course.

Within the Normal course, students have the option of taking the Normal (Academic) course or the Normal (Technical) course, both of which lead to the Singapore-Cambridge General Certificate of Education 'Normal'—GCE 'N' level examination at the end of four years. Those who do well on their 'N' level exams go on to take the 'O' level exams at the end of the fifth year. Approximately 80 per cent of the students do this.

Those students in the Special and Express courses will take their Cambridge General Certificate of Education 'Ordinary' (GCE 'O') level examinations at the end of their fourth year. After the secondary level, it's a selection whether to continue with:

- Junior colleges or centralised institutions to prepare for the Senior Cambridge General Certicate of Education 'Advanced' (GCE 'A') level examinations and later on, tertiary education.
- Polytechnics (Nanyang, Temasek, Ngee Ann, Republic, Singapore) to pursue diploma courses. They can also continue with tertiary education after that.
- Technical (ITE) or commercial institutes (MDIS, MIS, TMC, SIM).

The Singapore Management University (SMU) is the only tertiary institution that currently has a campus in the heart of town, along Victoria Street.

For tertiary education, the National University of Singapore (NUS), the Nanyang Technological University (NTU), Singapore Management University (SMU) and UniSIM (SIM University) are the local institutions.

FINANCIAL MATTERS

There are more than 140 commercial banks and 80 merchant banks in Singapore. Most offer full banking services, including savings and current accounts, ATMs (Automated Teller Machines), fixed deposits, safe deposit boxes, loans, overdrafts and transfers. Most banks are open from 9:30 am to 3:00 pm or 4:00 pm on weekdays, and from 9:30 am to 11:00 am or 11:30 am on Saturdays. Almost all the major foreign banks are represented in Singapore, including the ABN AMRO Bank, Bank of America, Wells Fargo International Banking Group, Bank of Nova Scotia, Bank of Tokyo-Mitsubishi, Banque Indosuez, Banque Nationale de Paris, Barclays Bank, Chase Manhattan, Citibank, Credit Suisse, First Boston, Deutsche Bank, Hong Kong and Shanghai Banking Corporation (HSBC), Moscow Narodny Bank, National Australia Bank Ltd, Standard Chartered Bank, Sumitomo and the Union Bank of Switzerland.

Local Banks

The major local banks are:

- Development Bank of Singapore (DBS)
  The Post Office Savings Bank (POSB) merged with DBS in late 1998 and, between them, they now have the most extensive network of branches and ATMs.
- Overseas Chinese Banking Corporation (OCBC)
  Keppel TatLee Bank (already a merged entity of two local banks) merged with OCBC in 2002.
- United Overseas Bank (UOB)
  UOB acquired Overseas Union Bank (UOB) in 2001 and both have been operating under the UOB since 2002.

The necessary requirements for opening an account varies from one bank to another, as well as minimum balances, account charges and initial deposit requirements but here are some likely standard requirments. You will need copies of your passport, employer's letter (endorsing your status), and a statement from a bank in your home country. Singapore has extensive facilities of ATMs and a cashless payment system called NETS (Network for Electronic Transfers) for your convenience. If you plan to stay in Singapore for an extended period, these facilities are highly recommended.

Singapore's regulations for issuing and cashing cheques are similar to those of Great Britain. In small print, near the payee line are the words 'or bearer', which means the cheque can be cashed or deposited by anyone presenting the cheque. Cross out these two words if the cheque is to be cashed or deposited only by the payee stated.

If a 'crossing' is made by drawing two parallel lines on the upper left corner, the cheque must be paid into a bank account and cannot be cashed. Never cross the cheque if you wish to receive cash.

The British system is also used for writing the date—day/month/year. On the cheque, lines are provided for writing the amount in words; you should put the word 'only' after the written amount. If in doubt, ask and do not make any corrections or extra markings on cheques—they will most likely be returned or rejected. Most local and European banks do not return cancelled cheques with bank statements.

Credit Cards

Credit cards are readily accepted in Singapore. Retailers, restaurants, hotels and even some taxis will accept international credit cards. Visa, MasterCard, Diners and American Express are all common here. Typically, to apply for a credit card, you will require an employment pass with at least 9–12 months' validity and an annual salary of S$ 30,000 for normal credit card and S$ 48,000 for a Gold Card.

In such a highly competitive, consumer society like Singapore, credit card offers are rampant with a multitude of rewards, benefits, points, promotions and offers that it can be mind-boggling at times. The good news is that this usually translates to excellent value and rewards for the consumer. Read your statements carefully, use your credit cards whenever possible and redeem your points on time and before you know it, you could be enjoying a relaxing weekend in Bali—on the house! This reward, bonus, loyalty system is not only popular with credit cards but also with your cable bills, phone bills, and almost every major shop in town. In Singapore, you will be accruing 'points' while you sleep and although it is bothersome at times to be asked for your 'loyalty' card at the petrol station, hairdressers, toy shop and the countless other places you go to, it's a huge part of Singapore society and one which is directly aimed at the *kiasu* mentality. Everyone loves a deal, and soon, you will too.

Capitalising on this last point, a number of the more aggressive banks organise roadshows where a special tent is set up in selected areas where there is high human traffic and bank representatives approach anyone in that vicinity to persuade them to sign up for a new card. On offer is more than just what the card can offer but other promotions and incentives e.g. free gifts as well as a waiver of the subscription fee for a certain period of time. One prime area for this is along Orchard Road so if you're the kind who doesn't like to be bothered, just sidestep them or politely decline and make your escape.

Taxes

Singapore has a well-regulated tax system, and personal income tax rates are generally lower than in other developed countries. The tax authority is known as the Inland Revenue Authority of Singapore (IRAS).

The amount of income tax one has to pay depends on two factors:

- Whether you are treated as a tax resident, or a non-tax resident of Singapore
- The income you earn

An individual's tax residence status is determined by his or her employment period in Singapore. Non-residents do not have to pay taxes on foreign income received in Singapore. The following table is a summary of the tax implications from 2003 year of assessment onwards:

Employment Period in Singapore	Resident Status	Tax Implications
60 days or less	Non-Resident	This is considered short-term employment and is exempt from tax unless you are a director, public entertainer or exercising a profession in Singapore.
61–182 days	Non-Resident	Employment income is taxed at 15 per cent or resident rates, whichever gives rise to a higher tax.
183 days or more	Resident	All income is taxed from 0–22 per cent.

You will be regarded as a tax resident if one of the following situations apply:

- You have been in Singapore for at least 183 days in a calendar year.
- You have physically been present or working in Singapore for three consecutive years even though the number of days in Singapore is less than 183 days in the first and third year.

As a tax resident, you will be taxed on all income earned in Singapore and any overseas income that is brought into Singapore in your current year of assessment (which you will only be filing for in the following year). You will also be given personal reliefs (earned income relief, wife relief, children relief, life insurance relief, course fee relief, etc.) and the tax rate is graduated (see next table).

Singapore has a progressive taxation system with a range between the minimum rate and maximum rate. The following table gives the tax rates for different levels of income earned. (As before, these are only applicable from the 2003 Year of Assessment onwards). For more information, refer to:

http://www.iras.gov.sg/ESVPortal/iit/
iit-se-a1.1.12 + foreigners + working + in + singapore.asp

Chargeable Income (S$)		Rates	Tax Payable (S$)
On the first	20,000	0 per cent	0.00
On the next	10,000	4 per cent	400
On the first	30,000		400
On the next	10,000	6 per cent	600
On the first	40,000		1,000
On the next	40,000	9 per cent	3,600
On the first	80,000		4,600
On the next	80,000	15 per cent	12,000
On the first	160,000		16,600
On the next	160,000	19 per cent	30,400
On the first	320,000		47,000
Above	320,000	22 per cent	

Singapore has entered into tax treaties with most of the Asian countries, several European countries and Canada. Most of the tax treaties reduce the rate of withholding tax in respect of interest and royalties, the most usual reduced rate being 10 per cent. To date, no tax treaty has been negotiated with the United States that allows for double taxation relief. However, there are foreign tax credits that can be taken which are significant. For further information and listing of Singapore's tax treaties with other countries visit:

http://www.iras.gov.sg/ESVPortal/
tax_resources/treaties/index.asp

The first step in filing your Singapore income tax return will be for your company to provide you with the IR8A form by 1 March, which contains your salary details. By 31 March, you should also receive an income tax form from the IRAS. Once you have these two forms, you will use your IR8A to fill in your income tax form and then mail both to the IRAS by 15 April. This can also be done online. At this point, no tax payment is due. After the IRAS has received and processed your forms, it will send you a bill for payment known as a Notice of Assessment (NOA). This could usually come between May and October. Once you have received your NOA, you then have two choices in making your payment. You can either pay the full amount within one month of the date of the NOA, or pay the amount due in 12 interest-free monthly installments. If you choose the latter method, the money will be deducted automatically through GIRO. A point to note: GIRO is quite convenient and can certainly alleviate the burden of having to pay a large lump sum, yet, it is important to realise that whenever you may be ready to leave the country, you will be responsible for immediate payment of the full remaining balance.

HEALTH

Not surprisingly, the health care system in Singapore is world-class and highly respected in Asia. Most doctors speak good English, have had training overseas and the facilities and technology used is up-to-date. There are a total of 11 private hospitals, seven public (government) hospitals and several specialist clinics, each specialising in and catering to different patient needs, at varying costs.

Patients are free to choose the providers within the government or private health care delivery system and can walk in for a consultation at any private clinic or any government polyclinic. All health care establishments such as hospitals, nursing homes, clinical laboratories, medical and dental clinics are licensed and regulated by the Ministry of Health (MOH).

Most housing estates are serviced by government polyclinics as well as private clinics. Government polyclinics were set up in the 1970s to provide subsidised and accessible health care to the population. As of January 2006, foreigners will no longer receive subsidies at the polyclinics. With this change in law, current fees at polyclinics will range from S$ 8 for a basic consultation for residents, S$ 12 for PRs and S$ 16 for foreigners.

Expatriates are usually given health benefits as part of their work contracts. This often means selecting a doctor or clinic from a list of managed health providers. The primary care physicians can also dispense drugs and medication so an additional visit to the pharmacist is usually not required, and the costs are all included in the coverage. Doctors here seem to be more liberal in dispensing medication, particularly antibiotics, than those in Europe or the United States.

Should you or a family member require hospitalisation, you can select (based on availability, of course) single-bed, two-bed or four-bed rooms of private hospitals. As for government hospitals, only a choice of single (A class) rooms or two-bed (B1 class) can be selected. Medical fees in government hospitals are relatively lower than in private hospitals but non-Singaporeans will pay a 30 per cent premium over the fees charged to the locals.

And if you are pregnant or considering having a baby while in Singapore, rest assured it will be no problem. In fact, many people from neighbouring Asian countries choose to deliver in Singapore with little or no trouble. Having had a baby in Singapore myself, I would say the only downside is perhaps the absence of family but then again, with household help, the logistics of a growing family are not as complicated... and soon enough, the grandparents will be arriving for their extended visit, anyway.

The procedure for having a child in Singapore is very straightforward. Basically, any child born in Singapore, of non-Singaporean parents, will have no 'nationality' at the time of birth. Usually, a birth registration needs to be completed and then one can apply for a passport and registration through your local embassy. Please check with your country's embassy for the procedure required for births in foreign countries. After the baby is delivered, his or her birth needs to be registered with the Birth Registration Centre and these are conveniently located within hospital premises at the following:

- K K Women's & Children's Hospital
- East Shore Hospital
- Gleneagles Hospital
- Mount Alvernia Hospital
- Mount Elizabeth Hospital
- National University Hospital (NUH)

- Singapore General Hospital (SGH)
- Thomson Medical Centre

For births in hospitals not listed above, the baby's birth has to be registered at the PR Services Centre on the 5th floor of the ICA in Kallang Road. For babies who are not born in hospitals (e.g. home or in cars), the mother has to obtain a Notification of Live Birth from the doctor, midwife or ambulance staff who delivered the baby.

Birth registrations must be done within 14–42 days (including Sundays and public holidays) from the date of birth. If registration is done after 42 days, a letter of explanation stating the reason for late registration must be submitted for the Registrar/Registrar General's approval. After approval has been given, the birth will be registered and the Birth Certificate will be issued.

Documents Needed

At the time of birth registration, the following documents need to be produced:

- Notification of Live Birth, issued by the hospital.
- Both parent's identity cards, if they are Singapore residents or both parents' passports, entry permit and embarkation/ disembarkation card issued by ICA if they are foreigners.
- Original marriage certificate.
- A letter of authorisation from the parents of the child (if someone else registers the birth on behalf of the parents.)
- A fee of S$ 18 is payable for the registration. Some hospitals may charge an administrative fee on top of this amount for the service provided.
- A child's name must be furnished at the time of birth registration. Ethnic characters of the child's name in Chinese/ Jawi/ Tamil can be included in the Birth Certificate.

And a word of warning, now that you have a Singapore-born child, don't be surprised when you receive in the mail a notification for vaccines and immunisations from the Ministry of Health (MOH).

Ambulance and emergency (A&E) care in Singapore is also top-notch. The number to dial for an ambulance is 995, which will transport your call to the nearest government hospital by the Singapore Civil Defence Force (SCDF) emergency ambulance. The SCDF also responds to traffic accidents and other medical emergencies. Note that the SCDF ambulance will not take a patient to a private hospital. However, once stabilised, a patient may choose to transfer to a hospital of his or her choice.

Several private hospitals (Mount Elizabeth, Gleneagles and East Shore) have their own A&E departments which will send an ambulance upon request. Please contact the hospitals directly for their specific A&E hotlines.

Traditional Chinese Medicine

Although Western medicine is the popular and common method of medicine in Singapore, about 12 per cent of the population does rely on Traditional Chinese Medicine (TCM) for much of their outpatient care.

TCM is an important part of the Chinese heritage which has maintained a following in modern society and with both Western and Asian cultures. TCM includes the practice of Chinese medicine, pharmacology/herbalogy, acupuncture, massage and *qigong* (a system of health using exercise and breathing control). Of this thousand-year-old practice, acupuncture (the insertion of needles into the skin) is the best known and most commonly used treatment. Its low cost, simplicity of application and rapid results enhances the practice of this form of medicine and encourage its use, alongside Western medicine.

To better appreciate and understand TCM and its importance in Chinese society, it is vital to know a little about its philosophy. TCM is based on *yin* and *yang*, which like all Chinese philosophies is based on the harmony and balance of life—on the belief that everything, including the universe, is interrelated and changing all the time. *Yin*—the dark, cold and inactive side—must always be balanced by *yang*, the bright, warm and active half. To maintain good health, one must have harmony (a balance of *yin* and *yang*) within oneself and with one's surroundings and peace of mind.

The human body is a microorganism like the world around us and it is believed that it contains the opposing and unifying forces of five interrelated elements: fire, water, wood, gold (or metal) and earth. One is healthy when there is equilibrium and one falls sick when there is an imbalance. The balance of the *yin* and *yang* (including the five elements) plus the proper and adequate flow of *qi* (Chi, life force or energy) is what every human being should strive for. When one's body is somehow imbalanced or has suffered some sort of injury (e.g. sprained ankle), TCM comes into play to get everything back on track again.

Something I encourage anyone visiting Singapore and definitely for anyone living here is to try out the Chinese foot massage and shoulder massage shops that can be found in

Health Tips

The good news, as you have just read, is that Singapore has excellent health care facilities and doctors. The bad news is that you will probably be seeing them much more than when you were in your home land. It is surprising the toll that living in the tropics, on a small, densely populated island, can take on the body. Below are a few tips on staying healthy and keeping your doctor's visits to a minimum:

- Drink lots of water. And more importantly, even if you are not feeling thirsty. Make it a habit and with Singapore tap water perfectly safe to drink, there is no excuse.

- Use sunblock and stay out of the sun during peak hours (11:00 am–2:00 pm). Being virtually on the equator, the sun is very harsh and can cause sunstroke or burning. And with the year-round sunny weather, you may find yourself outdoors more than usual. Do like the locals and carry always carry a tote umbrella most large shopping malls. If you don't believe in TCM, you may after this. But be forewarned, it can be painful but the relief and feeling of well-being are undeniable. And if you suffer from a chronic ailment, several sessions may certainly lead to some relief.

Traditional Chinese medicinal halls can be found all over the city (with over 500 listed in the *Buying Guide*!) but Chinatown is the best place if you want to see some of the well-established shops. Jars of unidentifiable things will line the walls and bins of dried animals, plants and herbs will surround you. Ask for some advice, and you can have a special remedy concocted to suit your ailments.

Alternative Medicine

For those who are interested and for the user of alternative medicine, it is also possible to find a variety of different

to protect yourself from the blistering sun or the unexpected shower.

- Have your vaccines updated and have the Hepatitus A and B shots. Singapore is a fantastic launching pad into the more remote and underdeveloped countries in Asia where food hygiene and diseases may not be as controlled as in Singapore.
- Take a vitamin C tablet or multi-vitamin daily to help boost your immune system.
- Be aware of mosquitoes and possible dengue. Spraying is done weekly at the large condos and in many areas, yet, mosquitoes can still pose a problem. Be sure to use repellent in the evenings and when going to parks and other densely green areas. Although you may not be allergic to mosquito bites in your home country, the heat often causes bites to swell out of proportion. Take necessary precautions in order to avoid later discomfort.

Asian forms of medicine such as Ayurveda, homeopathy and reiki, as well as a host of yoga, *taichi* (a type of Chinese martial arts), *qigong* and other ancient Asian forms of exercise. Morning exercise sessions can be seen along East Coast Parkway, at other public parks and on many HDB grounds.

Insurance

If you are not covered with group health care by your company, there are several factors to consider before taking on additional private insurance. Definitely, consider additional coverage:

- if you're only covered by a national health system or some other universal health system as these may not be adequate for your needs when you are here.
- if you would like to have the option for private care in your home country.
- if you think you might have to seek treatment for a specific problem in another country.

There is nothing to stop you from enquiring about the different insurance policies (some of which are tied to investment and savings plans) offered by the various companies. Before you start asking, just be sure of what you current policy allows and then figure out what you think you would need. Be specific when asking and don't let the agents run you down with their usual spiel. Unfortunately, there are many of such agents out to make a quick buck and haven't quite honed their listening and understanding skills. Be firm and take your time before you decide.

TRANSPORTATION

Getting around Singapore is a breeze, whether you have your own transportation or not. Primarily due to the short, geographical distances of the island itself, the controlled number of private cars on the road and the excellent public transport system, Singapore has established itself as yet another prime example of how to control and manage transportation in a thriving Asian metropolis.

For such a small island, Singapore has many vehicles on its roads. This junction along Orchard Road sees one of the heaviest traffic flows in the country, being the 'gateway' into the heart of town.

To help you better understand the distances, driving across the island from the south of the island to the Causeway in the north (to get to Johor in Malaysia) will take at the most one hour (in heavy traffic), most likely 40 minutes on excellent expressways. The expressways are well marked (all signboards are in English only), well maintained (I have never seen one pothole in seven years) and if it weren't for the incessant improvements and maintenance construction, they just may be the most desirable stretch of concrete in Asia! Even traffic jams and high-peak times may amount to an additional 15 minutes in your commuting time; however, nothing close to the massive traffic jam problems in other Asian cities. Once again, thank the Singapore government for planning things right and controlling not only the number of cars on the road but also installing Electronic Road Pricing (ERP) gantries across the island to help regulate the flow of traffic during peak times and into the CBD.

Owning a car in Singapore is very expensive, bottom line. In typical Singapore government style, several measures have been implemented to control private vehicle ownership and usage. In May 1990, the Vehicle Quota System was implemented and under this system, the Land Transport Authority (LTA) determines the number of new vehicles allowed for registration while the market determines the market price for owning a vehicle. The vehicle quota is, in turn, determined by the vehicle category's share of the total vehicle population, and the quota for a given year is administered monthly by the release of the Certificate of Entitlement (COE). It is that little piece of paper, the COE, that makes Singapore one of the most (if not the most) expensive places in the world to own a car. The cost of a COE can fluctuate quite a bit e.g. S$ 21,710 in March 2005 for a Category B (1.6-litre vehicles and above) car to S$ 9,000 for that same car in December 2005. For that reason, automobiles are a major display of status and wealth in Singapore. Add to that registration tax for new cars, road tax and ERP charges for road usage and the message is clear—the government wants you to use public transport.

And yet another unique aspect of cars in Singapore is that one will hardly ever see a car model that is older than ten years. Since the COE is for a ten-year period (it can then be renewed for either another five or ten years), cars usually reach a point where the scrap value is greater than the price for a new COE so it makes more sense to get the car scrapped.

Everything You Need To Know

Anything and everything you need to know about owning a car in Singapore can be found at LTA's website for car owners:

http://www.onemotoring.com.sg

But should you become a car owner, there are a few things to know. Firstly, a Singapore driver's licence is required if your stay here is more than six months. You must take a local Basic Theory Test before you are allowed to convert your foreign driving licence to a Singapore one. To take the theory test, you need to make an appointment (usually one month later), via the website or in person at one of the three driving centres on the island—Bukit Batok Driving Centre, Singapore Safety Driving Centre and Comfort Driving Centre. Be sure to study and read carefully the driving manual—questions can be confusing due to their wording and many times focus on the minute details of driving. If you are in Singapore for less than six months, you can obtain an International Driver's Licence from either your home country or the Automobile Associate of Singapore (AAS).

Secondly, now that you are ready to sit behind the wheel, be prepared for some pretty shocking road etiquette, or more precisely, lack of it! Tailgating, frequent and un-signalled lane changes, drifts into your lane, reckless motorcycles and not giving way are all common practice on the road. And not to be forgotten is the favourite Singaporean road rule—anything is OK as long as you have your hazard lights on e.g. coming to a complete stop on the main road, blocking an entrance or exit, taking a phone call. It seems like the government has also taken notice on these road practices since the LTA has launched road courtesy campaigns.

Some basic Singapore driving rules are:

- In Singapore, they drive on the left side of the road (meaning the driver sits on the right side of the car and you overtake in the right most lane).
- You must be at least 17 to qualify for an automobile driver's licence.
- The speed limit is 50 kmph on roads and 70–80 kmph on expressways.
- Seat belts and child seats are mandatory.
- All new Singapore driving licence holders are issued a one-year probationary licence, which allows up to a maximum of 12 demerit points in the year. (You get demerit points when you are caught for certain offences.) If you exceed this, you lose your licence. After the initial year, the demerit points allowable are increased to 24 points over a two-year period.
- Road markings galore. For the driving test you will need to learn all the road markings, so study up! Double white lines, zigzag white lines, single yellow lines, double yellow lines, etc., but the most helpful are, of course, the large directional arrows you will find on most roads—great if you are used to driving on the opposite side of the road.

- Do not drink and drive. There are severe penalties (first time offenders could be fined up to S$ 5,000 and jailed for up to six months) and the police tends to conduct many check points in the evenings.
- Do not use your mobile phone without hands-free equipment. If caught, you will be subjected to harsh penalties (fine of S$ 1,000 and/or six months in jail) plus 12 demerit points are taken.
- Beware and be cautious with red light and speed cameras. There are blue and white warning signs signalling an upcoming camera and if a violation occurs, you will receive a summon with the details of the infraction a few days later, in the mail.
- Get ready to be literally 'zapped' with another Singapore scheme intended to help keep the roads congestion-free. All Singapore registered vehicles are required to have an In-Vehicle Unit (IU) for paying ERP tolls. The unit is usually mounted on the dashboard, on the driver's side, so that it can be 'read' by the gantry. A cash card (with a healthy balance) must be in the machine every time you drive through an ERP gantry during peak hours; the toll will automatically be deducted from the cash card. The IU will beep and display the new value on the cash card. Should you not have enough balance when going through a gantry, the cameras will take a photograph of your licence plate and you will receive a fine in the mail a few days later, around S$ 10, depending on the time and location. This IU-cash card method is also being implemented in an increasing number of car parks, and the necessary payment is deducted upon exiting.
- Parking coupons are unique to Singapore and are mandatory when parking in public car parks, especially those maintained by the HDB and URA (Urban Redevelopment Authority). The coupons can be purchased at petrol stations and convenience shops, among other places, and must be properly perforated and displayed on your dashboard so they can be read through the car windscreen. Failure to use them correctly or not use them at all can result in fines

You will find multi-storey car parks like this one in almost all HDB housing estates and they serve the residents in the area as well as visitors. Residents can opt to buy season parking (paying monthly for the right to use the car park) but visitors will have to rely on the coupon system.

and/or wheel clamping. And yes, the 'meter ladies' (women and some men in uniform carrying a high-tech black box that issues your fine straight away) are pretty diligent about checking, so the need will soon be habit forming after a close call or parking violation that is for sure.

Should you decide to take the plunge and buy a vehicle in Singapore, definitely the best word of advice is ask a local colleague and car owner. They will let you know when the COE is up or down, whether to wait one month, maybe it's right before a holiday like Chinese New Year when car prices usually increase. While the vast majority of dealers are reputable, there are a few rogue ones who will try to scam you so if you can get a friend or colleague to recommend someone, so much the better. Since there are so many government regulations and restrictions and car inspections that must be adhered to, the dealer will be your best guide and walk you through all the daunting 'legalities' so getting one you trust is advisable.

There is also the option of leasing a car which is a popular choice with many companies that employ foreigners. Lease agreements include full and regular maintenance, 24-hour breakdown towing service and the responsibility of road tax renewal, insurance, radio licence and inspections is shifted to the company and not you.

And for those that just want a car, not a status symbol, there is the option to buy a car that has the COE expiring in five years or less, or one of the smaller, more economical models which are becoming increasingly available. In addition to the LTA website cited previously, the AAS has a good website (http://aas.com.sg) which provides plenty of background and sage advice on buying a car.

Public Transport

So it's clear the Singapore government doesn't really want you to own a car, but then again, you may not want one either. With the exorbitant cost involved in car ownership, many times it does not make economic sense to own a car. This is especially pertinent to those without children who don't have to juggle schedules, think about transporting strollers and extra equipment, and worry about using car seats. By most standards, Singapore's public transportation offers low prices, efficiency and reliability.

Buses

The least expensive, most extensive coverage of the island is provided by the bus system. Most of the buses are air-conditioned, many are double-decker and a growing number have television available. Buses run seven days a week, usually from 6:00 am to midnight, although those on longer routes might start from 5:30 am. On Fridays and Saturdays, some bus services end later for the benefit of late night revellers. There are also night services running through certain major areas.

Currently, the fare ranges from 64 cents to S$ 1.80, depending on the route, whether the bus is air-conditioned

Bus interchanges, like this one in Tampines, are found in all the larger housing estates, in a central location and usually close to an MRT station. This makes travelling easier as one can transit from one mode to another. At bus interchanges, you will be dropped off at a central point but you need to queue at the designated berths for the bus you want to get on. Some of the newer interchanges have screens which inform you how long you have to wait.

You will find orderly queues like this at an interchange but the situation tends to be a little more chaotic when you board at a bus stop. Some people (probably cut from the same cloth as those who drive) will try to squeeze past you even though there are only three people trying to get on!

and the mode of payment. If you use the EZ-Link card (the payment scheme that links the bus and MRT system), you not only pay less, you also get a small rebate when you transfer from bus to MRT and vice versa. (This also applies in some cases when transferring from one bus to another.) If you are paying by cash, you pay a slightly higher flat rate and will need to insert the exact amount as no change will be given. With the EZ-Link card, the exact fare will be deducted, minus your rebate if it applies. EZ-Link cards can be purchased or topped up at automated machines found at all MRT stations and bus interchanges.

There are also TownLink services that provide connects the different areas within a neighbourhood as well as to the bus interchanges and MRT.

MRT (Mass Rapid Transit)

The MRT (which runs underground and over land) offers a clean, fast, comfortable and convenient way to get around, although service is currently limited, with five lines covering the most densely populated areas of the city. The first MRT stations were opened in 1988 and steady expansion has

This area is monitored by CCTV camera for your safety.

71016

Inside the MRT train.

been underway ever since. By 2010, the Circle Line will be completed and will link all radial lines leading to the city. And more importantly for the handicapped and parents with prams, work is being completed to install lifts and ramps in all stations islandwide.

The MRT runs everyday from 5:45 am–12:15 am and with frequencies of 3–8 minutes. Currently, there are over 60 stations spread around the island serving almost a million passengers daily. The fare varies on distance and mode of payment but ranges from S$ 0.90–1.90, while children, students and senior citizens enjoy concession fares. There are fines for eating, drinking, littering and smoking in MRT stations and on board the trains.

An offshoot of the MRT is the Light Rail System (LRT) that serves a particular area. Currently, there are two: Bukit Panjang and Sengkang/Ponggol.

Taxis

With over 16,860 taxis roaming the city, they are a popular, convenient, fairly inexpensive (compared to many other large cities), fairly easy to hail (unless it's raining, a Friday evening or rush hour!) and impossible to overlook mode of transportation. (They are a favourite place for some very creative advertising campaigns.)

To help make your first taxi rides more enjoyable, here is a bit of helpful background:

- Your driver will be a local Singaporean, most likely male.
- They know the city very well and unless it is some very obscure place, you should be able to reach your destination with no major concerns.
- If they do not know the location, the street directory will not be the first resource; rather they will make a quick call to a buddy for directions—be patient.
- They speak English but of course, the Singaporean version called Singlish so communication may be a bit difficult. Having a written address will certainly help since reading English is not a problem. If you get stuck with communication, this is the time to use

your Singlish, stick a 'lah' at the end of your sentence! (*More on this in* Chapter Eight: The Different Tongues, *page 274.*)

- The driver may also ask which way you would like to go, "ECP or CTE to CBD?" Basically, he is asking whether you would rather have a possibly shorter ride with more tolls to pay, or go the longer, less expensive way.

- The taxi will be in excellent condition with air-conditioning and maybe even some magazines on board.

- Tipping is not required but rounding the fare up is always appreciated.

- Be prepared for an onslaught of personal questions, all intended in good jest and certainly not to be taken offensively or personally.

- And most importantly, be prepared for a bit of motion sickness as the on-off pressing of the accelerator is the preferred way of driving. Maybe it is believed to save petrol by accelerating, then coasting, accelerating and then coasting. Not sure, but it can be a bit nauseating if the traffic is heavy.

The best place to get a taxi, especially on busy, major roads is the designated 'Taxi Queue' locations outside every shopping mall, most office buildings and all hotels in town. Taxis may also be hailed on the road if there is no stand nearby and no disruption to traffic is posed. There are four main taxi firms: CityCab, Comfort, SMRT Taxis and Yellow-Top, as well as other individual taxi operators wich offer more 'prestigious' services such as Maxi Cabs, London Cabs and rides in a Mercedes Benz. A few other Singapore taxi must-knows are:

- The flagdown rate ranges from S$ 2.10–3.10 depending on which taxi you get into and the time you get in. This rate applies for the first 1 km (0.6 mile), and increases by 10 cents for every 240 meters thereafter (up to 10 km) and then 10 cents for every 225 metres (after 10 km) thereafter.

- There are additional charges for every trip from Changi Airport (S$ 5.00) as well as a S$ 1.00 surcharge when you board during the morning and evening peak periods. Peak periods are from 7:30 am–9:30 am and 4:30 pm–7:00 pm on weekdays, and 7:30 am–9:30 am and 11:30 am–2:00 pm on Saturdays.

- The passenger is responsible for any amount payable on the ERP, as displayed on the IU.
- You can call for a cab but that will add S$ 3.50 to your total fare. Booking half an hour or more in advance will set you back an additional S$ 4.80–5.00.
- If you take a taxi between midnight and 6:00 am (some taxis start at 11:30 pm), you will have to add 50 per cent of your fare to the total when you reach your destination.
- On public holidays, you will have to pay an extra S$ 1.00 if you take a taxi from 6:00 pm on the eve of the holiday to midnight of the holiday.

Shuttles

Another Singaporean mode of transportation that offers excellent service are the free shuttles that connect several major points in the city to other nearby popular destinations such as:

- City Hall MRT to Suntec City
- Orchard Road to Great World City
- Jurong East MRT to Science Centre

Help In Getting Around

Finding your way around this small, compact island can be surprisingly difficult! Many main roads tend to weave, change names, and one wrong turn can lead you directly into a never-ending maze of side streets, cul-de-sacs and ring roads. For this reason, nobody should be without the latest version of the street directory, which is available at all major bookshops, news stands and convenience stores. This detailed reference book lists everything including streets, government offices and every other Singapore building and park by name. The directory can also be found online at:

http://www.streetdirectory.com.sg/

SHOPPING

Singapore has been billed and seen as a shopper's paradise for as long as the country has been marketing itself. Asia has been rapidly changing and major international chain and luxury stores have now opened their doors in many of the region's neighbouring countries. The exclusivity that Singapore has had in the past seems to be fading and quite honestly, it's not the cheapest place in Asia when it comes to really finding a bargain. Nevertheless, shopping continues to be a national pastime and the abundance of shopping malls and neighbourhood shops is astounding for such a small island. The sidewalks on Orchard Road are some of the widest I've seen and are usually packed to the extremes on weekends and evenings. Orchard is even designed with underground tunnels that allow easy (if you can handle a few stairwells here and there) access to more malls across the street, MRT stations and refuge in case of the sudden and frequent tropical downpours. But just walk around Singapore's streets long enough and you will suddenly appreciate and understand the need for air-conditioned shopping havens. Like everything else about Singapore, it makes sense.

So as a shopper's paradise, I think that can be argued (especially with regards to price); but where Singapore truly stands out is the large and varied selection of Asian and European goods that can be found. Throw in the convenience and ease of getting around the island and maybe, shopper's paradise is appropriate after all!

Overall, Singapore is a cash and credit card shopping destination and not one big on bargaining because of all the established stores and chain stores. Having said that, however, I would not deter you from asking for a 'good price' in any of the mom-and-pop shops or the small independent stores. Many will give you a better price. And of course, if you are shopping for electronics, carpets, antiques or Chinese furniture, bargaining is a given. Take the cue from the shop owner and whether there is a price tag. With some luck, a 20–40 per cent discount (from the original quote) can be obtained.

If we split shopping into necessities and leisure, the common sense rule dictates—shop where the locals shop if you want the best price. The local Fairprice grocery chain found near most large HDB housing estates will have the lowest prices on toiletries and food, as will the wet markets and small fruit stalls. (*More on wet markets in* Chapter Six: Food Glorious Food, *page 196.*) There are great shopping finds and bargains to be found in the 'heartland' and more suburban/local neighbourhoods such as Ang Mo Kio, Tiong Bahru, Bishan, Bedok and Marine Parade. Explore during the weekends, walk around and observe the local lifestyle. I assure you, either a great food find will result or a great shopping find. It's worth it!

As for shopping for leisure, well, it is down to a science here. Most large malls have become 'entertainment complexes' and you will usually find cineplexes on the top floors, a multitude of shops in the middle floors plus a grocery and large eating area (known as a food court) in the basement. Additionally, the shopping malls tend to specialise in one target audience which makes it convenient and efficient when one is looking for a specific item.

Below is listed a rough guide of some of the large shopping malls. By no means is it meant to be an exhaustive list, rather I have just chosen to highlight the 'biggies' and a few of my personal favourites. The list is in geographical order, starting from the 'top of Orchard'—that is to say, Orchard is a one-way street, so from the furthest point at the top of the road and continuing to drive down towards the other end.

- Tanglin Mall (163 Tanglin Road)
  An expatriate haven with a large supermarket, Tanglin Market Place where an excellent selection of meats, cheese and deli products can be found, alongside an array of hard-to-find American and European food products. A range of excellent, European shoe shops (with large shoe sizes available) for adults and children, clothing stores selling Asian fashion for the Western taste, British India, small curio and Asian artefact stores, a large health

food shop plus Gymboree and KinderMusik outlets for doting parents.

- Forum the Shopping Mall (583 Orchard Road)
The large Toys "R" Us anchor store is the main attraction with a host of other child-oriented clothing, book/craft and toy stores. There are also several designer-label clothing shops on the ground floor to keep mom entertained (Emporio Armani, D&G, Max Mara) and a Coffee Bean where you can rest and rejuvenate your tired feet.

- Palais Renaissance (390 Orchard Road)
This shopping destination offers excellent eye candy or a well deserved splurge with such high-end tenants as Prada, Donna Karan, The Link (local luxury brand importer), Jim Thompson (exquisite Thai Silk, home furnishings and fabrics) and the 'ladies who lunch' favourite, the Marmalade Pantry restaurant in the basement.

- Wheelock Place (501 Orchard Road) and Liat Towers (541 Orchard Road)
Adjacent to each other, these shopping malls offer plenty to see with Wheelock housing Borders book store, the new, large AppleCentre, Marks & Spencer and a host of restaurants and boutique shops, while Liat Towers is home to the widely popular, Spanish clothing stores Zara and Massimo Dutti with clothing for women, men and children. There is also a Starbucks for a quick pick-me-up, plus a Burger King for the kids to grab a bite.

- Far East Plaza (14 Scotts Road)
A large, bustling shopping mall that specialises in independent, budding local designers and everything for the young and trendy. In the basement is Level One where one can find a unique array of street fashion, accessories and knick-knacks.

- C K Tangs (320 Orchard Road)
The grandaddy of local department stores (founded in 1932), Tangs has made its mark as an Asian lifestyle store with an international appeal. Be sure to check out its extensive kitchenware department in the basement.

An aerial view of Orchard Road which is the tree-lined strip in the middle of the picture. Scotts Road branches off to the left (bottom of picture). C K Tangs is the building on the left, the one just in front of the tower with the Oriental roof (which is Mariott Hotel).

- Wisma Atria (435 Orchard Road)
  The large Japanese department store Isetan houses its exclusive designer boutiques in this complex while the remaining floors showcase more designer and high street fashions such as French Connection, Anteprima, Paul & Joe, Topshop and Warehouse.
- Lucky Plaza (304 Orchard Road)
  A magnet for domestic workers on the Sundays, this houses shop upon shop of tourist trinkets, curios, electronics and clothing. This is a good place to try your bargaining skills, especially fo electronics.
- Ngee Ann City (391 Orchard Road)
  Besides the giant Japanese department store Takashimaya, this massive complex houses over 100 other speciality stores ranging in everything from books (Kinokuniya, the largest bookstore in South-east Asia), to housewares, designer clothing, jewellery and a newly expanded fourth floor complete with excellent art supply stores, beautiful paper shops and children's boutiques. Practically everything you can imagine can be found here: supermarket, library, post office, art gallery, a plethora of excellent restaurants and one of the busiest and popular food courts (eating area, *see* Chapter Six: Food Glorious Food, *page 188*) on Orchard. Plus the large, open outside area (the Civic Plaza) in front of the building hosts all sorts of events like fashion shows, contests, concerts and weekend entertainment.
- Paragon (290 Orchard Road)
  Across the street from Ngee Ann City, newly revamped, renovated and expanded, Paragon is the place for more upmarket designer boutiques such as Gucci, Kenzo, Ermenegildo Zegna and Prada. There are also large outlets of department stores UK chain Marks & Spencer and local chain Metro, together with a host of speciality, boutique accessory and home shops.
- The Hereen (260 Orchard Road)
  Home to the large HMV music store (the largest in Asia), this shopping mall is known for the Annex on the fourth and fifth floors. The Annex presents a new shopping

concept similar to Harajuku in Tokyo or Island Beverly in Hong Kong, where shops sell street and vintage fashion wear, unique accessories, quirky toys and comics.

- Centrepoint (176 Orchard Road)
  One of the largest and most popular centres, here you will find something for everyone. The large Robinson's department store is the anchor tenant here, and stands beside stores specialising in classical music, casual clothing, electronics, furnishings, Oriental rugs, sporting goods, fine arts and Asian antiques, books and much, much more.

- Plaza Singapura (68 Orchard Road)
  Recently, new life has been breathed into the oldest multi-storey shopping centre (built in 1974) on Orchard with the arrival of the French hypermart, Carrefour, and the Australian craft and material store, Spotlight. Other attractions include a large cineplex, music, book, clothing, home furnishing and electronic stores, as well as a range of other speciality shops.

So that is an edited overview of the iconic Orchard Road but of course, there are many other interesting and worthwhile shopping destinations around the island. The other area worth noting is the Raffles City Shopping Centre that is connected via an underground shopping mall (Citilink) to the neighbouring Suntec City and Marina Square shopping areas. Raffles City is located next to the City Hall MRT station.

Places to Shop

The following websites offer a more complete and detailed listing of places to shop:

- http://www.visitsingapore.com/publish/stbportal/en/home/ what_to_do/shopping/where_to_shop.html
- http://www.entersingapore.info/country/Shopping/shops A_Z.htm

---

Currently, there are several great new shopping guides e.g. City Scoops has an interesting list of more specialised shops. Of course, word-of-mouth is good too, especially if this comes with recommendations. More importantly, discovering a shop and area on your own adds immensely to the reward of buying and finding something new. Not to take away from the hunt, but to enhance your experience, here is my guide to the best Singapore shopping destinations (in no particular order):

- Holland Village

    A widely popular shopping and eating destination, for both expatriates and locals, because of its unique independent outdoor shops and small shopping arcade with a good and wide, albeit expensive (aimed at foreigners) selection of Asian artefacts (porcelain, batiks, wooden accessories, furniture) and souvenirs. Along the road are news vendors carrying a huge selection of international magazines and behind the arcade is PariSilk—the insider's place for cheap electronics that has knowledgeable staff. Across the road is Jalan Merah Saga (part of Chip Bee Gardens) which has evolved into an eclectic mix of interesting art galleries and speciality stores (Galerie Cho Lon is known for its interesting and quirky mix of books, music, furniture, accessories and curios from India, China, Vietnam and beyond). There is a row of excellent eating establishments and food related supply stores, among them Da Paolo (which has wonderful gourmet takeaway delicacies), The Butcher and Phoon Huat & Co for ingredients and baking supplies. The only drawback to this unique area is the lack of parking, now made worse by the construction work for the upcoming Circle Line station which has eaten into space normally allotted for car parks. It is hoped that once the MRT is up and running, this problem will be alleviated.

The various ethnic enclaves are also wonderful places to visit and shop. The book, *Discover Singapore on Foot* by Dominique Grêlé is an excellent guide, packed with history, architecture and interesting facts on the Lion City.

- Chinatown

    This small ethnic enclave is still a popular destination for its unique Chinese shops, medicinal halls, eateries and

Part of Smith Street in Chinatown comes alive with local food every evening. During the day, you can still visit the shops in the area.

old Singapore charm that it has tried hard to retain. This is a must-see during the major Chinese festivals of Lunar New Year and the Mid-Autumn Festival. Any other day, it's still very worthwhile visiting the Chinese Heritage Centre on Pagoda Street and the Yue Hwa Emporium (at intersection of Cross Street and Eu Tong Sen Street), the local branch of the Hong Kong department store that offer all things Chinese—five floors of everything from Chinese herbs and medicine to clothing for the entire family, household items, musical items, arts and crafts, porcelain and furniture. Chinatown is also well known for its beautiful shophouse architecture and colours, as well as being the home of two of Singapore's oldest places of worship—the Masjid Jamae at 218 South Bridge Road is one of the city's oldest mosques (built between 1827 and 1835) and, not far from it at 242 South Bridge Road, the Sri Mariamman Temple is Singapore's oldest Hindu temple (established in 1827 and completely rebuilt in 1843).

RISHI
HANDICRAFTS
リシ・ハンディクラフト
58. ARAB STREET

TOKO PULICAT CHOP GADJA
GOODWILL TRADING CO,

BAGHDAD ST

Arab Street has many speciality stores that offer great bargains.

The stalls along Serangoon Road in Little India hold wonderful treasures for both the locals and expatriates. Take your time and explore.

A short walk from the centre of Chinatown is the intersection of Club Street and Ann Siang Road, where you will find picturesque two- and three-storey shophouses, unique home stores and a thriving evening restaurant scene. In the other direction, towards the famous Maxwell Food Centre is Erskine Road which is quickly developing into a must-see destination with the chic Scarlet Hotel (for decadent rooftop drinks) and a few interesting, quirky home and accessory stores.

- Little India
  A must-see during Deepavali when the streets and shops are lit up with lights, decorations and packed with artisanal decorations. Explore all the alley ways, historical shophouses and authentic Indian flavours and smells. And one place you have to go to is Mustafa Department Store (corner of Serangoon Road and Syed Alwi Road)—the only major store that is open 24 hours a day, seven days a week in Singapore—the shop destination for bargain hunters and those patient enough to navigate the four floors of packed merchandise and aisles.

- Arab Street
  Part of Kampong Glam (just off Beach Road and Ophir Road), this Middle Eastern Muslim neighbourhood has

seen many changes in recent years. With the arrival of several small, independent cafés and restaurants, the area has been rejuvenated with nightlife and an easy, laid-back feel. The streets are short and some are for pedestrians only which encourage you to meander and step into the little shophouses with stores of baskets, material, ribbons, oriental perfumes, fabrics, carpets, second-hand finds as well as Singapore souvenirs and curios.

SAFETY AND SECURITY

In this day and age, security and safety for one's family is neither a given nor a ridiculous consideration. It is a fact of life and when you are lucky enough to have it (or more importantly, feel it) you don't want to take it for granted. In Singapore, one feels the security. It may just be a state of mind since after all, where is one really safe and secure? There are no guarantees. But the safety

Since December 2001, Singapore security services have detained more than three dozen members of Jemaah Islamiyah (JI), a terrorist organisation with links to Al Qaeda.

is there, be it in the form of the proactive government, the non-aggressive nature of the people, the tolerance for racial and religious differences and the sheer geographical size of the country.

In a Feedback Unit poll of 519 Singaporeans in July 2005, following the London bomb blasts, 74 per cent of those polled believed that despite the threat of terrorism, Singapore remained one of the safest places to live in the world. And a large majority (88 per cent) was confident that the government had taken the necessary measures to ensure national security. As a follow-up to the increased terrorists acts in the region (Indonesian blasts in October 2002, August 2003 and September 2004), Singapore has increased its security measures in the country. The government has increased the number of police patrols in MRT stations, tightened scrutiny of air cargo, regulated the sale of pre-paid mobile phone cards (in terrorist incidents abroad, militants have exploited the anonymity offered by pre-paid cards to carry out their

This building houses one of the divisions of the SCDF (there are a total of four) plus the fire station. The police centre is to the left (not in picture). Strategically located defence forces around the island are part of what makes the country so secure.

deadly missions), and installed radiation detection devices at container ports. In January 2006, a full-scale mock terror attack drill was held by the SCDF, with encouraging results. Clearly, the Singapore policy of 'emergency preparedness' is taken seriously.

This leads to me another important aspect of Singaporean life that is taken very seriously—all the laws governing this tiny city-state. For such a small country, it seems like its laws and reputation are known the world over as either an exemplary case of how to do it right, or as an example of how to take away freedom from individuals. The debate will continue for a long time that is for certain; however, after living here, the question seems to be, are you really taking away freedom when you are giving back so much security and safety to the society and individual? It's a price many people are willing to pay in this day and age.

One has to understand and see the point of view of the people in charge. They have forthrightly taken away anything and everything which, in their eyes, could upset the tranquility and safety of the society. Through fines, imprisonment, caning and the death penalty, the Singapore government has managed, with great success, to maintain the balance and order it desires in the society.

A popular T-shirt design reads, 'Singapore is a fine city. We have fines for everything'. This is absolutely true, and the fines are not small either e.g. first-time offenders can be fined S$ 500 or more for littering or jaywalking. Below is a list of some uniquely Singapore offences and punishments:

- It is illegal to use a toilet and then not flush it.
- You will be fined for spitting.
- The sale, importation and possession of chewing gum is banned and subject to heavy fines. This was done as the result of the high cost and difficulty of removing chewing gum from the street.
- Litterbugs who are caught more than once are issued with a CWO (Corrective Work Order), made to wear bright jackets and to clean up a public place. The media may even be invited to cover the event.
- Items such as bullet-proof clothing, toy guns, pistols, weapons or spears cannot be brought into the country without authorisation from the government.
- Chewing tobacco, toy currency and obscene materials are strictly prohibited.
- Smoking is not allowed in public buses, taxis, lifts, theatres, cinemas, government offices, air-conditioned restaurants, shopping centres and some of the newer bus stops. (This is expected to extend to more areas over time.) First time offenders are fined S$ 1,000.
- Flicking a cigarette butt on the ground could easily get a smoker a fine for littering.
- Eating or drinking is prohibited in MRT trains and stations. It carries a minimum fine of S$ 500.
- Driving while using a mobile phone carries a fine of up to S$ 10,000.

After the Michael Fay (the American teenager caned for vandalism) incident in 1994, it seems that the world is more familiar with the Singaporean policy of caning. This is done by a martial arts expert with a six-foot-long piece of rattan that has been soaked in brine. Caning is carried out for vandalism offences, immigration violations and other offences. It is a mandatory part of the sentence for rape and many drug-trafficking offences.

And for persons caught trafficking large amounts of narcotics, the punishment is the death penalty which was introduced in 1975 for persons convicted of trafficking more than 15 g of heroin, more than 30 g of morphine, 30 g of cocaine, 500 g of cannabis, 200 g of cannabis resin, or 1.2 kg of opium. The law is very straightforward—if you possess these quantities, you are deemed the trafficker and therefore, subject to the death penalty. Per capita, Singapore has the highest number of death penalties in the world.

With all the petty laws, strict punishment and lack of personal freedom that may be absent in Singapore, you have, on the other hand, one of the lowest crime rates in Asia, beautifully maintained public gardens and parks, clean streets, beaches and public transport, safe streets and neighbourhoods and you will never have the horrible sensation of sticking your fingers in someone's old chewing gum. And don't believe that because you are a foreigner or tourist you are exempt from the law, it applies to everyone on Singapore soil. In the end, strict yes, but more importantly, effective.

FOOD
GLORIOUS FOOD

CHAPTER 6

MAN AT WOK

'And it is not just sustenance; eating is a social occasion
and celebration for Singaporeans. They love their food—
the different ethnic cuisines as well as the variety
of ingredients and preparation styles that have
become signature Singaporean dishes.'
—*Not Just a Good Food Guide: Singapore*

SINGAPORE PRIDES ITSELF ON BEING A FOOD LOVER'S PARADISE, having practically every kind of cuisine on this small island. This is not surprising given the country's multi-racial ethnic mix and its position at the crossroads of Asia. The sheer variety that is available will astound you—everything Asian from Chinese to Indonesian to Indian to Thai to Japanese, and international cuisines such as French, Italian, Egyptian and Russian can be had if you just know where to go.

While we are on the topic of international food, let's explore this a little bit. You will not have to worry if you have a craving for food from home because you're likely to find it here, either in its pure form or mixed in with something a little Asian. There are tonnes of food guides at the local book stores and just as many write-ups in the local newspapers on where you can find what. If you enjoy eating, keep your eyes and ears open for these and you'll be able to pick out a favourite restaurant sooner than you think.

Most international food is served at restaurants and it is only recently that a number of outlets have opened in food courts and coffee shops (*more on what these are a little later on in this chapter*). What this means is that international food is comparatively more expensive. You will, however, be treated to some of the best cuisines in the world as a number of renowned chefs have outlets here. On the whole, your taste buds are in for a treat.

A TASTE OF LOCAL FOOD

So, what if you're the adventurous kind and want to try some of the local food? You're in luck! Singapore has much to offer by way of its own cuisine, which consists mainly of Chinese, Malay, Indian and Peranakan dishes. As you already know, the Singaporeans of today are descended from immigrants who came mainly from China, Malaysia, Indonesia and India, so of course, the food they have today is what was brought over by their ancestors. However, what came over has not been in a vacuum and many of the dishes have evolved to suit local tastes. Living with other cultures also means that one culture will adapt or adopt culinary aspects from another. For example, many Chinese dishes in Singapore have chilli or other spices added while the original dish tends to be lighter or blander; the Malays and Indians have taken a page from Chinese food and incorporated the different types of noodles into their cuisine.

To get into an in-depth discussion of local food would take too long and too many pages so here are just certain main characteristics to keep in mind. If you really want to try the entire spectrum, take your time and get a local person to help you out. There are so many outlets around the island that you might like to visit different ones to try different dishes, or even the same type of dishes for a different taste. Another good source of information is the book, *Not Just a Good Food Guide: Singapore* which gives pretty detailed descriptions of all the popular local dishes from the different ethnic groups plus a couple of suggestions where you might try them.

Staple Foods

Considering their ancestry, it isn't really surprising that the staple food for most Singaporeans is rice, with noodles coming a close second. Steamed white rice is probably the most popular and regardless of whether Singaporeans are eating out or at home, steamed white rice is usually eaten with a number of savoury dishes from a few food groups i.e. vegetables, seafood, meat, etc. If you'd like to eat as the locals do, try ordering something from the economical rice (strange term, but true) or *nasi padang* stall—the latter is similar in nature but is normally a Muslim stall so the food is *halal*. There are also a number of one-dish meals using rice as a base e.g. fried rice, chicken rice (a hot favourite but cholesterol laden!), roast meat rice, *nasi lemak* and *nasi bryani* (*see the list of typical dishes in this chapter for an explanation of what these are*). Oh, and some of these dishes use a variation on steamed white rice. For example, in chicken rice, the rice served is aromatic and a little oily from having been cooked with *pandan* (screwpine) leaves, butter and chicken stock. Similarly with *nasi lemak* where the rice is cooked with coconut milk. In *nasi bryani*, basmati rice is cooked with spices to give it a yellow colouring.

Rice comes in other forms as well. The Malays frequently make *ketupat* (sometimes also known as *lontong*), where raw rice is wrapped in leaves and steamed. As it expands and has little space to move, the final appearance is very compressed. This is normally eaten with another dish, either savoury and/or spicy e.g. *rendang* or *satay* sauce.

The Chinese also use rice as a base to make other dishes. For example *chwee kueh* is a small steamed rice flour cake eaten with a fragrant vegetable topping. *Bak chang* or rice dumplings makes use of white glutinous rice.

Noodles, which you probably know, are Chinese-style pasta and they come in a host of different types. Here are some of the more common:

- There are basically two types of egg and wheat noodles: the thin noodles are known as *mee kia* while the fatter flat ones, *mee pok*. (In case you're wondering, *mee* is noodles in Hokkien and Teochew.)
- Bright yellow noodles are known as Hokkien *mee* or *sek mee* and its colour comes not from eggs but from the alkali that is added to the wheat-based mixture.
- Flat rice flour noodles are known as *kway teow*. Sometimes people call this *hor fun*, especially those that are broader.
- *Bee hoon* are very thin rice flour noodles that are rather translucent before they are cooked. They are also known as rice vermicelli and are often mixed up with the glass noodles that is often found in Thai food. Incidentally, glass noodles are made from mung bean.
- *Chor bee hoon* is also made from rice flour but it is long and round in shape like Hokkien *mee*.

Wanton mee is very popular in Singapore and can be eaten for breakfast or lunch. (Some people don't mind it for dinner either!) *Wanton* is a small meat dumpling normally served in soup. It is eaten with noodles served with some vegetables and roast meat.

These basic noodles can be combined with all manner of ingredients for a large selection of dishes. The Chinese have a long list of dishes such as *wanton mee* (see picture above), beef *hor fun* and fish ball noodles, while the Malays have *mee siam* (*bee hoon* in a sweet-sour gravy) and *mee soto* (Hokkien *mee* in a soup made from chicken stock), and the Indians have *mee goreng* (noodles fried with chilli and some vegetables). In many cases, you can specify which type of noodles you want. For the Chinese noodles dishes, many come in either the soup or the dry versions so you need to indicate which you want. Keep in mind that the dry versions often come with a dollop of chilli so if you aren't used to spicy food yet, make sure you tell them not to add this.

For Indians, breads are also a staple. These aren't your usual sandwich loaf type of breads but Indian breads— basically dough made from different quantities of ingredients, kneaded and cooked in various ways. Some of the popular ones include *roti prata* (a crêpe-like bread), *naan* (leavened flatbread cooked in a tandoor) and *chapatti* (wheat-based flatbread cooked over a griddle).

Meats and Seafood

Most of the other foods in Singapore aren't really that exotic so you don't have to worry too much about trying fried silk worms, sautéed cockroaches or braised fish eyes. What will or won't make you squirm will depend on what you're used to before and how daring you are when it comes to food. Among some of the more 'unusual' dishes you will come across are gizzards and innards, raw cockles, frogs (bull frogs and padi frogs), bone marrow, pigeon, sea snails and black chicken (cooked complete with the feet).

"We Throw Away the Heads"

In the 1980s, a British gentleman was sent here for six months by his head office to oversee the operations of the local factory. The factory manager, a Chinese man, took him out in the first few days, just to get him used to the place and the local cuisine. The British man was keen to try the food here and professed a fondness for spicy food. When the Chinese man suggested going for fish head curry, he was surprised at the puzzled look on the Brit's face. The latter explained, "We don't eat fish heads back home. We thrown them away and just cook the main body of the fish." It took some convincing but the British man was finally persuaded to go along and try it for himself. He was amazed at how wonderful it tasted and kept going back whenever he could.

So what can you look forward to? There's a lot of fresh seafood as fishermen still go out to sea every day. These are sold are the markets and to restaurants. Smaller outlets still tend to use frozen seafood (fish in particular) so if you are sensitive about the taste and smell, just be more cautious. As far as meats are concerned, there is a wide variety. For poultry, chickens and ducks are the most common; for red meats, pork, beef and mutton. Remember, Muslims don't take pork but they're quite happy with beef, mutton, chicken and seafood. Hindus don't eat beef and a good majority are not too keen about pork either so you find that most will eat mutton, goat meat, chicken and seafood. The Chinese eat almost all types of meat but there is a small minority who do not take beef as a sign of respect for one of the gods they pray to.

Vegetables and Fruits

In Singapore, there are a number of green leafy tropical vegetables and most are more well-known by their local names. Among these are *chye sim* (Chinese mustard greens), *kang kong* (convovulus), *dou miao* (snow pea shoots) and *gai lan* (Chinese kale). These are normally sautéed, fried or cooked in soups. Other Western vegetables are also available, like broccoli, cabbage, carrots, iceberg lettuce, potatoes, okra, aubergines and spinach.

There are also a number of Asian fruits which you may have heard about but not actually seen. These include *rambutans*, dragon fruit, mangosteens, *cempedek*, jackfruit, lychee, longan, soursop, star fruit, *chiku*, rose apple and, of course, durian.

Amazing Strength

For many Singaporeans, the durian is the king of fruits. Native to the region, this fruit has a strong and distinctive odour which you will either love or hate. Its green and thorny husk belies the soft succulent flesh that can be found on the inside. Once you crack open the husk, you will find that each of its compartments (there could be six or eight) contains several pieces of yellow flesh. Each of these pieces comes with a seed in the centre and if the fruit is of high quality, you will find a lot of creamy flesh and a very small seed.

It does take some skill to open the husk and the thorns do not make it any easier. Most people will use a knife to cut slits in the back end of the fruit before prying it open. Seet, an experienced fruit seller, once had a customer who claimed he could open a durian with his bare hands. In all his years selling durians, Seet had never been able to open one without the help of a blade and he really doubted anyone could. He told this customer, "If you can open it using only your hands, you can have the durian for free." Five minutes later, Seet found himself short of a durian as the man first made slits at the back of the fruit with his thumb nail and then pried the husk open. The fruit seller could not believe his eyes; but he respected the man for his ability and gladly let him have the durian for free. Every time this customer returned to buy fruits, Seet would ask him to demonstrate his bare-handed skills.

Vegetarian Food

There are a number of outlets that sell vegetarian food and these are either Chinese vegetarian or Indian vegetarian, of which the latter uses mainly vegetables, lentils and beans. Chinese vegetarian food sees a lot of fried local vegetables as well as a number of mock meats made out of bean curd. For example, the stall may have goose, fish or *char siew*, but even though they may look very much like the real thing on the outside, there are actually made out of soya bean curd. In some cases, the taste of a dish may even be similar because the texture of the mock meat is very much like the real thing.

Constant Craving

One thing you will notice after your first few weeks here is that Singaporeans love to eat, at all hours of the day. That explains why there are so many food outlets and snack stands all over the island, sometimes even in places where there doesn't seem to have much human traffic. Singapore is so small that it isn't really that difficult to travel from side of the country to the other just to get a taste of your favourite food. And yes, there are places that are open 24 hours a day so you can never really go hungry here.

Some of the snacks are worth a try as they can be as delicious as main meals. You don't really need any one to help you here. Visit a shopping mall or walk along Orchard Road and you will find stalls that sell small items which you can munch as you walk. After a while, you find one that you will really like.

Desserts and Drinks

You will be spoilt for choice when it comes to desserts. Lots of *kuehs* (local cakes), hot 'soupy' desserts, as well as desserts with fruits and ice on top. One of the most popular, especially among the younger children, is *ice kachang* which consists of a mountain of flavoured and coloured ice sitting on top of 'hidden' treasures in a bowl: red beans, diced jelly, sweet corn, rice-flour 'worms' and *attap chee* (the unripe fruit of the nipah palm). The latest twist on this age-old recipe is to add a dollop of durian or strawberry purée or a scoop of ice cream on the top of the ice mound. This is great to have on a hot day but it can leave your mouth rather numb. Another popular Singaporean way to eat ice cream is tucked into a slice of bread. There are a number of ice cream vendors (with a portable ice box on wheels) along Orchard Road who have this local speciality.

Fruit juices and fruit-based drinks are common here, and you might like to try some using some of the local fruits. One of the most popular is sugar cane juice where the sugar cane is passed through a press and the juice is collected. It is normally served with some ice which makes it more cool and refreshing. And another popular favourite for cooling the mouth after some spicy food is a kalamansi lime drink. Kalamansis are small, sour lemons that are combined with lime and perfectly sweetened with sugar syrup for a refreshing drink. If you like beverages, beware that if you are ordering coffee and tea at place other than a restaurant or a coffee or tea specialist outlet, what you get is made local style and may be stronger and much sweeter than what you are used to.

Some Popular Dishes

Chinese

- chicken rice: fragrant rice (raw white rice sautéed with pandan leaves and margarine then steamed with chicken stock) served with pieces of chicken which has either been boiled, braised with soya sauce or roasted
- *wanton mee*: noodles served with *char siew* (roast pork, with the red colouring) and *wanton*, a little meat dumpling that's either boiled or fried
- chilli crabs: chopped up crabs (usually the Sri Lankan variety) fried in a spicy chilli concoction
- *char kway teow*: literally 'fried kway teow', this is rice flour noodles fried with egg, some vegetable and meat as well as black soya sauce and sweet flour sauce
- *bak chor mee*: this means 'minced meat noodles' when literally translated; noodles mixed with fermented black rice vinegar and oil and served with pork in various forms, minced being one of them. A soup version is also available.

(Continued on the next page)

(Continued from previous page)

Chinese (continued)
- carrot cake: a steamed cake made from rice flour and radish (known as 'white carrot' in Chinese; aha, the light dawns...) is broken up and fried with eggs, chopped spring onions and *chye poh* (preserved radish). Some places add sweet black soya sauce to give it a brownish appearance.

Malay
- *nasi lemak*: rice cooked with coconut milk, served with small helpings of *sambal* (chilli mixed with other ingredients), crispy *ikan bilis* (anchovies) and peanuts, fried omelette and fried *ikan kuning* (gold-banded scad); sometimes chicken wings and *otah otah* (barbecued mixture of fish paste, chilli and starch).
- *mee siam*: *bee hoon* and bean sprouts served in a sweet and sour gravy
- *rendang*: meat (usually beef) slow-cooked in spices, coconut milk and water
- *satay*: barbecued meat on skewers eaten with a spicy peanut sauce
- *roti john*: a local inventon, this is minced meat, egg and sliced onions on a baguette and fried face-down on a griddle

Indian
- *nasi bryani*: basmati rice cooked with spices and meat
- *roti prata*: a type of thin crêpe-like Indian bread eaten with curry gravy
- Indian *rojak*: deep-fried flour-based batters (with and without fillings such as potatoes) eaten with a peanut-based sauce
- fish head curry: a local invention, this is a complete fish head cooked then served drenched in a thick spicy curry sauce

Peranakan
- *laksa*: noodles and some meat served in a thick and spicy curry soup; also known as *laksa lemak* (rich *laksa*)
- Penang *laksa*: noodles and fish meat served in a sour but spicy fish stock; also known as *assam laksa* (sour *laksa*)

EATING, SINGAPORE STYLE

Unless they are being invited to a formal meal, most Singaporeans are quite casual in their eating style. Many Malays and Indians prefer using their hands, especially when eating at home, while Chinese are as comfortable and adept at using forks and spoons as they are with chopsticks. Here are some areas that you should pay attention to.

Communal Dining

In most Asian cultures, communal dining is common, whether it's at home or at a restaurant, whether the occasion is formal or not. Basically the main dishes are placed in the centre of the table and everyone helps themselves to however much they want. The Health Promotion Board (HPB) has been trying to encourage all food outlets to provide serving spoons but some places still don't. You can always ask for extra spoons or forks if you are not comfortable with everyone dipping their own cutlery into the communal dish. Also, when using the communal cutlery, make sure that it does not come into contact with anything on your plate.

If you are invited to a Chinese banquet, each dish is brought out one at a time and is served to all diners at the table. In some nouveau Chinese restaurants, the dish may be divided in the kitchen and individual portions will be served to you.

For a typical meal, there could be anything from three to eight dishes depending on how many diners you have at the table. If you are the one tasked with ordering the food, try to make sure you have a good mix, preferably one from each of the major food groups.

Halal Food

As mentioned before, Muslims will only eat *halal* (permitted) food. If you are eating out with Muslim friends and have ordered non-*halal* food, make sure you do not mix up the cutlery or put non-*halal* food onto the crockery from a halal stall. A big faux pas would be to use the fork and spoon from a *halal* stall to eat the Chinese food you had ordered, just because you have problems using a pair of chopsticks. Unless, of course, the cutlery is disposable.

Eating with Your Hands

You might like to 'do as the Romans do' and use your hands to eat. All fine and good and the locals are likely to applaud your effort. Just remember to always use your right hand to touch the food. How do you eat with your fingers? Normally you use the cutlery to dish what you would like onto your plate first. Then use your fingers to take a little bit of one dish and put that together with some rice. Make it into a small ball before using your thumb to push it into your mouth. The goal is to only have your fingertips touch the food. It is considered bad manners to have the entire hand covered or food dripping down to your elbow. It sounds more complicated than it is and the more you practise, the better you will get.

Some places will have a wash basin nearby so clean your hands before and after the meal. Muslim outlets also have a kettle and washing bowl and you're welcome to make use of these.

Sometimes you might be required to use your hands to eat certain types of food e.g. crabs or prawns. Don't be shy; go ahead, use your hands and enjoy yourself. You will be given wet towels or a small bowl of water with lemon or lime to wash your hands at the end of the meal.

Using Chopsticks

This, too, takes time to master and you shouldn't bother what people tell you about technique. As long as the food gets to your mouth without too much trouble, you're on the

Another very Asian technique for eating which is quite novel for foreigners is to eat with the fork in the left hand and the spoon in the right. Pushing with the fork!

right track. Couple of things to keep in mind. Don't transfer food from one pair of chopsticks to another. And don't stick chopsticks upright into a bowl of rice as this is reminiscent of funeral rites. Some people also consider it impolite to cross your chopsticks. If you are dining at a restaurant that provides chopstick holders, make sure you rest your chopstick on these holders if you have finished eating. This is a sign to the wait staff that he or she can remove your crockery.

EATING PLACES

Compared to many other cultures, Singaporeans eat out frequently. Lunch is normally taken at eating places around the workplace and few people bother to bring packed lunches from home. After a hard day at the office, the last thing anyone wants to do is slave over a hot stove when he or she can buy a tasty and satisfying dinner for just a few dollars. Many families with school-going children will try to have dinner at home, with food usually being prepared by the domestic help or a stay-at-home parent.

Dining Do's and Don'ts

Do's

- Use serving spoons when taking food from a communal dish.
- If you'd like to, learn how to use your hands to eat as the Malays and Indians do.
- When eating seafood such as crabs and shelled prawns, you're welcome to use your hands.
- Make the effort to use a pair of chopsticks.
- To signal that you have finished with the dish in front of you, place your chopsticks on the holders if they are provided and not across the plate or bowl.

Some (with children or otherwise) also order from catering services which offer a different menu (meals consisting of rice plus meat and vegetable dishes) every day and this rotates on either a bi-weekly or monthly basis. For many, this is one way to have a 'home-cooked' meal without the hassle of having to cook or burning a hole in their pockets.

So where do Singaporeans go when they do decide to eat out? There are a few places depending on what you want to eat, the atmosphere you want and how much you want to spend. Here's a quick guide.

Hawker Centres

One of the oldest types of eating place in Singapore having being around for decades, this is a collection of stalls in a large sheltered complex. Be prepared to sweat it out if you want to eat here as all of them only have ceiling or wall fans. If the centre is fortunate to be at the confluence of winds, then it will probably be cooler. If you're planning to attend some high-powered meeting, think twice about eating here as you're likely to smell like a hawker centre once you leave the place. This is because

Don'ts
- Don't let the serving spoon touch anything on your individual plate.
- Don't use cutlery from a *halal* stall to pick up food on non-*halal* food.
- It is taboo to use your left hand to handle food that you put in your mouth.
- Don't mistake the washing bowl for a soup or drink.
- It is impolite to transfer food from one pair of chopsticks to another.
- Don't stick chopsticks straight up in a bowl of rice as this is reminiscent of Chinese funeral rites.

the ventilation doesn't allow the smoke and oil from all the cooking to dissipate so it clings to you.

Hawker Centres to Visit

Every housing estate will have several hawker centres and each one will have one or two stalls that offer pretty outstanding food. If you have the time, you can try all of them. However, if you'd like to get the most of out each experience, here are some that have a number of 'good' stalls each:

- Newton Food Centre
- Tiong Bahru Market and Food Centre
- Maxwell Road Food Centre
- East Coast Lagoon Food Village
- Chinatown Food Street
- Lau Pa Sat Festival Market
- Tekka Market and Food Centre
- Adam Road Food Centre
- Old Airport Road Market/Hawker's Food Centre

There will be rows of stalls selling all manner of food. Walk around to see what interests you before you make your order. Most stalls will have pictures of the dishes or a list of the dishes available as well as the price. If you see a sign saying '$3/$4/$5', this refers to the prices for a small, medium and large serving respectively. If you are not sure what the dish is called, just point to the picture. Most stall owners can speak some English, or at least enough to understand what you want. For those you have problems understanding, you may have to rely on a mix of sign language and pointing, but chances are someone else nearby can interpret and place the order on your behalf.

Tables and chairs in hawker centres are usually mounted to the ground, with most tables designed to accommodate four or six people. All tables will have a number and you need to remember this number when you order your food, particularly if the food will be delivered to you. You only pay for your food when it is delivered. Some stalls will have a 'self service' sign and for those, you will have to order, wait

Lau Pa Sat Festival Market is a hawker centre set within an enormous cast-iron Victorian filigree structure (originally built in 1894), one of the last remaining in South-east Asia. It is situated in the CBD area and draws huge lunchtime crowds.

and pay for your food before carrying it back yourself. At some of the larger hawker centres, you may encounter some problems ordering from a stall far away from where you are sitting so be prepared to wait and carry.

During meal times, hawker centres can get quite crowded and the more popular stalls are likely to have a long queue. This may not be a physical queue but one where you have to wait a long time for your food to be delivered. If you are in a hurry, you might want to ask how long it will take. If you don't have enough time, think about ordering from another stall or eating something else.

When the place is crowded, you may have to share tables. If you are in a group, it is advisable to leave someone at your table while the rest make their orders. Some people will just assume that empty seats means there is no one there and sit down. The person left behind can then tell them the seats are occupied. Another way of reserving seats is to leave something behind on the seat. No, definitely not your mobile phone. The most common items are umbrellas and packets of tissue. (Packets of tissue, by the way, are commonly sold by roaming salespeople in the hawker centres as the food stalls do not provide napkins.) This is a predominant trend in the CBD areas because everyone breaks for lunch at about the same time. Make sure you respect this unspoken law and not take a seat if something is lying on it. It is also not wise to buy your food then look for a table as you may end up walking around aimlessly with a tray of food.

Coffee Shops

Known locally as *kopitiam*, this is usually an eating place located at the ground floor of many HDB blocks. Some are located in shophouses or other types of developments and may also be called eating houses. Despite its name, the coffee shop is like a small-scale hawker centre and boasts several stalls selling a variety of foods, usually Chinese and *halal* Muslim or Indian. Of late, coffee shops have started to offer fancier fare such as Japanese food and even pizza.

One other thing that many coffee shops have is a *cze cha* stall. These normally operate only for dinner and start about 5:00 pm or so and open till 11:00 pm or midnight. *Cze cha* stalls are like smaller scale restaurants which serve one dish meals as well as a variety of dishes which can be eaten with rice. These are usually Chinese but over the last decade of so, a few Muslim stalls have adapted this same concept and set up their own *halal cze cha* stalls. The dishes are similar; they just use permissable meats (e.g. chicken) instead of pork.

Cze cha stalls tend to be a little more expensive than economical rice stalls. Another difference is that you don't get to point at the food you want. Instead, you will get a menu, but most don't have pictures. Try asking the person who takes your order what they recommend and ask what the dish is. Also ask the price. Some of them may suggest the more expensive dishes knowing that you are a foreigner. Most dishes are S$ 6 and up, with vegetables and tofu being the cheapest and seafood or speciality dishes the most expensive.

Literally, *cze cha* translates into 'cook fry' from Chinese. And this is precisely how the food is prepared as almost all the dishes you find at these stalls are fried. Very rarely will you have braised or steamed foods.

If you plan on patronising a *cze cha* stall and there are only two in your party, try to order less or you may have to ask for a doggy bag. You can order two one-dish meals or rice with two or three dishes. The best way to experience a *cze cha* stall is to get a larger group of friends and you can order more dishes.

The coffee shop is essentially another no-frills eating place as it is not air-conditioned and because of its locality, very convenient for people staying in that neighbourhood. On the whole, people eat and go; diners do not linger. However, once the lunch and dinner crowd disperses, the 'lingerers' appear. These are usually the older folks who meet up with their friends at the coffee shop for a quick bite and lots of drinks, either beverages, home-made drinks, beer or stout. Most coffee shops have television sets mounted at strategic locations so patrons can catch up with the news or local drama while having a bite. This is another attraction for those who stay for a while at the shop.

At coffee shops, there is one central drinks stall and you can order at the counter or wait for one of the roving assistants to come by and take your order. When it gets crowded, some save time by shouting your orders to the counter so it can be prepared immediately. Drinks assistants can easily be identified by the waist pouch (containing spare change) they wear. In some coffee shops (and even at some hawker centres), you will see beer ladies in the evenings. These women are employed by

Geylang

Singapore's famous red-light district is also the best place to check out delicious food. From early evening to the wee hours of the morning, the streets that make up the Geylang area are teaming with foodies in search of great food. Everything from simple *dim sum* to delicious beef *hor fun* can be found here, even unusual dishes like frog's leg porridge and Taiwanese smelly bean curd. Then there are also the roadside fruit stalls that sell durians and other tropical delights. Little tables and stools allow buyers to enjoy a fruit feast al fresco style.

Football Fever

On days when there are important football matches—English Premier League, FA Cup or even the S-League (Singapore's football league)—fans will gather at coffee shops, order drinks and watch the game together. This is probably the closest thing to being at the game itself and the atmosphere in a crowd can be electrifying, especially when a goal is scored.

beer companies and will come round to take your orders for beer or stout. They can be identified by the uniforms or T-shirts they wear which are usually in the colours of the beer they are selling.

Food Courts

The food court is an air-conditioned version of the hawker centre—much cleaner, and more brightly lit. These are often located in shopping malls, and almost all are part of a chain e.g. Food Junction and Kopitiam, so you will find the same variety at different places although the people running the actual stalls might are not the same. The most recent additions are *halal* food courts, Banquet and Fork and Spoon, where the variety and type of dishes offered is similar to other food courts but pork has been substituted with permissable meats. The one drawback of food courts when compared to hawker centres is that the stalls are controlled so you will only get one stall selling one type of food. In a hawker centre, you may sometimes get two or three stalls offering the same dishes. This is advantageous for the diner as he or she has more

The Pioneer

The first food court in Singapore was Scotts Picnic in the basement of Scotts Shopping Centre. When it opened in the 1980s, it was perpetually packed. Picnic has gone through several renovations and still manages to hold its own against the competition.

Food courts are air-conditioned, clean and bright, and normally found in shopping malls.

choice, especially if the quality of food at one stall isn't quite up to standard.

Expect to pay more at a food court as the rent is higher and the amenities are better. While you can get S$ 2–3 meals at hawker centres, you normally have to pay at least S$ 3.50 and above at a food court. It is mainly self service at food courts, even for drinks. While tables are still shared, 'reservations' by personal belongings are less common.

Opening Hours

Most food courts are open for lunch and dinner from 10:00 am or 11:00 am to 10:00 pm. For the stalls at coffee shops and hawker centres, the opening hours will vary and this depends on the stall owners and in some cases, what they are selling. Some open for the breakfast crowd and stay open through lunch, closing some time in the afternoon. Others open for the lunch crowd and stay open till just after dinner. But of course, when the food is finished, it's finished! On a busy day, the more popular stalls may run out of food and close up before the closing hours. If you really want a specific popular dish, come early and be prepared to stand in queue. There are some who only open for dinner but operate till the wee hours of the morning. While stalls in a food court tend to be open seven days a week (in certain areas, some food courts close once a week), most stalls in hawker centres or coffee shops close at least one day in a week (some close once in two weeks) so they can have a well-deserved rest. And this may not be at the weekend. As these tend to be family-run businesses, they may close for a week or two in a year for a longer vacation. It will take a bit of time but after a while, you will learn the operating hours of your preferred stalls.

Restaurants

The selection of restaurants range from casual dining to classier places set with fine china and crystal, serving all types of cuisine, from international to Asian. The décor usually gives an indication of price, in that fancier places charge more; but there are a number of expensive but casually

Lunch is a good time to try new restaurants as there is usually a luncheon set that is affordably priced. If you like what being served, come back and try the full menu for dinner.

chic places. There is usually a menu at the door so you can easily get an idea of the price and the fare it offers. Most places accept walk-ins but for busy periods such as weekends or occasions such as Valentine's or Mother's Day, reservations are advised.

Most restaurants do expect you to dress pretty decently when you dine there. Normally, the more upmarket the restaurant, the more you should dress up; but smart casual is acceptable at almost all places. What is usually frowned upon is shorts and T-shirts. When in doubt, call ahead to ask. A few places are not very keen to have children in their restaurant, although this will not be stated anywhere. Feel free to call and enquire. If they beat around the bush or tell you 'no' straight out, you can always take your family to another place where children are welcome.

With such a wide range of restaurants available, you may be stumped on where to go. Ask your friends for suggestions and start there. The local newspapers has food features on the new eateries and the flavours of the moment. There are also a number of restaurant guides published by *Wine and Dine Singapore* and *Singapore Tatler*. If you have a credit card, you are likely to receive booklets or flyers every month on the special promotions your card provider is running with various restaurants.

Fast Food

If your children or teenagers crave for fast food, they will have enough choices to choose from; and the list seems to be growing. The golden arches of McDonald's are all over the island as are other chains such as Pizza Hut, Kentucky Fried Chicken (KFC) , Long John Silver's and Burger King. Taco Bell hasn't quite taken off while A&W and Wendy's have closed their outlets here. On the other hand, Carl's Jr opened its first outlet here in 2005. Mos Burger, the burger chain from Japan, started here in 1992 and has more than 15 outlets.

While the choice of menu may not be as extensive as back home, the staples like the Big Mac and Whopper are all there. There are also 'special' food items which cater to local tastes so Burger King has a *rendang* burger (your basic burger with a thick spicy sauce), Pizza Hut has spicy chicken pizza, McDonald's has McSpicy chicken and occasionally brings back the Samurai Burger (burger with teriyaki sauce) while KFC has two types of chicken, original and crispy, of which the latter spicy.

Delis and Coffee Places

There are many delis serving great sandwiches, cakes and coffee. Among them are the international chains, Starbucks and Spinelli's for coffee as well as Subway and Oliver's for sandwiches. There are also a number of home-grown places such as Coffee Club, Coffee Connection, Delifrance and Bakerzin. Many bakeries also offer a variety of breads, cakes and pastries and some of these can be rather exotic, using many local ingredients like *sambal* (a type of chilli condiment), *floss* (shredded dried meat with a fluffy texture) and *bak kwa* (barbecued pork).

As mentioned before, if you order coffee and tea at hawker centres and coffee shops, you're likely to be served a local blend. Some food courts have more upmarket blends but many have what is known as local coffee as well. If you want a branded cup of java, visit the various coffee places but be prepared to pay about ten times the amount you would for a cup of local coffee.

Kaya Toast and Coffee

One local breakfast favourite (that is also considered a snack) is *kaya* toast with coffee. *Kaya* is an aromatic egg and coconut jam and in this dish, the *kaya* and a thin slab of butter is spread over slices of toasted bread. If made in the old-fashioned way, the bread would be toasted over a charcoal fire before the *kaya* is spread. The butter slab is placed on last and allowed to melt from the heat of the toast. For many, the taste is heavenly, especially when taken with a cup of freshly brewed local coffee. The most famous place for this concoction is Killiney Kopi Tiam but many people are now flocking to Ya Kun Kaya Toast which has branches all over the island. Many others have sprouted on the scene and are fairly decent.

TAXES, TIPPING AND OTHER CHARGES

When you buy food at the hawker centre and coffee shop, don't expect to get a bill or receipt. The prices are usually stated on a sign and customers are expected to know how much the dishes are. The good thing is these prices are nett and no taxes are added on. The only time you pay extra is when you ask for something different e.g. extra cockles for your *laksa* or sometimes when you want takeaway.

At the food court, the price stated is also nett but you will get a receipt. If you scan this receipt, you may discover that the 5 per cent Goods and Services Tax (GST) has been included into the 'nett' price. This also applies to some delis and coffee places.

When you dine at a restaurant, however, the scene changes. There is no tipping culture in Singapore but the restaurant automatically slaps a 10 per cent service charge onto your bill. This service charge does not always go to the staff and some restaurants actually take it as part of their revenue. Other than the service charge, there is also the 5 per cent GST and 1 per cent government tax. Normally, this is written as ' + + + ' after the price. So if the menu price of a dish is '$29 + + +', you will need to factor in the taxes and the total comes close to S$ 34.

Even though it is not compulsory to tip, nor does anyone expect you to, if you think that the service you received has been exceptional, there is nothing to stop you from leaving a little something behind for your server. The only problem with this is that some establishments have an in-house policy that all extra money received goes into a common till to be shared out between all the staff working that shift.

At some outlets, there are a number of hidden charges which may pack quite a hefty punch if you are caught unaware. These include the appetisers (e.g. Chinese restaurants have peanuts or pickles, Indonesian and Thai restaurants have crackers), the tea (you get one pot of tea and water is continually added throughout the meal; this is usually provided when ordered and billed on a per head basis) and the towel charge (the wet ones in a foil or plastic packet). The last is something you will incur at certain

cze cha stalls so you might want to keep this in mind if your sums don't add up.

ALL MANNER OF SIGNS
Grading
As you walk around from one stall to another at a hawker centre or food court, you may notice that each stall has a piece of coloured paper with a letter of the alphabet on it. This is actually the grade given by the Ministry of Environment (ENV) to denote how hygienic a food outlet is and you will find them even at the most upmarket restaurants. There are four grades, A to D, with A being the most hygienic. Checks are conducted periodically so the outlets have to ensure that they are vigilant in this area. What seems rather strange to many people, though, is that not all those who are graded well have the best tasting food. Perhaps this is just a case of one man's meat being another's poison.

Healthy Lifestyle
An increasing number of stalls have a small sticker stating that they offer 'less oil, more greens'. This is in line with the government's healthy lifestyle programme and if you see

this sign, you're welcome to ask for less salt, less oil and more vegetables.

MUIS Certified

For those who are concerned about whether the outlets they patronise serve *halal* food, there is an easy way to tell. All food outlets that serve *halal* food will carry a certificate from MUIS, Singapore's Islamic religious council. This certificate is renewed on a yearly basis and must be prominently displayed. The MUIS website (http://www.muis.gov.sg) carries a list of certified outlets and the certificate's expiry date.

Accolades

Since eating is, in many ways, a national pastime, it is not surprising that there have been so many television

MUIS is very particular about the food sold to Muslims and make every effort to ensure that *halal* stalls and food are certified. When shopping for groceries, any food item bearing the above mark means that it has been passed by MUIS as safe for consumption for Muslims.

programmes, newspaper articles, Internet listings and write-ups about the food in Singapore and which stalls have the best tasting dishes. Stalls will milk this publicity for all it is worth and these press clippings or stickers would be proudly pasted on the showcase of the stall. Remember that taste is very personal and what other people like might not agree with you. However, this is a good way to get introduced to the local food until you discover your own personal favourites.

DRINKS
Free Water?
Most restaurants will serve water on a complimentary basis. And yes, tap water is safe to drink. However, fancier places may only serve imported bottled water and this can be quite pricey. Bottled water can easily go at S$ 10 a pop so unless you need it, just specify that you want normal water, the complimentary sort. If you are Caucasian, the waiter will automatically try to offer you bottled water by asking if you want sparkling or still water. My American friend was most impressed when dining at the five-star Oriental Hotel, the waiter proudly announced that they had 14 varieties of bottled water and proceeded to rattle their names in a single breath. Unfortunately for him, my friend opted for the normal iced water which was refreshingly thirst quenching.

Don't bother asking for complimentary water at coffee shops, hawker centres or food courts. If you want water at those places, it's a given you will have to buy a bottle. Thankfully these are not as expensive and you should be able to get a 500 ml bottle for less than S$ 2.

Some fast food outlets do provide free water as well but you will have to ask for this specifically. These will be served in a small cup as they would rather you bought a drink or a bottle of water.

Wines/BYO
Wine-drinking has become more popular in Singapore and many restaurants offer a decent selection of wines that are priced competitively. While not all places have an extensive list, there should be a few reds and whites for your selection.

Keep in mind that some places levy a corkage charge if you bring your own wines. This amount varies but is normally between S$ 15–35. So, unless you are drinking the good stuff, the corkage may cost more than the cheap wine!

In recent years, there has been a growing number of shops selling wines from all over the world. The major supermarkets will have a range, no matter how small, but if you have premium tastes, look out for a speciality shop. You can do a search for wine shops or wines/liquors at the E-Guide website (http://www.eguideglobal.com/sg/) or join a wine club which will point you in the right direction.

Beer and Alcohol

Expatriates are often surprised by how much beer costs in Singapore when compared to back home. While beer and alcohol are not that cheap, there are happy hours with one-for-one offers and other great deals. You can find great Irish brews here at the Irish pubs such as Muddy Murphys in Boat Quay and Father Flanagan's at Chijmes, and there are also specialist beer outlets such as Paulaner Brauhaus and Brewerkz. There are also a number of great places to enjoy cheap beer if you are not too particular about the surroundings. A jug of beer on tap can cost anything from S$ 13–45 depending on where you go, although most are priced around S$ 25. If you drink, remember that there are heavy penalties for drink driving so leave the car at home if you are planning a big night out.

Home-grown Tiger

Launched in 1932, Tiger Beer is Singapore's home-grown beer and the flagship brand of Asia Pacific Breweries (APB). This pale lager is loved by beer drinkers all over the world and what better place to enjoy a Tiger than in its birthplace.

SHOPPING FOR FOOD

Where does one go to shop for groceries? The freshest produce can be had at the wet market which normally operates from 6:00 am–10:00 am but this is not for the faint-hearted. There is a reason why the locals call this a 'wet market'. Don't expect things to be clean and tidy. While there are different sections for different types of food, everything is fresh and raw so

you will have certain smells in the air which you might not be used to and the floors are usually not dry.

Why would anyone want to put themselves through this, you might ask. Well, many want to get their food as fresh as possible and at wet markets, you get to pick the choicest cuts. You come face to face with the various types of fish and can check their gills and eyes for freshness. Looking at the various cuts of meat hanging from hooks at the stall, you can point to exactly which you want and ask the butcher to trim the fat. At the dried goods stalls, you can gesture to what you want and if you are on good terms with the proprietor, bargain for a 20-cent discount. You smile at your usual vegetable stall owner and ask for 50-cents worth of chillies which is wrapped up in newspaper and placed in a small bag. You guessed it; this is as much a social occasion as it is a shopping expedition and many people relish the chance to buy food the way their parents and grandparents did.

Almost every housing estate has a wet market but these days, the prices vary depending on the area. Vegetables that would normally cost S$ 1 in the Queenstown area (one

If you like things clean and dry, prepare yourself mentally before visiting a wet market or you may be repulsed. It is advisable to dress casual (shorts and T-shirt are fine) and make sure that your footwear gives you enough traction so you don't go sliding on the wet floor.

of the oldest housing estates in Singapore with a much older demographic) are likely to cost twice that amount in Tampines, one of the newer estates which is home to many of today's upwardly mobile and affluent middle class.

It is advisable that the first time you venture into a wet market, take a 'veteran' with you. Many of today's younger Singaporeans feel like a bull in a china shop when at a wet market so make sure you go with someone who has been a number of times and knows his or her way around. Also, be prepared to jostle with overzealous housewives and, on occasion, busy executives on their way to work.

If a wet market is really not your cup of tea, a more comfortable approach is the supermarket. There are two main players in Singapore: FairPrice and the Dairy Farm Group. The former is a co-operative and their branches are located literally everywhere. Prices are competitive and selected branches also stock gourmet items to meet the demands of residents in the area. Their website (http://www.fairprice. com.sg) includes an online store.

FairPrice supermarkets are co-operatives run by NTUC (National Trades Union Congress), the largest union in Singapore. Because it has so many outlets, it is able to keep its prices affordable, especially for the those in the middle and lower income groups.

The Dairy Farm Group operates several chains covering all price points but the better one to shop at is Cold Storage which includes Market Place. These offer quality produce sourced from all over the world. What you can find back home is probably available although sometimes, prices may be slightly higher. Check out http://www.coldstorage. com.sg for the listing of branches and an online shopping store. Note that not all Cold Storage branches carry the full range of merchandise and smaller ones may have a limited selection. In addition, not all branches accept commercial credit cards. In the Orchard area, the branch at Ngee Ann City, Paragon and Tanglin Mall accept credit cards but not the one at Centrepoint which only accepts their in-store card other than cash and NETS.

Carrefour (the French-based hypermart) is a relatively new addition to the scene and currently has only two outlets which seem to have a constant stream of customers. They are slightly different from FairPrice and Cold Storage in that they tend to be more of a one-stop store with more than just groceries. If you'd like to buy everything under one roof, then this might be the place of choice for you.

For those who are looking specifically for items from Japan, there are a few Japanese supermarkets in Singapore. These are located in the same building as the largest Japanese departmental stores and it is very convenient to get all types of shopping done at the same time.

Mustapha Grocery Store in Little India has a large selection of pulses, grains, spices and *halal* food.

Kosher Food

Unfortunately, there are no outlets which sell kosher food in Singapore. However, you can buy your own ingredients and these can be obtained at the major supermarkets run by FairPrice and Dairy Farm. Alternatively, you can buy supplies from the Maghain Aboth Synagogue which has a shop in its compound at 24/26 Waterloo Street. The synagogue also serves kosher meals on Sabbat and the holidays.

There are also a number of speciality establishments from butchers to gourmet shops to check out.

- Swiss Butchery at Greenwood Avenue offers many choice European-style cuts. What's more, the butchers will prepare the meat according to your instructions.
- The Butcher, located at Holland Village, is an Australian butcher specialising in marinated meats and barbecue cuts.
- Another good butcher is Espirito Santo-Latin Deli & Butchery, in Upper Thomson and the Parkway Parade Shopping Mall, for a wide selection of meats and Brazilian speciality items and cuts.
- Culina (http://www.culina.com.sg) is a supplier of Italian speciality food and has two outlets: Park House at Orchard Boulevard and Bukit Timah Road.
- Tierney's Gourmet at Serene Centre along Farrer Road has many hard-to-find European food items, Mexican and Latin ingredients, and an excellent selection of chocolates and speciality items come holiday time.

- German Food Shop which specialises in (what else?) German items and sweets.
- If you are a fan of New York-based chichi supermarket Dean and Deluca, you can find some of their products at Front Row at Club Street.
- So Delicious, on South Buona Vista Road, for Danish cheeses, meats and other food items.
- Cellar Door along Bukit Timah Road for New Zealand and Australian cheeses, wines and speciality items.
- IKEA has a small grocery store where Swedish and Scandinavian items are available.

But what if you've forgotten to buy a loaf of bread for the next day and the nearest supermarket is more than 15 minutes away? You turn to the 7-Elevens, neighbourhood shops and convenience stores at petrol stations. Like all of their other stores worldwide, 7-Elevens are open 24 hours a day and carry some of the basic necessities including sandwiches and microwaveable food. All housing estates have little neighbourhood stores either as part of a row of shops at the bottom of a HDB block or as a stand-alone stall in the void deck. (The latter is sometimes called a 'mama shop' because these were traditionally run by Indians who were known locally as 'mamas'. This term for the ethnic group is fading but the name for this type of shop is still being used.) They don't have the full range of items but they carry all the basics and are wonderful to have around when you find you've forgotten something very ordinary like milk, eggs, rice, soya sauce, shampoo or bread. Most petrol stations have a little convenience store and if you are filling up on petrol on your way to work or home, you can pick up what you need. Anything from ice cream to drinks to pet food.

ENTERTAINING

Singaporeans entertain both at home and in restaurants. In both scenarios, it's always polite to bring a gift or token for the host or hostess. Chocolates, wine and flowers will always be appreciated but do not expect that your chocolates or wine to be offered to the guests on that day. Chances are the hostess has already planned the menu carefully and your gifts will be enjoyed on another day. If you are visiting friends who are Muslims, make sure there isn't any non-*halal* elements in any of the food items you are giving. For the Chinese, make sure you don't bring a bouquet of chrysanthemums as these flowers are only given when someone has passed away. Similarly, should your hosts be Hindus, avoid anything related to the sacred cow.

While Singaporeans are notorious for being late for a number of social functions, they do tend to be rather finicky when it comes to a sit-down lunch or dinner at home. Try to be punctual or arrive within 15 minutes of the stated time as the meal has most likely been planned accordingly. The exception to this is when cocktails or drinks are being served beforehand; then you often have a wider time frame.

When visiting a Singaporean home, you will be expected to take off your shoes and leave them at the door, so wear something that can be easily removed. However, there is a increasing trend for guests to wear their shoes in. Just take the cue from your hosts. If they are wearing footwear, then follow suit. In terms of dress, it's normally smart casual; if there is a dress code for the event, your host is likely to mention it. Otherwise, just ask to be sure you and your spouse don't turn up in chinos and a sundress while everyone else is in a lounge suit or cocktail dress.

If your host has an elderly parent or relative at home, acknowledge their seniority by calling them 'Auntie' or 'Uncle' instead of calling them by name, even if you are introduced to 'my father, Brian'. It may not be part of your culture to do so but Brian will think well of you. It's just part of the Asian way of life that elders are respected.

After accepting several invitations, you may want to reciprocate and invite your friends for a meal. Either at home or outside is fine, but again remember that most social occasions are fairly casual unless you choose to dine in a formal restaurant. Most Singaporeans you are likely to come into contact with are rather worldly and are likely to feel at home in any situation. Just bear in mind people's dietary restrictions due to religion.

As always, be considerate, use your common sense and if any mishaps or unforeseen accidents happen, have a good sense of humour and file it away as something to be mindful of for the next party.

ENJOYING SINGAPORE

CHAPTER 7

IT'S NICE TO BE WARM

'Unique is the word that best captures Singapore,
a dynamic city rich in contrast and colour where you'll
find a harmonious blend of culture, cuisine, arts and
architecture... Brimming with unbridled energy and
bursting with exciting events, the city offers countless
unique, memorable experiences waiting to be discovered.'
—Singapore Tourism Board (STB) website

Now that you have all the basic information out of the way, you can sit back, relax and discover what other things Singapore has to offer.

CLUBS AND GROUPS

One simple way to find out what's going on is to get in touch with other people who have been in a similar situation and are now experts in finding their way around. There are a number of expatriate associations and clubs which you can join who will gladly point you in the right direction. Some of these are listed in our Resource Guide at the back of the book. Another avenue to find out more information is your local embassy.

There are also a number of women's groups who help ladies meet other ladies with similar backgrounds, language, interests. Again, ask your embassy for the contact person and get in touch to find out what they have planned. These groups normally organise coffee mornings at least once a month where members gather to get to know each other better. This could be at someone's home or at a club or community hall. Sometimes, guest speakers are invited to these mornings to talk about the classes they run. This is a good source of information if you are looking to meet people or for new hobbies or pastimes to engage in, nor just for yourself but also for the children. Clubs and women's groups also organise a number of activities to tie in with

The Queenstown Community Centre (above) may not be the most modern but it still offers a fairly wide range of activities, both indoor and outdoor (below). Its proximity to a number of condominiums, all with expat populations, makes it an ideal place to start looking for things to do.

various events throughout the year. These could range from bake sales to mini funfairs to day tours to charity events. As a member, you will be on the mailing list so will get to know the details in due course.

Local community centres or clubs (e.g. Cairnhill, Ang Mo Kio, Marine Parade, etc.) are also an excellent place for meeting people, learning a new activity (they offer exercise, art and cooking classes, for example) and becoming better acquainted with your neighbours and community overall. One friend even went a step further and began teaching French cooking classes at the local centre. They were a success and a great source of cultural exchange for all the parties involved.

PLACES TO VISIT, THINGS TO DO

By world standards, Singapore probably has much fewer attractions than most large cities but when you consider its size, everything becomes relative, and you might even be pleasantly surprised at the number of activities that are available. The following is just a small cross-section. To find out what else is in store, ask your friends and colleagues, look through the Life!Events section of the local newspapers or check with your expat group.

Zoo and Night Safari

Finding Out More

For more information about the zoo and the Night Safari, visit:

- http://www.zoo.com.sg
- http://www.nightsafari.com.sg

This is a world-standard open-concept zoo that was first opened in 1973. The standard favourites are all there, including a small petting area for children who want to get up close and personal with chickens, ducks and the like. The young (and brave) at heart can touch a yellow python, or let it be draped over them for a picture. The polar bear exhibit is a hot favourite, especially during feeding time, and one of the proudest moments of the zoo's history was when the first male cub, Inuka, was born in the tropics in 1990. Despite Singapore's hot and humid weather, these bears (as well as the emperor penguins in the next enclosure) are kept happy. And don't forget to bring swimsuits for the children—there is a water play area near the petting zoo where the children can really enjoy themselves and cool off.

Opened in 1994, the Night Safari is the first wildlife park in the world to be built primarily for night visits and only opens its doors from 7:30 pm to midnight. If you have the time, take the tram ride around the entire place first then pick which one of the trails you'd like to follow. It is while you are on the tram that you can also appreciate the immense variety of flora that has been meticulously cultivated for the zoo. As you travel on the tram, you will see nocturnal animals out to feed and some may come right next to the tram. But don't be foolhardy and try to touch them—these animals may be kept in captivity but they are still semi-wild; one never knows what might happen. Walk the trails to take in the details: see nocturnal animals grazing in their pens; take the children on a walk across the suspension bridge; come face to face with a tiger or leopard with only a thick sheet of tempered glass between you.

Having Fun

Tina, a British expatriate, tells of the time she and her family took a friend visiting from the States to the Night Safari. "It wasn't our maiden visit but it was the first time they were all going as a family. We got there just after the park opened and hung around for the first animal show. We were adults and knew what to expect but for the kids, it was great! What we liked most was getting to see a tiger up close. You really don't realise how big that animal is until you come face to face with it. One of its paws was as big as my face! Walking through the aviary was interesting as there were a number of fruit bats hanging upside down from the low-hanging branches. I know we aren't supposed to touch them but my brother decided to have some fun and pulled one of its wings outward to see how long it would stretch. Surprisingly, the bat let him. At the end of a long hot night, we were thrilled with what we had seen and our friend enjoyed himself immensely. Needless to say, he was really impressed with the whole set-up. The icing on the cake came right at the end when we bought our ice-cold beers from the F&B outlet next to the exit!"

Mandai Orchid Garden

Located just off Mandai Lake Road, on your way to the zoo and Night Safari, is the Mandai Orchid Garden, a joy for all those who love flowers, especially orchids. About 200 varieties of orchids can be found on the open hillside with pockets of other flora nestled elsewhere on the grounds: an herb and spice garden, a water garden as well as a tropical fruit orchard. For more information, refer to the website at:

http://www.mandai.com.sg

Jurong BirdPark

This attraction has been in existence since 1971 and has grown in proportion and standard. Currently the largest park in the Asia Pacific, Jurong BirdPark specialises in South-east Asian birds and has a total of 600 species. Its four aviaries include the largest walk-in aviary with a man-made waterfall. Like the zoo, there is also a playground and a water play area for the children. To find out more about what it has to offer, refer to the official website at:

http://www.birdpark.com.sg

These beautiful macaws await your arrival at the Jurong BirdPark. Make a trip out with the family and enjoy yourself.

Botanic Gardens

It was Sir Thomas Stamford Raffles who first mooted the idea of a botanical gardens in 1822 and this was initially started in Fort Canning. The current site only came into being in 1859 and has grown in stature, size and standards. Today, the gardens—which includes a National Orchid Garden—are under the purview of the National Parks Board, and is the choice site for many outdoor events such as band performances. It is constantly upgrading its services and even welcomes volunteers, especially those who have a love for nature. To keep in the know, look up its website at:

http://www.sbg.org.sg

HSBC TreeTop Walk

The first of its kind in Singapore and South-east Asia, the TreeTop Walk consists of a 250-m free-standing suspension bridge spanning the two highest points in the MacRitchie Catchment Area. There are two way of getting to this bridge: from one of the walking trails at MacRitchie Reservoir or from Venus Drive, off Upper Thomson Road. Either way, be prepared for a long (and often, uphill) walk before you actually get to the bridge. Make sure you go in walking attire and shoes, and take a leisurely walk. Otherwise, the heat and humidity will get to you and you won't enjoy it as much. It's not really suitable for the elderly as the terrain isn't that smooth and there is a lot of climbing (up and down) to be done. You also might want to think twice about bringing very young children as you may have to carry them most of the way.

Finding Out More

For more details on the TreeTop Walk, visit the National Parks Board webpage on the walk at:

http://www.nparks.gov.sg/nparks_cms/
display_level2.asp?parkid = 8&catid = 9

The TreeTop Walk really does take a lot out of you. If you are planning to bring children, make sure they can walk on their own or be prepared to carry them, like this lady in the picture.

Sungei Buloh Wetland Reserve

Officially opened in 1993, this wetland reserve is located way in the north, and depending on where you are on the reserve, you will be able to see a small section of the state of Johor in Malaysia. This place is a paradise for birdwatchers in particular because a number of bird species e.g. the egrets and plovers stop here as part of their migratory pattern. In addition to the mangrove swamps, there are some 'resident' birds like the herons and kingfishers. This is a great place to plan a group outing, especially for children. Find out more at its official website:

http://www.sbwr.org.sg/

Bukit Timah Nature Reserve

Originally established as a forest reserve in 1883, the Bukit Timah Nature Reserve (BTNR) is one of the four gazetted nature reserves in Singapore, the other three being the Central Catchment Nature Reserve (the area around MacRitchie Reservoir), Labrador Park Nature Reserve and Sungei Buloh Wetland Reserve. The BTNR has an area of 164 hectares (405.3 acres) of which a significant portion is primary rainforest. It also contains more species of trees than can be found in North America. The reserve has well-marked trails so there's no danger of losing your way. You can also hike up Bukit Timah Hill, the highest point in the country at 164 m (538.1 ft).

MacRitchie Reservoir

Singapore's first reservoir was completed in 1868 and today, holds more than just water for the small island. It is a catchment reserve area with a number of boardwalks and walking trails for those who wish to explore nature. You can take your time and walk the trails yourself or join one of the free guided tours.

Chinese Gardens and Japanese Gardens

Two great places to relax at the weekends, the Chinese Gardens and Japanese Gardens are situated next to each other and are sprawling gardens with either Chinese or Japanese landmarks. A good way to get away from the hustle and bustle of city life when you don't have too much time. The gardens also hold a must-see Lantern Exhibition during the Mid-Autumn Festival sometime around mid-September and

Lush greenery and Chinese architectural landmarks are some of the elements that make the Chinese Gardens ideal for a quick relaxing weekend getaway for the family.

again during the Chinese New Year. (More on these festivals a little later on in this chapter.) This is a great outing for the entire family as there usually is a special amusement area for the children.

Ethnic Enclaves

With its multi-ethnic background, its quite natural that each major group has a spot in Singapore where it is predominant. The Malays have Kampong Glam and Geylang Serai, the Chinese have Chinatown, the Indians have little India. Each is distinctive in its own way, either in the architecture, history or the types of business that you find in those areas. Explore at your leisure.

Finding Out More

You can find more information of each of these at the Singapore Tourism Board's website:

http://www.visitsingapore.com/publish/stbportal/en/

home/what_to_see/ethnic_quarters.html

The Peranakans may not have been given an area of land but they tended to congregate in the East Coast, particularly in the Katong area. The area still has many Peranakan-style buildings like this one (that sadly is now closed) which sell many of the foods, arts and crafts of the Peranakan people.

The cable car is a great way to get a bird's eye view of the area and of Sentosa Island. Now you can even book the cable car in advance for special dinners in the sky—a great way to spend Valentine's or have some family fun.

Sentosa

The island previously known as Blakang Mati has, since 1972, grown into a full-fledged island resort and is set to develop even further with the construction of an Integrated Resort (IR) in the near future. The monorail that had been running since 1982 was decommissioned in 2005 to make way for the light rail system that will link the island with the mainland via the current North-East Line (NEL, part of the MRT) underground system. This is expected to be up and running by the end of 2006. You can also get to Sentosa by driving, taking a bus or via cable car, the last of which is a popular choice of those who want to get an overview of the area. Currently, Sentosa has hotels, chalets, spas and resorts as well as a host of attractions that keep people coming back again and again. Some of these attractions include a musical fountain, beaches, Carlsberg Sky Tower (at 131 m above sea level, Singapore's tallest free-standing observation tower with a panoramic view), Underwater World and Fort Siloso. Find out more, including its future plans, at:

http://www.sentosa.com.sg/

> **For War History Buffs**
>
> If you are interested in Singapore's war history, there are a number of places you can visit:
>
> - Fort Siloso on Sentosa island is a 120-year-old coastal fort that played a vital part during World War II. Today, it serves as a museum of World War II history.
> - Battle Box, located at Fort Canning, is the largest underground operations complex of the British Malaya Command Headquarters during World War II.
> - Changi Chapel and Museum: see http://www.changimuseum.com/ for more details.
> - Labrador Tunnels at Labrador Park were the underground tunnels used in the British strategic defence of Singapore during World War II. It was only opened to the public in 2005.
> - Kranji War Memorial honours people from Australia, Britain, Canada, India, Malaya, the Netherlands, New Zealand, Pakistan and Sri Lanka who gave their lives during World War II.

Pulau Ubin

On an island just north-east of Singapore, one can almost discover what life was like back in the 1960s. That is the beauty that is Pulau Ubin, Malay for 'Granite Island'. You can take a guided tour (this is recommended for first-timers), cycle with a group of friends, camp on the beach or stay at the chalets. Not something you should do on a whim though so find out more before you embark as Singapore's wilderness are still subject to much of the country's famous bureaucracy. You might like to check out these websites:

- information from the National Parks Board
  Website: http://www.nparks.gov.sg/nparks_cms/display_level2.asp?parkid = 6&catid = 1
- Focus on Ubin
  Website: http://www.focusubin.org/

Singapore Science Centre

If you're looking for something to feed the mind, visit the Science Centre. Officially opened in 1977, it was set up with the aim of promoting science and technology mainly through live exhibits. Since then, the centre has become a popular destination for schools and students and its portfolio has grown to the point that it now produces its own range of books on life sciences. It has played host to a number of travelling exhibits including the Lord of the Rings and The Art of Star Wars. To find out the exhibits on display, visit:

http://www.science.edu.sg

G-Max The Ultimate Bungee

If you need an adrenalin rush, try the reverse bungee, G-Max, located at Clarke Quay. You are strapped into a seat and thrown up into the air to a height of 60 metres, going from zero to 200 kmph in a matter of seconds. Scream all you want as you feel the blood rush to your head; no one's really going to mind. Get more details at:

http://www.gmax.co.nz

Duck and Hippo Tours

A first of its kind in Asia, Duck Tours makes use of an amphibious vehicle—a boat on wheels that can travel both on land and sea—to take you on a tour of the city (land) and the harbour (sea). Find out more at:

http://www.ducktours.com.sg/

Run by the same company, Hippo Tours takes you on a ride to various famous landmarks in an open-top double-decker bus. You can find out the exact route, as well as buy your tickets, from the Visitor Information Centre along Orchard Road.

Heritage Trail

The National Heritage Board (NHB) has introduced a number of heritage trails to help locals and expatriates alike learn more about the past and the remnants that have been left behind. You can discover more about the different trails at:

http://www.nhb.gov.sg/discover_heritage/
discover_heritage.shtml

You can also sign up with the Board for email alerts on the various activities they run throughout the year. Some

The trishaw is another leisurely way to explore the sights. Unfortuantely, this is a dying trade in this fast-paced city.

of these are archaeology workshops while others are night trails to lesser known spots in Singapore.

SPORTING ACTIVITIES

You can take part in almost any kind of sports in Singapore except for maybe skiing or ice skating. But wait a minute, that's not quite true. Singapore does have a snow slope and an ice skating rink—all artificial, of course. Snow City in Jurong, next to the Science Centre, is an artificial snow slope that is open to the public every day except on Mondays. They allow skiing and snowboarding but only for the experienced and at set times in the evenings only. You do have to book in advance though. During the day, the slope is opened to the public for snow tubing. For those who have experienced the real thing, this might not be too fun but anyone coming from a tropical country or for children, this can be a pleasant way to spend the afternoon. Find out more at:

http://www.snowcity.com.sg/

Toddling in the Snow

It was obviously the little boy's first time and he didn't really know what to expect when mom and dad brought him to Snow City. They were a Korean family and from the looks of things, the parents had experienced snow before and wanted to take their son out for a good time on a Sunday morning. He was about two or three years old and a little unsteady on his feet. Wrapped up in his warm jackets, boots, gloves and helmet, he looked like a round ball walking in the common area. He gamely climbed up the stairs to the top of the slope and let his dad hold him as they tubed their way down. Wheeee!!! With the wind in his face, the cherubic little boy was all pink from the excitement and ready for another round.

Located at the Jurong Entertainment Centre, Fuji Ice Palace is currently the only skating rink in Singapore. You can go with friends for a good time or you can opt to take lessons. The rink may be closed for private functions and practices from time to time so it is advisable to call and enquire before going down. For more information on fees and lessons, look up their website at:

http://www.fujiice.com.sg

Water Sports

Singapore is surrounded by water so it's only natural that there are lots of opportunities to indulge in sea sports such as windsurfing, canoeing, kayaking, boardsailing, water skiing, sailing, etc. And this is likely to increase with the development of the Marina Bay area, with which Singapore is hoping to encourage more international events in this arena. For those who want to engage in these sports for fun, there are centres (mainly on the east coast) from whom you can rent the equipment (some may require you to be a member). A good place to find out more about this is the People's Association which currently runs five sea sports clubs. Check out their website at:

http://pa-online.pa.gov.sg/ NASApp/maps/online/
sscms/common/OSK_SCCIndex_A01.jsp

But that's not all. Singapore has produced Asian champions in swimming and water polo, a glowing testament to public and private swimming pools that pepper the various housing estates, condominiums, hotels and clubs. If you're into serious training and need a standard Olympic-size pool, you can visit a number of the swimming complexes. To find out the facilities each one has, log onto the Singapore Sport Council (SSC) Sportsweb website (http://www.ssc.gov.sg) and look under 'Sports Facilities'.

Other Sports

Back on land, there are tonnes of sports you can engage in; you just have to find the right group of people. It might take a little longer to find people for group sports but you can always get a group of friends together for those that require two or four people. Depending on your sport of choice, you can find out about and book facilities online at the Sportsweb site (http://www.ssc.gov. sg). Some sports are more popular than others so you might have to book in way in advance if you want to ensure that you get your play time in.

Some of the more popular sports in Singapore are:

- Football (soccer)

  This is an all-time favourite in Singapore and has as many players as spectators. In 2000, the Football Association of Singapore (FAS) launched the National Football Academy to help aspiring footballers realise their dream. The association also runs a number of other programmes and courses. Street soccer is fairly new but gaining popularity.

- Golf

  Would you believe there are about 14 golf courses on this small island and more than half of these are 18-hole courses? Most are part of membership clubs but there are four—Tanglin Golf Course, Seletar Base Golf Course, Green

Fairways and Executive Golf Course—which are open to walk-in bookings. All have nine-holes except Tanglin which has five.

- Table tennis
  Singapore's recent medal wins at international and regional events have raised the profile of this sport in the last few years.
- Badminton
  A sport that has had a strong following for years.
- Tennis
  A perennial favourite but in Singapore's rather unpredictable weather, your game can get rained out quite unexpectedly.

- Rockwall climbing
  A recent addition to the sports scene, this is popular among men and women.
- Inline skating/rollerblading
  Despite being a relative newcomer to the sports scene, inline skating has garnered a wide following over the last five years or so. You will see many people, young and not so young, donning their skates for a roll in the neighbourhood parks or at East Coast, along the paved walkways next to the beach.

Asian Sports

For those who might like to pick up or watch some of the local or other Asian sports, here are some you might want to consider:

- *Sepak takraw*
  A popular game in South-east Asia, *sepak takraw* is like playing volleyball with your feet and using a rattan-like ball. Ask around at the local community centres.

- *Wushu*
  This covers a range of Chinese martial arts, of which *taichi* is one. A good place to start is:
  http://www.singapore-wushu.com

- *Silat*
  Malay martial arts which are predominant in South-east Asia. Contact the Singapore Silat Federation (http://www.persisi.org) to find out more.

- *Aikido*
  Japanese martial arts which has been gaining popularity among the locals and expats. Best place to start is the Aikido Federation (Singapore) website at:
  http://www.aikidofederation.com

Keeping Fit

If you are one of those who isn't really looking for a rigorous sport but more of a keep-fit regime or workout, you can opt to join a gym such as California Fitness (http://www.californiafitness.com) or Planet Fitness (http://www.planetfitness.com.sg). Alternatively, you can check out any of the 14 ClubFITT gyms in neighbourhood estates. Find out their locations at the SSC Sportsweb site (http://www.ssc.gov.sg).

More than a decade ago, the locals bought into the aerobics craze and many joined classes held at the community centres and clubs. These days, more people are getting into yoga and pilates, with a growing set taking up *qigong*. And yes, the community clubs are still conducting classes. The People's Association website (http://www.pa.gov.sg) would be the ideal place to start looking.

Extreme Sports

This has been slow to make headway in Singapore for a number of reasons. One has been the lack of space. Even for something relatively tame as motocross, it was difficult for riders to find the right kind of terrain to be much of a challenge. Skateboarding had been around for some time but try riding your board on the streets or on the well-maintained pavements and you're likely to have disgusted looks and frowns thrown your way. Add to this the element of danger and over-protective parents and you get an overall atmosphere that's not very conducive for sports of this kind to grow. This is likely to change as the Ministry of Community Development, Youth and Sports (MCYS) has been conducting more feedback sessions with youth and are implementing youth projects to raise the status of the sports and public awareness. The going will be slow but it is a start especially when groups and institutions such as the National University of Singapore (NUS) are willing to challenge the norm and advocate such sports as mountaineering.

AFTER DARK ENTERTAINMENT

While it cannot be denied that the nightlife here isn't as vibrant as Bangkok, there has been a visible improvement in the past five years. Pub crawlers should visit the Mohammad Sultan area for its numerous bars and pubs that are crowded almost every night of the week. Another favourite area is Chijmes, where you can meet your friends for a great dinner before unwinding at the entertainment outlets there. For those working in the CBD, ask your colleagues about the watering holes nearby. Orchard Road has a number of establishments scattered along its stretch. Walk the length and you will discover them. The more popular ones are in the Emerald Hill area, near Centrepoint Shopping Mall.

The good news for those who like to move with the music is that bar-top dancing is now allowed at a number of outlets. You can always try; the worst that could happen is that you will be asked to come down. For those

One place that always comes highly recommended is the Long Bar at Raffles Hotel. This is supposedly the place where the Singapore Sling was invented. Located on the second floor of the hotel and accessible from the side facing the Raffles City Shopping Centre, the Long Bar's décor reeks of old world charm with its wooden panels and rattan seating. You get groundnuts with your drinks and you're welcome to throw the shells on the floor.

into more serious moves, the more popular discos are Zouk, in the River Valley area and the newly opened Ministry of Sound in Clarke Quay offers the largest dance floor in town. If, on the other hand, you prefer something a little more sedate, a dinner show might be the answer. The world-famous Paris peek-a-boo show Crazy Horses is now playing at Clarke Quay. If that's not quite your style and you want something more local yet risqué, visit either the Gold Dust Theatre Bar at Orchard Towers or the Boom Boom Room at Amoy Street. Here you will get to see Singapore's very own motor-mouth drag queen Kumar in his element. Bring your sense of your humour with you though, as the audience is sometimes pulled into the act.

TRAVELLER'S TALES
The truth is that Singapore can get a little claustrophobic and everyone needs to get away every now and again. Even the locals do, every chance they get. The most convenient place to visit is Malaysia. You can pop into Johor for a day or zip to Malacca for a weekend. The more time you have, the further you can go. For a free and easy 'adventure' into Johor, take a ride on any of the three local buses from Kranji MRT station. They will stop at the checkpoints for the necessities so be sure to have your passport and immigration card ready. This goes via the Causeway and one big drawback of this is that you can get caught in an enormous queue if you go at the wrong time. The funny thing is that any time seems like the wrong time! If the traffic is heavy, and you are fit and able, and the weather is fine, consider walking across the Causeway. You'll still have to queue at Customs but you're likely to get across the bridge a lot faster than the bus.

If you want to go further—even to Thailand—you can opt to drive or book your seat on one

Island Retreats
Two other popular places are the islands of Bintan and Batam, both of which have resort hotels and are a short ferry ride away. Many businessmen enjoy visiting Batam for a weekend of golf while those who wish to relax tend to head for Bintan. Ask your friends, do a search on the web or check the local newspapers for the best deals.

Sail into the Sunset

Looking for a little R&R and don't really want to drive, fly or sit for long periods of time? Try going on a cruise. You get away for a few days and depending on which package you choose, get to visit another port of call. You also have all your meals catered for and lots of activities on board. Sit back, relax and just enjoy yourself.

of the numerous coaches that travel up every day. (You can also take a train but these are not as frequent. Check either the KTM website at http://www.ktmb.com.my or th Orient Express website at http://www.orient-express.com.) Many of these companies also have package deals for coach and hotel rooms so be sure to do your homework before deciding. Quality varies from one company to another and you might want to ask around before making up your mind. Some have excellent 'in-flight' services (e.g. light meals, onboard toilet), some have an express travel time, and others have lots of leg room and huge chairs. Much will depend on who are a travelling with, how pampered you want to be and how much you want to pay.

Budget airlines are a relatively new phenomena in Singapore but have certainly picked up speed. There is now even an entire airport terminal dedicated to traffic from these airlines. Some of the popular destinations are Bangkok and Hong Kong. Check out their websites for prices:

- Valuair
  Website: http://valuair.com
- Jetstar Asia
  Website: http://jetstarasia.com
- Tiger Airways
  Website: http://www.tigerairways.com
- Air Asia
  Website: http://www.airasia.com

The local newspapers carry classified ads daily on the various offers and promotions the different companies have. NATAS (National Association of Travel Agents Singapore) holds an annual travel fair and is a good place to pick up deals. Some of the major travel companies such as Chan Brothers and S A Tours organise their own travel fairs and these are normally advertised well in the local papers. Keep a look out for them.

THE CULTURAL SIDE

As recently as a decade ago, many people (locals and foreigners) have moaned about the dearth of culture in Singapore. But it has certainly improved tremendously. The arts in Singapore are, and will always be, a mixture of old and new. With a nation of people that hail from different ethnic backgrounds, it is a given that many cultural traditions would be passed down through the ages. But Singapore is also a young and growing country and, like most children, it's easily influenced by outside forces. Not surprising that you find so many elements of Western culture e.g. its style of painting, drama, music, literature and dance in this small space, so much so that it often overshadows the ethnic arts. And that has been much of the debate for years. While purists lament the influx of outside influences, progressives welcome the exchange of ideas between cultures. While traditionalists cling to their tried and true ways of thinking and doing things, visionaries embrace the possibilities and look to create fusion. There really is no right or wrong; just what the public wants to accept.

The National Arts Council (NAC), the statutory board set up in 1991 to 'nurture the arts' in Singapore, is constantly finding new ways to raise the profile of visual arts, dance, music, literary arts and theatre among all members of the community so you never really know what they might come up with next. Keep up with the latest at their website:

> The Arts Central channel on television includes slots for the 'advertising' of ongoing arts events so you can watch out for these.

http://www.nac.gov.sg/

Art and Sculpture

Just over a decade ago, the art scene in Singapore consisted mainly of a couple of choice galleries and a handful of established artists. It has also progressed from paintings and sculpture to performance and installation art. Some galleries periodically bring in pieces from overseas so there is always something to view and, if you are so inclined, to buy. Here are two websites that can point you in the right direction:

- Singapore Art Museum (SAM)
  Website: http://www.nhb.gov.sg/SAM
  One of the first fine art museums in South-east Asia, SAM moved into the refurbished premises of the old Saint Joseph's Institution in 1996. Today, its permanent collection numbers in the seven thousands and is currently the largest owned by any museum in the region. The website is a good starting point to find out what's going on there.

- Singapore Art Gallery Guide
  Website: http://www.sagg.com.sg
  This is a monthly publication helmed by expatriate René Daniels and it lists exhibitions, artists and venues that have something going on for that month. You can buy the guide at major bookshops or through subscriptions via the website listed above.

- Singapore Art
  Website: http://singaporeart.org
  A comprehensive website that has everything you need to know about local artists, venues, arts supplies and organisations.

- Sculpture Square
  Website: http://www.sculpturesq.com.sg
  Singapore's first (and currently, only) space dedicated to three-dimensional art pieces and sculpture. Located a short walk away from SAM, Sculpture Square has two galleries, one of which is a converted 19th century Baba Methodist Church—its 9-m-high pillar-free space is ideal for the purpose at hand.

Asian Art Fair

ARTSingapore is an annual fair for contemporary Asian art, a five-day event that showcases art from the Asian region. It was launched in 2000 and has been gaining popularity ever since. You can find out more at its website:

http://www.artsingapore.net

Performing Arts
Music

Western-style music is everywhere and you can probably get your favourite artistes at the local stores. You have your worldwide chains like HMV and Borders, as well local ones such as Sembawang Music Stores, Gramaphone and Music Junction. Walk into any shopping mall and you will find at least one music outlet there.

Local music consists of a lot of Western influences and you will hear pop, hip-hop, rap and jazz, some original and some covers. According to some, the Chinese music scene is more vibrant with many artists from the Asian region, particularly Taiwan and Hong Kong. A number of Singaporean singers have also ventured to these two places to make a name for themselves before returning back home. For record labels, this just makes commercial sense because of the size of the population—no matter how many fans you have in Singapore, the base is still small compared to what you have in other Asian countries. The situation is similar for Malay singers, many of whom have a strong following in Malaysia. Conversely, many Malaysian and Indonesian singers are very popular here.

If you enjoy your music live, there are a number of bars and pubs that have live bands playing. If you like the more laid-back sounds of jazz, Boat Quay would be the place to start (try Harry's Bar). And not far from that is Clarke Quay with a couple of clubs that have live rock bands on certain nights.

Live Entertainment

Check out the STB's Visit Singapore website which has a list of some of the more popular night spots with live entertainment. The website is:

http://www.visitsingapore.com/publish/stbportal/en/home/what_to_do/nightlife_in_singapore/nightspots/experiences/live_entertainment.html

---

Those who are more classically inclined will not be left out either. The Singapore Symphony Orchestra

(SSO) has regular performances, sometimes with guest artists. These are usually advertised in the local newspapers but you can plan ahead by logging onto their website at:

http://www.sso.org.sg

For something more ethnic, check out the following:

- Singapore Chinese Orchestra
  Website: http://www.sco.com.sg
- Orkestra Melayu Singapura (Singapore Malay Orchestra) or OMS
  Website: http://omsyouth.blogspot.com/
- Singapore Indian Orchestra and Choir (SIOC)
  This currently doesn't have a dedicated website but it comes under the purview of the People's Association (PA) so you can contact them for more information. The PA website is:

  http://www.lifeskills-lifestyle.pa.gov.sg/
  html/services/box_office.htm

Incidentally, you can also contact the PA about the Malay Orchestra.

Dance

Obviously Western-style dance dominants here and you will also get performances by famous companies from other countries such as the Russian Ballet. A number of ethnic dance groups do exist and performances are often listed in the Life!Events section of the local papers. These are likely to incorporate ethnic elements of dance into modern Western-style dance or vice versa. There are also some performing arts companies that conduct classes. Here are just a few to get you started:

- Arts Fission Company
  Website: http://www.artsfission.org
- Attitude Dance Studio (Latin American)
  Website: http://www.asiasalsa.com/
- Bhaskar's Arts (Indian)
  Website: http://www.bhaskarsartsacademy.com
- Country Line Dance Association (line dancing)
  Website: http://www.cldas.com/

- Dance Ensemble Singapore
  Website: http://www.des.org.sg/dance.htm
- Ecnad
  Website: http://www.ecnad.org
- John & Josephine Dance Creative (ballroom)
  Website: http://www.johnjosephinedance.com.sg
- Odyssey Dance Theatre
  Website: http://www.odysseydancetheatre.com
- Singapore Dance Theatre
  Website: http://www.singaporedancetheatre.com/
- Sri Warisan Performing Arts (Malay)
  Website: http://www.sriwarisan.com
- Temple of Fine Arts (Indian)
  Website: http://www.templeoffinearts.org/sg/

Dance Classes

Some community centres and clubs conduct dance classes in social, ballroom and line dancing. They also have ballet and some Indian classical dance classes aimed at children. Look up the People's Association CC Online website if you're interested:

http://160.96.187.35/NASApp/cconline/main.do

Just click on courses and do a search for 'dance' under the community club or centre of your choice.

Theatre and Drama

There is a thriving local theatre scene in Singapore with many new making their mark overseas and locally. There are a number of local theatre companies (for English, Chinese, Malay, Indian and Peranakan drama) which perform local and foreign productions. The NAC website carries a comprehensive list. Check it out at:

http://www.nac.gov.sg/the/the07.asp

Moving Pictures

Local Chinese-language serial dramas for the small screen have been produced for decades and are now being exported to other countries. English-language dramas have lagged far behind and these have not enjoyed as much success as their

An actor in a Chinese *wayang*, complete with face paint, headgear and costume. For those who aren't used to loud cacophonic and often discordant sounds, this type of opera is usually an acquired taste.

Mandarin counterparts. (One exception has been *Growing Up*, which had a strong viewership during its run.) Sitcoms fair a little better, with some such as *Under One Roof* and *Phua Chu Kang Pte Ltd* gaining iconic status.

Locally produced movies are a fairly recent phenomenon, and this was started by a number of short and independent films. Commercial success for films only started in 1998 with Jack Neo being the man with the vision and Raintree Pictures, the production company with the golden touch.

Saturday Night Fever, Singapore-style

In 1998, local talent Glen Goei wrote and directed his first movie, *Forever Fever*, which had many elements from *Saturday Night Fever* (including John Travolta's trademark dance move) and *Strictly Ballroom*. Marry that with a typical Singapore roughneck with a heart of gold and choice comedic scenes, this became an instant hit with many Singaporeans. It was shot entirely in Singapore and employed many well-known local names. In addition, it had a popular soundtrack. Soon after its local release, it was picked up by Miramax International and screened in the United States under the title, *That's the Way I Like It*.

Opera

There really isn't that much by way of Western-style opera in Singapore, unless you get a visiting diva performing with the SSO. Singapore's equivalent of the opera is the *wayang*, or Chinese street opera. This form of art was brought over from the mainland when Chinese immigrants came here to work in the 1800s. A stage was erected, about 2 m above the ground, and people would crowd around (or sit if seats were available), talking at the top of their voices while watching the opera unfold on stage. And this was no mean feat as the music accompanying Chinese opera is usually loud and deafening, consisting mainly of gongs, drums and one or two stringed instruments. The music and the movements haven't changed, and in some cases, neither has the noise from the audience.

In the beginning, all opera performers were male but over time, women have gotten into the act as well. Their faces are usually heavily made up with opera paint and they dress

Completed in 2005, the National Library is located along Victoria Street.

in elaborate Chinese costumes that come complete with ornate headgear. There are usually few players on the stage at one time, and they interact with each other in sing-song Chinese and in song. Occasionally there would be mime and acrobatics as well.

Chinese *wayang* does take some getting used to, especially more if you don't speak the language (normally performed in Cantonese, Hokkien or Teochew). Even many of the local Chinese can't stomach them! Nevertheless, it is an experience to catch part of a performance.

Where to Start

A good place to begin your journey is to find out more about the various types of operas and the different companies in Singapore. The NAC website has a list of these at:

http://www.nac.gov.sg/the/the07.asp

Literary Arts

The standard of literacy may be very high in Singapore, in the 90 per cent range, but strangely enough, they aren't really a

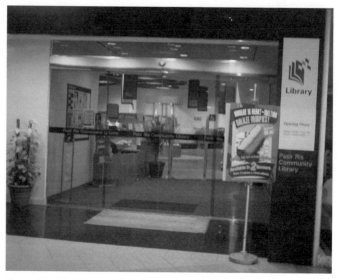

The Pasir Ris Community Library is conveniently located within a shopping mall that is centrally located.

nation of readers. The National Library Board(NLB) has been trying to reverse this trend by making reading more fun and accessible vis campaigns and special events The main library (Lee Kong Chian Reference Library) is a 13-storey building located in Victoria Street, its new premises as of July 2005. There are numerous regional and community libraries around the island. Check the NLB website (http://www.nlb.gov.sg) to find one near you.

The literary arts in Singapore has flourished over the years, in all four official languages. The National Book Development Council of Singapore (NBDCS) has been instrumental in encouraging the writing, publishing and reading of more local works. As usual the NAC has a list of literary arts groups and you can begin your search at:

http://www.nac.gov.sg/lit/lit07.asp

A YEAR OF CELEBRATIONS

There are ten official public holidays during the year, and not surprisingly, they represent the various cultural groups plus some Western holidays that have found a place in the yearly calendar.

National Public Holidays

The following are legal public holidays as set down by
the government.

New Year's Day	1 January
Hari Raya Haji	variable, dependent on Islamic calendar
Chinese New Year	variable, two days, usually some time in late January to early March
Good Friday	variable, usually some time in April
Labour Day	1 May
Vesak Day	variable, usually some time in May
National Day	9 August
Deepavali	variable, usually some time in October or November
Hari Raya Puasa	variable, dependent on Islamic calendar
Christmas Day	25 December

Secular Celebrations
New Year's (1 January)

Singapore rings in the New Year much like the rest of the world, with a big bang at midnight on 31 December. There's always a big countdown show featuring local celebrities and, if you're lucky, foreign artistes (i.e. those from Asia) as well. This will usually be televised live on Channel 5 and in recent years, also on TV Mobile that goes out on all the public buses.

Dancing the Night Away

New Year's has always been a joyful time for Singaporeans, even in the 1950s and 1960s. A Singaporean lady in her 70s recounted how there was always a great celebration on New Year's Eve at the Victoria Memorial Hall. Many people would dress up to the nines and gather to count down to the new year, complete with party hats, drinks, music and lots of dancing. One year, she and a group of friends were invited to a private celebration at a bungalow thrown by the uncle of one in the group. It was a lavish party with food, drinks and music. But it was the dancing they enjoyed the most—waltz, cha-cha, foxtrot and quickstep among others. And at the stroke of midnight, they toasted the new year with champagne.

The venue for this big countdown varies from year to year (in 2005, it was held at Seah Im Car Park, across the road from Harbourfront) but all the major 'hot spots' will have a big bash going on. One of the most popular events in the recent past has been the foam party on Sentosa beach that starts in the late evening on New Year's Eve and goes on to the wee hours of the morning.

Labour Day (1 May)

The first of May is Labour Day but there isn't really much in the way of a celebration. Most people look forward to it because it's a day of rest and if it comes near a weekend, all the better—they take off for a long vacation! If you're the kind who likes great deals, check the local papers for what's on as many of the larger departmental stores and supermarkets will have special offers to tie in with this event.

Istana Open House

The Istana is the official residence of the President of Singapore and is situated in the Orchard Road area, next to the Plaza Singapura Shopping Mall. While entrance is restricted, the Istana is open to the public on certain days:

- Labour Day
- National Day
- Chinese New Year
- Hari Raya Puasa
- Deepavali

Admission for Singaporeans and PRs is free and foreigners have to pay an entrance fee of S$ 1. However, this is mainly for the grounds and you will be treated to band performances and, depending on the time you are there, be able meet and take pictures with the president and his wife. Also on display are the special commemorative gifts from other foreign government and dignitaries.

For an additional S$ 2, you will be able to view official staterooms within the building itself. There will also be souvenirs on sale. All monies collected (including entrance fees) are donated to charity.

National Day (9 August)

This marks the day Singapore broke away from the Malaysia and became an independent nation. The one thing many people look forward to on National Day is the parade, held on the day itself, usually in the evenings. It is a spectacular event that starts with sombre proceedings—inspection of the guard by the president, march past of the military and civilian contingents—and continues with an extravagant outdoor 'concert' that usually touches on Singapore's history and its achievements since independence. The concert always culminates in stunning fireworks, a hot favourite of young and old. It is always interesting to see how innovative and colourful the creators get each year. After all, in how many ways can you recount history? Plenty, it would seem, as the parade proves year after year. And it is a matter of pride to be involved in any part of these events. The various participants, be it for the more serious or fun-filled portion, practise for months just to get things right.

Tickets for the parade are free but may not be easy to come by. The good thing is there is usually a dress rehearsal about two weeks before so even if you can't get tickets for the actual day, you can try for the one before. And every spectator gets a goody bag—a medium-sized knapsack filled with everything you would need during the parade (water, light stick for waving) and memorabilia you can take home with you.

The Padang was traditionally the place for the parade (although it was held at the soon-to-be-under-renovation National Stadium in Kallang for a number of years; it will be held at the current stadium for the last time in 2006) but 2005

National Songs

About a month before National Day, you're likely to hear a song being broadcast on television with some regularity. This would be the national day song for that year. Before you raise your eyebrows in cynicism or disbelief, the songs are generally very well received. Some say that this started in the early 1990s when Singaporeans in general received some backlash (from other Singaporeans no less) about not having any national pride or patriotic spirit. Next thing you knew, there was a national song. While the national songs of the 20th century were about Singaporeans being proud to have achieved so much and being Singaporean, those of the 21st century are more about feeling at home in Singapore and looking towards the future.

was slated the last year this would happen as the parade gears up to move to the waterside arena in Marina from 2007 onwards.

Another keenly anticipated event that occurs during National Day is the Prime Minister's National Day Rally speech which is televised live on all the major channels. It is during this speech the prime minister takes stock of the situation in the country and maps out some of his plans for the year ahead. I suppose some people might equate this to the State of the Union address in the United States; and in Singapore, this is much fodder for talk for weeks to come.

Other Festive Celebrations

A number of other Western celebratory days seem to have gained some prominence over the last few years.

- Valentine's Day (14 February):celebrated in much the same way as the rest of the world, with the prices of flowers (especially red roses) skyrocketing.
- Saint Patrick's Day (17 March): usually celebrated by the Irish in Singapore and there's usually some wonderful festivities at the various Irish pubs on the island.
- Mother's Day (second Sunday of May): families normally take the family matriarch out for a delicious meal.
- Father's Day (second, sometimes third, Sunday of June): much like Mother's Day.
- Halloween (31 October): celebrated by pockets of people. Unfortunately, children don't really go trick-or-treating here unless you live in a large private condo or want to go to the Woodlands area where many American families reside and where it is a huge neighbourhood affair.

School Celebrations

If you've enrolled your children in a local school, you will soon be familiar with three school holidays on which your children get to stay home. Youth Day is celebrated on the first Sunday in July, which means that the following Monday is also a holiday, and all children in school—from primary, secondary, college, polytechnic—get the day off. Tied in with this is the Singapore Youth Festival which holds a number of different competitions (mainly in the music and dance genre) and all schools are encouraged to participate.

Teacher's Day is on 1 September and it is used to honour all those who impart knowledge to the next generation. Children's Day (1 October), on the other hand, is for all the children still in school. However, it's only a holiday for those in primary school. In some schools, students are encouraged to showcase other talents outside the academic arena so you have special concerts and shows put up by the students themselves, usually under their teacher's supervision.

Chinese Celebrations
Chinese New Year

The most important celebration for the Chinese population— not just in Singapore but around the globe—is Chinese New Year which marks the start of the New Year according the Chinese lunar calendar. Usually this takes place some time in late January to early March and lasts for 15 days, even though only the first two are public holidays. Before the actual day, Chinese will already have been getting ready for the event by spring cleaning the home and buying new clothes and New Year goodies.

Even these apples are all geared up for Chinese New Year. Each apple gets a Chinese character which people can use to assemble auspicious proverbs and sayings so as to bring in good luck and fortune for the new year.

Festive Foods

New Year goodies will be on sale and no Chinese home would be complete without some or all of the standards.

- love letters: also known as *kueh belanda*; these are crisp rolls made from batter than have been poured onto specially designed moulds.
- pineapple tarts: open faced or totally wrapped, this is a specially prepared pineapple jam on or in a slightly savoury crumbly pastry.
- *kueh bangkit*: a white baked coconut biscuit that melts in your mouth.
- *kueh baulu*: baby sponge cakes with a crisp outer shell and a less dense consistency.
- *bak kwa*: barbecued meat (usually pork) that have people lining up for hours at some of the more popular stores in Singapore.
- groundnuts: meant to symbolise health and longevity.
- sweets: a symbolic item; its sweetness is meant to signify that the eater would be blessed with a sweet year ahead.
- chocolates: these would often be made in the shape of coins—these days you get them in nuggets and groundnuts as well—to symbolise money; you also get them shaped like eggs to symbolise new life.
- prawn rolls: a relatively new addition to the list of favourites, this is usually a fried paste of dried shrimp and chilli that has been wrapped in a small piece of egg-roll skin and deep fried.

During this time, Chinatown will take on a life on its own. The whole area will be strung up with lights and buntings, and stalls are set up along the streets to sell all sorts of Chinese New Year paraphernalia, everything people would need to make their new year more festive, from goodies to delicacies to decorations to clothes. You name it, they have it. If you don't mind crowds (and even if you do), take a trip down and experience it for yourself, especially in the evenings when the atmosphere is turned up a notch. Don't bother to drive though because you won't be able to park in Chinatown itself, and all the roads around the area will be packed. Take a taxi or take the MRT to tthe Chinatown station.

Visit Chinatown before Chinese New Year and you will find the entire place transformed with makeshift stalls selling all sorts of festive goodies you won't normally find during the rest of the year.

While some of the items are sold at a bargain, the prices of others have been jacked up. In general, if the offer is a few for a set price (e.g. buy one at S$ 4 but buy three for S$ 10), then you shouldn't insult the owner by bargaining. Not unless you intend to buy a huge bundle. But in the spirit of the season, the owner is likely to offer a further discount on their own accord. Shop around and have fun.

Those with nerves of steel might even like to visit on Chinese New Year's Eve, after nine or ten at night. Prices tend to be cut after a certain time as this is the last chance the owners will have to sell their stock before they close the stall after midnight. (And you will be surprised how fast they will have to clear out of there.) The only drawback of this is that the prime stock will probably have been sold by now and varieties may no longer be available. The choice is yours.

What Will The Locals Buy?

The times are a-changing and many of the younger families don't bother too much about getting their homes decked out for the season. They will, nonetheless, stock some goodies in the house just in case people come to visit. The more traditional folks will make sure that there have certain items to ensure they are endowed with the best for the coming year. The following is a sampling.

(Continued on the next page)

(Continued from previous page)

- Chinese sausage, waxed duck
  As strange as this might sound, these were actually leftovers from the long winter months that came before. In China, people would preserve their meats in this manner and once spring arrived, they had to find a way to get rid of them. The tradition has carried over to overseas Chinese like those in Singapore. You can only get waxed duck during the New Year period but the Chinese sausage (*larp cheong*) is now available all year round and makes a fragrant addition to many a fried dish.
- candied sweets and fruits
  These are usually served in a dish (lacquer or otherwise) with eight compartments, the number eight being auspicious of course. It signifies having a 'sweet' year ahead.
- *nian gao* (literally 'year cake')
  This is a steamed glutinous rice cake in banana leaf and plays an important part in sending the Kitchen God back to heaven on the 23rd day of the 12th month during the lunar year. Legend has it that the Kitchen God was privy to everything that went on in the household and would carry tales back to heaven thus determining the fate of the family for the coming year. *Nian gao*, being sweet and sticky, had a two-fold purpose. It would be sticky enough to 'seal' the mouth of the Kitchen God so he would not be able to speak; and if he could speak, the cake would be sweet enough to ensure he would only say 'sweet' things.
- New Year goodies
  As mentioned previously, most families try to have a little bit of everything, whether this is to serve to guests during the 15 days, to give away to family and friends, or to cook for reunion dinner or other feasts during the season.
- peach blossoms
  Believed to bring luck in romance.
- kumquat trees
  The Chinese word for gold (*kum*) sounds the same as that for oranges, of any kind.
- water narcissus
  These are bought before the actual day and people would wait for it to bloom. If it is does so on the first day of the New Year, it is meant to be very auspicious, even more so if the plant bears white flowers.
- phoenix tail
  A favourite for Chinese businesses, this plant is meant to foretell how well the business will do in the coming year. The number of blooms it contains on the first day of the New Year will signify the number of times the company will succeed.
- pussy willows
  Another symbol of longevity. Sometimes, other auspicious items such as *hong baos* (more on this later) are hung from the branches.

ussy willows adorned with all the trappings of the Lunar New Year: fans, pineapples, lanterns and kumquats. The Chinese couple, lion, drum and firecrackers at the base of the vase only add to the festive air.

On New Year's Eve, there is the all-important reunion dinner. This is a throwback to the olden days in China when families in different parts of the country would reunite for the start of the new year. This still holds true today except that Singapore is a lot smaller so it is much easier for families to get together. Another major change that is gaining popularity is the change of venue from the home to the restaurant. In the past, mothers and daughters used to slave over a hot stove for an entire day or more to cook up the elaborate meal for the entire family. And of course, tradition dictates that there had to be plenty for everyone to eat till their heart's content, plus leftovers. This is so that the family will never want for food in the coming year. These days, though, many families have their reunion dinners at restaurants or *cze cha* stalls; and many of these eating outlets now have special menus for this evening meal that include fish, prawns and other dishes, all which have some sort of significance when uttered in the Chinese tongue.

Auspicious Dishes

Whether you are eating at home or outside, there are certain dishes which traditional Chinese will always try to incorporate into their meals because of the significance they carry. Here are some of them.

- abalone: significant in that it is expensive; the Chinese don't believe in holding back during the dinner as a full and prosperous table would auger the same for the year to come.
- *fatt choy*: a type of seaweed that looks like hair when cooked. It is considered auspicious because its name in Chinese sounds like 'to prosper'.
- *serng* (Chinese leek): the Teochew believe that eating this vegetable during the dinner will ensure that money comes in during the year.
- fish: the Chinese term for fish (*yu*), especially in Cantonese, sounds like the word for 'extra'. If you 'have fish' (*yao yu*), you will have 'extras' in the coming year.

(Continued on the next page)

(Continued from previous page)

- prawns: the Cantonese word for 'prawn' is *har* and so prawns tie in with the Cantonese proverb, *hee har dai siu* which signifies that you will laugh the whole year through i.e. have no worries and be happy.
- *yu sheng*: this is the raw fish salad which only used to be available from the first to 15th days of Chinese New Year. Nowadays, many outlets offer it at least five days earlier and families opt to have this for the reunion dinner. Each ingredient is meant to represent an auspicious trait and when tossing the salad, the higher you toss the better as it signifies that whatever you do will reach new heights.
- *nian gao*: some people have this for dessert. Besides feeding this to the Kitchen God (see before), the name of this sweet cake signifies that you will be promoted in the coming year.

Another change is that many younger couples tend to have two dinners, one with the husband's family and one with the wife's. In the past this rarely happened as a woman was not considered part of her own family once she was married off so she was not obligated to be 'reunited' with her own family.

For those who are up for the experience, try visiting a wet market on the eve when it is open all night long. The market will be closed on the first day of the New Year (and for most of the stalls, likely to be closed for at least three days) so people want to stock up on enough food. Despite the fact that supermarkets are open all the time and you can buy food even during the first three days. But old habits die hard and many Chinese prefer to buy fresh food. Keep in mind that if you do decide to buy something that prices at these midnight wet markets will be a lot higher than at normal times.

The first day of Chinese New Year dawns and most families are up and about very early. Some will pray and offer food sacrifices near their homes; you may see huge bins near some HDB flats for the burning of 'paper money', to those who have died so they have something to spend in the afterlife. For

All stocked up and ready for guests. Just a little bit of everything will do, plus lots of mandarin oranges.

others, the first day is usually for visiting relatives. But people never go empty-handed. They must bring along mandarin oranges and present two to the host or hostess of the home they are visiting. These symbolise prosperity and it is a token gift that wishes upon the family good fortune in the coming year. And this is not one-way; the host or hostess will have to present you with two in return. The Chinese believe in the philosophy of 'got come, got go', or to put it very simply, tit for tat. To just take without giving is selfish and does not bode well for the first day of a brand new year.

New Year Greetings

Even if you don't visit your friends, you're likely to hear some auspicious New Year phrases being uttered, in all the different Chinese dialects. One of the most common would be *gongxi facai* which is Mandarin for 'wishing you prosperity'. Another phrase is *xingnian kuaile* which is 'happy new year' in Mandarin. Someone might say to you, "*niannian youyu*", which is their way of wishing you abundance and 'extras' every year. To the older generation, one might say, '*suisui pingan*' meaning that one wishes them lasting peace from age to age.

Most children love Chinese New Year because they receive *hong baos* (also called *ang pows* or red packets) containing

Some families arrange for a lion dance to be performed at the home as this seen as a good start to the new year.

money. This originated from days of old when *hong baos* were given to young people to wish them good luck and safety. While the meaning seems to be lost these days, the tradition lives on and technically, any unmarried person qualifies. Most of the time, there seems to be an implicit understanding that once you start working, you will stop receiving *hong baos* even though you may still be single. Nonetheless, there are exceptions, especially among family members.

The amount given varies but is always an even number. Inflation has its effect on *hong baos* as well and the least amount one should give these days is S$ 4. (To some, that too is a measly sum and definitely not an auspicious sounding number.) *Hong baos* are normally given out by the females in the family and you often see them with different stacks in their bags, each bundle with different amounts of money in each packet. What each child receives often depends on how well the person or family knows the child's family, or in some cases, how much the giver wants to impress the parents of the child. If your child receives a *hong bao*, you should also give one to the child of the giver, unless this person's children are all grown or she has not started her own family.

Superstitions

There are certain superstitions connected with Chinese New Year. One major one is that you should pay all your debts before the start of the new year so that you will be debt-free throughout the coming year. Another one is that if you want to cut your hair, you must get this done before the new year. This is because the Chinese word for 'hair' sounds like the Chinese word for 'prosper' so cutting this means you are cutting off your wealth or prosperity.

On the first day of the new year, you should not do any sweeping in the house and this is symbolic of sweeping all your luck away. Children, especially, are told time and again that they should not squabble or quarrel with anyone on the first day as this will represent disharmony among people—definitely not a good sign. A topic that is taboo at this time is death as it is not auspicious to speak of ends at the beginning of the new year. Strangely, some Chinese believe that if someone is gravely ill before the start of the new year, this is a hurdle for them to cross. If they make it past the first day, the next hurdle will be the 15 days of the season. If they can live through that, they will be able to last through at least another year.

While everyone is encouraged to buy and eat some sweets during this period so that their year will be sweeter, they are discouraged from buying shoes and trousers; if they do, they have to buy them before the start of the new year. Some people say this is because the Cantonese word for shoes sounds like that for 'rough' while others say is sounds like someone sighing. Either way, it doesn't bode well for a new beginning. Trousers has similar connotations; the Chinese word (in at least two dialects) for 'pants' sounds similar to the Chinese word for 'bitter'. I'm sure you've already started to see a pattern emerging by now.

Traditionally, Chinese businesses tended to close their doors for about ten days (some still do) or for the whole 15 days of the festive season. Some will open for an hour or two on the second day, mainly for prayers, otherwise they will not be able to do business until the fourth day as it is inauspicious to do business on the third day. Why this is so has been hard to discern but possibly because the third day is often thought of as a day when people tended to quarrel or be at odds with others. Of course, this is never a good sign during the New Year period.

Some companies also believe in hiring a lion dance or dragon dance troupe to visit the business premises. (Some homes do this too.) One belief is that the lion and dragon were the only animals that Nyan, a mythical predatory beast that roamed the earth at one time, is afraid of. With the amount of noise the dancers make, it's more likely that they will scare all the bad luck way!

The seventh day of the Lunar New Year is the common man's birthday (or everybody's birthday). In ancient China, this was often more important that an individual's birthday so of course, noodles must be eaten as its length symbolises longevity. In Singapore, many people still eat noodles but they also partake of *yu sheng*. Some people, however, turn vegetarian for the day.

Hokkien New Year

A number of people are not aware of this but the ninth day is the start of the new year for Hokkiens. This goes back to ancient times in China. One version of this story tells of some soldiers from another province (some say they were Manchu, some say they were Cantonese) who were travelling through the Hokkien province just before the start of the new year. They asked for directions but no one could understand them. Their frustration then led to anger as they felt the villagers were making fun of them on purpose so they lashed out at the Hokkiens, who fled to the sugar cane fields. The soldiers terrorised them for days, but the Hokkiens hid in the fields, using the sugar cane growing there to keep themselves alive and praying to the Lord of Heaven for help. The foreign soldiers finally moved on, and the Hokkiens emerged from the fields. They realised it was already the ninth day of the Lunar New Year and also the feast day of the Lord of Heaven. What better offering than the sugar cane that kept them alive during their time of trial? Since that time, sugar cane has always featured prominently for the Hokkiens during this festive period.

Chinese New Year is not just about visiting friends and relatives. Many people look forward to two events which occur during this time. The first is the Chingay, a vibrant colourful parade along Orchard Road that is similar to the Rose Parade of the United States. The first Chingay was introduced into Singapore in 1973, seemingly, as a substitute for firecrackers which had been banned the previous year. The first parade was simple and involved the People's Association (PA) and the various pugilistic associations in Singapore. It has since grown to gigantic proportions and consists not just of the floats and performances but also involves people from different ethnic groups and different countries. Held in various housing estates for the first 20 years or so, the parade moved to Orchard Road in 1985 and, except during the 2000 millennium year, has been held in that prime spot ever since. For more information about the chingay, log onto:

http://www.chingay.org.sg

While the Chingay is a one-evening affair (two, if you count the full-dress rehearsal as well—and lots of people turn up for that too), the Singapore River Hongbao normally lasts for slightly more than two weeks, starting just before Chinese New Year and ending about the same time or just after. It was introduced in 1987 as a way to revive interest in Chinese culture and put some oomph back into the new year celebrations. It has grown from strength to strength and features different arts and folklore e.g. calligraphy and palm reading, mini floats, cultural performances such as folk dances and acrobatic acts, as well as kiddy rides and food. For years, it was held at Marina Promenade but moved to the Esplanade Park to mark its 20th anniversary in 2006. To find out when the next one will be held, check out the STB's Visit Singapore at:

http://www.visitsingapore.com/cny/

The 15th and last day of Chinese New Year is called *chap goh mei* (literally, '15th night') and is sometimes known as Chinese Valentine's. By this time, everyone should have visited all their relatives and friends and had their fair share of food and New Year goodies. In ancient China, single girls were supposed to throw oranges into the river on this night in the hopes of snagging a husband (perhaps someone rowing a boat on the river?) in the coming year. These Chinese of today's Singapore don't keep up this tradition but some familities choose to have another reunion dinner while many others make it a point to eat *tang yuan* on this day.

Qing Ming

Literally meaning 'clear and bright', this is the Chinese version of All Soul's Day. It is celebrated 106 days after the Winter Solstice (see section on 'Dong Zhi') which coincides with the 4 or 5 April, depending on whether it is a leap year. During

Qing Ming, families visit the cemetery and columbariums to clean the graves and niches of the dearly departed. Because of this, Qing Ming is also known as Tomb Sweeping Day in some countries. They also pay their respects, offer food and prayers and burn joss sticks.

Duan Wu Festival

What do rice dumplings have to do with dragon boats? Plenty, if you ask the Chinese. Many believe that it all started when the patriotic poet-minister Qu Yuan threw himself into the river after he became disillusioned with the corrupt government of his time. The villagers were distressed at what their beloved minister had done that they rowed out to the river and beat their drums in an effort to keep the fishes away from his body. Sadly they failed so the next thing was to throw raw rice to 'feed' Qu Yuan's spirit. In doing so they hoped to keep him alive. It is said that Qu Yuan then appeared to some fisherman and informed them a dragon had been eating their rice offerings and he was starving. He advised them to wrap the rice in a three-cornered silk package to prevent the dragon from stealing his food.

This legend lives on today in the Duan Wu Festival which is celebrated on the fifth day of the fifth lunar month. The three-cornered silk packages have become rice dumplings (*bak chang* or *zongzi*)—meat encased in glutinous rice which

Dragon boat races are held In June every year to tie in with the Duan Wu Festival.

is wrapped into a pyramidal shape using bamboo leaves then steamed. You can buy this at many outlets during the year but during Duan Wu Festival, many people make their own, some using a secret family recipe.

Tying in with this is the Dragon Boat Festival. In Singapore, boat races are held at Marina Bay and teams from all around the world are invited to compete. If you'd like to find out more, log onto the Singapore Dragon Boat Association website at:

http://www.sdba.org.sg/

Hungry Ghosts Festival

The seventh month of the Chinese lunar calendar is considered an inauspicious time as the Gates of Hell are open and spirits are allowed to roam the earth. This usually coincides with late July and most of August, and children (and youngsters) are warned not to stay out late during this period as you ever know what the spirits might be up to. Be prepared to encounter more 'haze' than usual as people burn more paper money and joss sticks. Even if you don't believe in the presence of spirits, it is advisable to watch where you step during this time as it is unlucky to step on the ash or remains of joss stick. You may not incur the wrath of the spirit, but you might upset the person who was praying at that spot.

One of the highlights during the Hungry Ghosts Festival is the presence of outdoor performances called *ge tai* (literally meaning 'song stage'). From out of nowhere, you will find performers of all ages

Getting Married

Naturally, the seventh month is not a good time for getting married. Many will arrange for the ceremony to take place before or after this month, the latter being a more popular choice. In this modern day where many young adults have converted to Christianity, this mindset still prevails mainly because their parents (or their relatives, or parents' friends) still hold to this belief. Traditional parents will object vehemently to any wedding held in this month, and even those who don't may find that relatives and friends will not turn up. Either way, it would not be an auspicious start for the happy couple.

If you really have no qualms about having your wedding during this period, it is likely you will get a pretty good deal from the hotels as they will be starved for business on this front. Keep in mind that your Chinese friends and colleagues may beg off attending though.

belting out all sorts of, mainly Chinese, songs, from oldies to the latest hits. People believe that this is meant to entertain the spirits, although judging from some of the singing that goes on, it would seem they were trying to scare the spirits away! *Ge tai* is normally organised by a community of Chinese in a particular area. These could be certain families or businesses that have banded together, or even someone who is 'paying back' for a petition answered from the previous year.

While some opt for the modern *ge tai*, others prefer the traditional Chinese *wayang*. Auctions are also held during this festival to raise funds for charity.

Mid-Autumn Festival

Also known as the Moon Cake or Lantern Festival, this is celebrated on the 15th day of the eighth lunar month, which falls some time between mid-September and mid-October. The Chinese believe that on this day, the moon is the fullest and brightest. In China, this day coincided with harvest time in the middle of Autumn.

There are many romantic stories associated with this festival. One has to do with Chang-Er, a woman who drank the elixir of immortality and floated away to the moon. Some people believe that if you gaze at the moon on this night, you will catch a glimpse of her with her pet rabbit. Another story tells of rebels who hid secret messages inside round cakes urging their fellow sufferers to rise up at a certain time and place and overthrow their oppressors. Because the uprising was so successful, the people commemorate their victory on this day by eating round moon-like cakes.

The tradition of eating moon cakes has been passed down through the ages. Previously you could only buy moon cakes filled with red bean or lotus paste. Today, the variety of moon cakes available is only limited by your imagination.

Lanterns abound during this time, being a beacon to light your way as well as a symbol of good luck and prosperity. They come in all shapes, sizes and varieties, from small lanterns that open up in an accordion-like

fashion to translucent decorated plastic stretched taut over wire bent in certain shapes such as rooster, rabbits, to more sophisticated ones in the shape of your children's favourite characters (e.g. Hello Kitty) or super hero. This is also an opportune time to visit the Chinese Gardens in Jurong as it usually has a wonderful display of lanterns, large and small, modern and new.

Dong Zhi

This day marked the start of winter for farmers of ancient times, as well as the end of another harvest period. This was the longest night of the year, known as the Winter Solstice in the Western world, and usually falls on 21 or 22 December. This festival is not as widely celebrated as Chinese New Year but traditional Chinese families will make the effort to get together for a sumptuous meal and *tang yuan*, glutinous rice balls (plain or filled) served in hot soup. These signify unity within the family.

Festival of the Nine Emperor Gods

One of the lesser known festivals, celebrated mainly by Taoists, pays tribute to the nine Emperor Gods who are believed to have healing powers and can bestow longevity and good fortune. The venue is the Jiu Huang Da Di (meaning 'Nine Emperor Gods', of course) Temple in Upper Serangoon Road. While the actual feast day is on the ninth day of the ninth lunar month, festivities span a total of nine days, and the temple compound is transformed into a place of joyous celebration with chants and Hokkien opera to entertain not just the emperor gods but also the mortals who come to pray. On the final day, the gods are given a spectacular send-off as they return to heaven. The gods are 'invited' to sit on sedan chairs which are carried by four men around the compound and then towards Sungei Serangoon (water is supposed to be significant as this is how the gods came to earth). The sedan chairs are placed on a platform raft which is later lit and sent out to sea.

Buddhist Festivals
Vesak Day

While the Buddhists celebrate a number of festivals throughout the year, the most important is Vesak Day, which commemorates the birth of Buddha, his enlightenment and attainment of nirvana. It is celebrated on the day of the full moon in the lunar month of Vesakh, and usually falls some time from end April to May. On this day, Buddhist temples will be decorated with lights, flowers and flags, ready to welcome the devotees who come to pray, meditate and make offerings, while the resident monks chant sutras. Many will observe the ceremonial ladling of scented water (or 'bathing') over a statue of the baby Siddhartha—Buddha's earthly name before he was enlightened—meant to symbolise the purifying of one's thoughts and deeds. Captive birds are released into the air to symbolise the liberation of captive souls.

All Buddhists turn vegetarian for the day (if they are not already) and a good number of them partake of the meals offered at the temples. Acts of generosity (known as *dana*) are encouraged and Buddhists will help the poor and needy in cash or kind, organise or participate in blood donation drives at the hospitals or spread the joy of the occasion with the less fortunate in hospices, old age homes, prisons and rehabilitation centres.

The end of the celebrations are marked by a mass candlelight procession through the streets culminating in a huge gathering at a public place. Non-Buddhists are welcome to join in the celebration at the temples.

Other Buddhist Festivals

- Dharma Day commemorates Buddha's first sermon and is celebrated on the day of the full moon in July.
- Sangha Day, normally in October, is a time for people to reflect on their commitment to the Buddhist way of life. Monks and nuns are known to go for a retreat during this time to reaffirm their beliefs.

Muslim Celebrations
Awal Muharram

This is the first Day of the Islamic New Year (obviously falling on the first day of the first month of the Muslim calendar). The Islamic calendar first came into being in 622 AD when the Prophet Muhammad continued his journey to Medina from Mecca after escaping from his enemies. This was taken to be a good omen and the start of a new beginning. In the same way, Muslims view the new year as the start of something new but unlike many other ethnic groups, they mark the day with solemnity. Many will visit for mosque for prayers and religious lectures.

Maulud Nabi

This commemorates the birthday of the Prophet Muhammad and is celebrated on the 12th day of the third month of the Islamic calendar. This day is marked by prayers and talks at the mosque.

Ramadan

The ninth month of the Islamic calendar is Ramadan and this is a time for reflection, abstinence and charity. During Ramadan, Muslims practise one of the Five Pillars of Islam—*sawm* or fasting—and anyone who has reached puberty is required to fast for as long as he or she is able. Exceptions are made for those who are sick, mentally ill, pregnant or nursing. Menstruating women are not obligated to fast, although they will need to 'repay' those days after the month of Ramadan.

Fasting—from food, drink and worldly pleasures—is from sunrise to sunset. In most families, someone will wake up in the wee hours of the morning to cook the morning meal (known as *sahur*) which must be eaten before the sun rises. The actual time for sunrise and sunset, as determined by MUIS, will be announced in the papers and over the news every day. MUIS also publishes a yearly calendar for prayer times (also posted on their website at http://www.muis.gov.sg) which one can also use as a guide. In general, one must stop eating about 15–20 minutes before morning prayers (*subuh*) in the morning and can break fast at the time of the evening prayers (*maghrib*).

During the fasting month, Muslims reflect on their good fortune and look towards attaining peace of mind. By abstaining from food and drink, they remember those who are hungry and thirsty. By abstaining from other pleasures, they practise self-control and strive to cleanse their bodies. It is also at this time that Muslims will practise *zakat* (another Pillar of Islam), and through this action, they learn to think about and help the less fortunate. Another avenue for them to do charitable acts is by placing donations into the boxes and tins that can be found at Muslim establishments.

If you happen to be out with your Muslim friends at fast breaking time, you might like to

The Islamic Calendar

Based purely on the cycle of the moon, the Muslim calendar consists of 12 months in a year. Each month begins at the sighting of the new moon and will last either 29 or 30 days. As such, the Islamic calendar is shorter than the Gregorian one so it may 'appear' that major festivals such as Hari Raya Puasa occur earlier and earlier on the latter from one year to the next.

Even if you are non-Muslim, it is advisable to remember which month is Ramadan and be more sensitive to your friends and colleagues who are Muslim. In this case, it is not polite to offer them any food or drink during the day, or insist that they have lunch with you.

wish them 'selamat bebuka puasa'. To break their fast, Muslims will try to eat three to six dates before going for prayers. If dates are not available, they will try to take something sweet. A proper dinner will follow only after that. Some will also break fast with a rice porridge that is cooked and provided by the mosque. This is normally available from after the mid-afternoon prayers are said.

During Ramadan, prayers known as tarawih will be said every night at the mosques. All Muslims are encouraged to read the Qur'an during this period and to help them towards this end, a small section is read every night at the mosque so that by the end of Ramadan, the Holy Book will have been read through once.

Ramadan is the month before Hari Raya Puasa (more on this in the next section) and Muslims spend quite a bit of time preparing for this celebratory occasion. The house will be cleaned and new curtains are often made. The whole house will be decked out with lights and these sometimes extend to the outside of the house, giving the home and its surrounding a festive air. Lots of different types of goodies are also made, some of which are similar to those found during Chinese New Year (e.g. pineapple tarts and nut-based biscuits). Most of these will be home-made and even if they are bought, will tend to be purchased from a friend of friend of a friend's relative who makes them at home. New clothes are needed and these can either be bought or tailored.

For this purpose, a number of Muslims will visit the Geylang Serai or the Kampong Glam areas which become hubs of activity during this period, especially in the evenings. These two areas will be decorated and lit up for much of Ramadan as well as a good part of the Hari Raya season. Huge tents are set up and stalls selling traditional Malay kuehs, delicacies, clothes and home furnishings will open for business sometime in the afternoon till well past midnight.

The festive atmosphere only begins in the evening, just before the time for breaking fast. Many Muslims, usually in groups, will visit the area early and do their rounds at the food stalls, buying different items for dinner. But they wait for the call to break fast and will do so quickly before taking turns to say their prayers before eating some more and taking a tour of the area to look for items to buy for Hari Raya.

To truly experience the festive air for yourself, do as the locals do and have dinner in the area. Then you walk the streets to soak in the atmosphere. Be warned though, the whole place gets more crowded as the night wears on and the closer it gets to Hari Raya, the more people go down. You will find everything: all sorts of traditional costumes like Punjabi suits, *baju kurung* and *sarong kebaya* next to modern clothing like jeans and T-shirts; Persian and Turkish carpets; shisha pipes; arts and crafts, costume jewellery; henna paint; curtains, pillows and pillow cases; and tonnes more. And if you didn't have a proper dinner, you can also munch your way from one end to the other as food stalls are scattered throughout all the tents. You'll find burgers, fish balls on a stick, honey chicken wings, grilled seafood, shish kebab, and even Turkish ice cream.

Hari Raya Puasa

The end of Ramadan marks Hari Raya Puasa or Adil Fitri, one of the important days in the Muslim religious calendar. In Malay, *hari raya* means 'day of celebration' and *puasa* means 'fast or abstinence' so this occasion is the day of celebrating the fast. Hari Raya Puasa normally lasts for a month, although it is usually the first three to five days that are the most festive.

In the morning on the first day of Hari Raya Puasa, Muslims will visit the mosque for prayers after which some will visit the graves of departed loved ones, offering prayers to Allah on their behalf as well as doing some housekeeping of the grave site. Some families will have already tended to this matter a few days before and may spend the time after visiting the mosque cooking a feast in preparation of the people expected during the day.

The visiting of family and friends usually occurs in the afternoon. While some wait at home for relatives and friends to drop in, others will have a list of homes they want to cover in the space of a day. Dressed up to the nines in festive finery—some families even colour co-ordinate their clothes in a show of unity—Muslims visit the homes of family members to give thanks for familial bonds as well as seek forgiveness if any transgression has been committed in the previous year. Children, too, look forward to this time as they receive *duit raya*, token sums of money which, these days, are put into little green packets.

Food abounds during this time of celebration and it is considered an affront if someone visits a Muslim's home and is not shown hospitality in the form of food and drink. Some of the wonderful dishes you're likely to find are *ketupat*, *sambal sotong* (chilli squid), deep fried chicken, *rendang* and curry chicken.

If you have been invited for a visit, take a gift along. Obviously alcohol is out of the question, so are any food stuffs made from or with non-*halal* items, and anything made out of pork skin (this includes bags, purses and the like). Something for the home would be appreciated e.g. a set of pretty glasses, a tea set, or even something from your home country. When in doubt, ask your friend or colleagues, preferably another Muslim or someone who has been in such a situation before. If you know that a group of colleagues from the office has been invited, find out if they are all chipping in for a group gift and if you can participate.

In some years, Hari Raya Puasa (also known as Eid el-Fitr in some countries) in Singapore is sometimes celebrated one day earlier than in other Muslim countries. Technically, Hari Raya starts from the sighting of the new moon and in many Muslims countries, an announcement is made by the leading religious body of that country once the new moon has been sighted and thus Ramadan ends. If there is no sight of the new moon, Ramadan continues for another day. This will, of course, change depending on where the sightings are taken from—the country itself or Mecca. In Singapore, MUIS has slightly different criteria and looks at the moon on the 29th day of Ramadan to determine when Hari Raya starts. For more accurate dates, check the MUIS website at http://www.muis.gov.sg.

While most Singaporean Muslims are open-minded, it is still best to dress modestly when visiting someone's home as a sign of respect to the older folks who may still reside there. They probably won't say anything in front of you but their children or grandchildren are likely to get an earful after you have left. Do your friend or colleague a favour and mind your dressing and manners.

Hari Raya Haji

Celebrated on the tenth day of the last month of the Islamic calendar, this marks the annual pilgrimage or *hajj*, another Pillar of Islam, which all physically and financially able Muslims must undertake at least once in their lives. It is also on this day that Muslims commemorate the sacrifices that Prophet Abraham made to his god. After congregational prayers at the mosque, there will be the *korban*, a ritual and symbolic sacrifice of lambs which have been supplied by individuals and families. Two-thirds of this meat is then distributed to the poor while the remaining one-third is returned to the person or family who donated the meat. In this manner, the Muslim community is united and looks after each other, especially the less privileged. Muslims spend the rest of the day visiting family members.

Hindu Celebrations

Tamil New Year

This is the first day of the Tamil calendar which corresponds to a date in April on the Gregorian calendar. The Tamil calendar is a solar calendar of 12 months, with the days in each month varying between 29 and 32. Legend has it that this was the day that Hindu god Brahma begin his creation of the world and thus the new year signifies a new beginning for the Hindus. In the same tradition that the Chinese celebrate Chinese New Year, Hindus make sure that the first day of the new year is spent in harmony and joy so that the rest of the year unfolds in the same manner. In the weeks leading up to the actual date, homes are cleaned, new clothes are purchased, delicious snacks and goodies are made or

Kolams

Believed to bring prosperity and longevity to the home, *kolams* (also known as *rangoli* in some parts of India) are symmetrical patterns drawn in front of the main door of the house using powdered rice. In southern India, the lady of the house would draw a *kolam* every morning and allow it to dissipate naturally—by people walking over, rain, wind—only to redraw it the next morning. In Singapore, *kolams* are normally drawn on special occasions such as weddings, birthdays and festivals. These days, many use vinyl stickers of *kolams* instead of rice powder.

bought. The first day of the new year begins with the lighting of the traditional oil lamp which is then placed on the family altar. *Kolams* decorate the floor in front of the main door while mango leaves are hung from the doorway. Hindus will visit the temple for prayers and turn vegetarian for the day, if they are not already. They also spend the time visiting relatives in much the same way the Chinese and Muslims do on their respective new year days.

Deepavali

Also known as the Festival of Lights, this falls on the 14th day of the seventh month according to the Tamil calendar, usually some time in October or November. There are a number of legends surrounding this festival but most of them stem from the Indian epic Ramayana and each one celebrates the triumph of good over evil, of light over darkness. To signify this momentous event, homes are usually brightly lit during this time. Hindus from southern India start the day off by taking a ritual 'oil bath'—a drop of oil is dabbed on each person's forehead before he or she takes a bath and this is a symbol of purification. After the bath, the family makes their way to the temple to offer prayers.

During this festive occasion, *kolams* are drawn at the threshold to the home and mango leaves adorn the doorway. Lighted oil lamps are found in every Hindu home and when family and friends come to visit, they are served with delicious food and goodies such as *murukku* (a crunchy, spicy but tasty snack) and *vadai* (a type of cake made from lentils).

During Deepavali (also known as Diwali), Little India comes alive with lights in the form of lighted *diyas* or clay pots, and modern light bulbs, as well as street stalls selling garlands, foods, jewellery, fragrant spices and spectacular *saris*. There will also be traditional Indian dancing to add to the festive mood.

Navarathiri

The term Navarathiri means 'nine nights' so it's not surprising that this festival spans nine nights and ten days some time in October. Through traditional songs and dances, Hindus honour the Mother Goddess who takes three forms: Dhurga, Lakshmi and Saraswathi. Dhurga is the goddess who represents power and protects Hindus from evil and the first three days are devoted to her. Lakshmi is the goddess of wealth and from the fourth to sixth days, devotees pay tribute to her. Saraswathi is the goddess of knowledge and wisdom and the last three days are in honour of her. The tenth day, known as Vijaya Dasami, celebrates the Mother Goddess' triumph over a demon king. Austerity and abstinence is observed during this time so Hindus take only one meal a day during the ten days. One of the highlights during Navarathiri is the *golu*, a display of the various Hindu gods and goddesses, and important personages at the temples. Another element of this celebration is the giving of *thambulan*—betel nuts and leaves, fruits, turmeric, vermilion, flowers and sometimes trinkets—which are placed alongside the *golu*. On this last day, a beautifully decorated statue of the Mother Goddess is paraded on a chariot led by a silver-haired horse around the temple grounds.

Theemidhi

This Fire-Walking Festival is held during the eighth month of the Tamil calendar, sometime in October or November. As the name implies, this is when devotees walk across a bed of hot coals. This is meant to honour the goddess Draupadi who is believed to have walked barefoot across hot coals to prove her innocence. The act itself may not take too long but devotees who choose to partake in this ceremony must prepare for weeks in advance through fasting and austere living. On the day itself, they have to walk about 4 km from one temple to another before the coal walking actually takes place.

Ponggal

Lasting over four days, Ponggal is a harvest festival that is celebrated predominately by the Hindus from southern India on the first day of the tenth month of the Tamil calendar, usually sometime in January. The word *ponggal* means 'to boil over with happiness, prosperity and success' and early in the morning on the first day, a sweet rice (traditionally, new harvested rice mixed with milk and sugar) is cooked in new pots and allowed to boil over as a sign of prosperity. Vegetables, sugar cane and spices are offered to the gods and later eaten by the family as part of a purification ritual. The rituals on each of the four days are different. The first day is spent with the family while the second is spent in honour of the god of rain, Lord Indra. On the third day, cattle are washed, painted with bright colours and adorned with sheaves of corn and garlands. On the last day, females feed rice to crows and birds as an offering for the welfare of their brothers.

Thaipusam

Celebrated in the tenth month, usually January or February, Thaipusam or Day of Thanksgiving is a processional event in which Hindus offer thanks, ask for blessings and fulfil vows, all in the name of Lord Subrahmanya, the destroyer of evil and representative of virtue, power and youth. Festivities begin one day before Thaipusam when a finely adorned statue of Lord Subrahmanya together with his consorts are carried on a chariot in a procession from one temple to another to symbolise the blessings he sought from his older brother. On Thaipusam itself, another procession ensues from this second temple to a third. Some carry milk in pots, the milk being an offering to Lord Subrahmanya for blessings and purification. Other devotees in the procession choose to pierce their tongues with skewers and carry decorated wooden arches on their shoulders. The supreme act of devotion comes from those who opt to carry *kavadis*, a decorated semi-circular metal structure with spikes that pierce into the skin of the carrier. To prepare for this act, devotees must live an austere life at least one month before

A Hindu man prepares himself for the fire-walking ceremony during the festival of Thaipusam.

Thaipusam and cleanse himself from all impurities of heart and mind. Only fortitude and faith will help him to endure the pain inflicted by the *kavadi*.

Christian Celebrations
Good Friday and Easter

This is celebrated in much the same way as it is in the rest of the world: Lent starts with Ash Wednesday (this can fall some time from end February to early March) and lasts 40 days, ending with Palm Sunday. The following Friday will be Good Friday, a solemn day that marks the crucifixion of Jesus Christ. Regardless of denomination, all churches will hold a service (usually in the afternoon) to mark the occasion. Saturday is a day of reflection and a lead-up to Easter Sunday, a joyous time and most important event in the Christian calendar.

Like elsewhere worldwide, this event has spun off a number of secular celebrations such as Easter bunnies and egg hunts. While some traditionalists may feel that this is an affront to the sobriety of the occasion, others feel it is for the benefit of the younger children who have not fully grasped the idea of Easter. A number of hotels will have Easter egg hunts and other activities for the children while shopping malls will have special events to tie in with the Easter bunny or egg theme. The same goes for some expat clubs and country clubs, and almost all of these are targeted at families.

Unlike many other countries, Monday is not a public holiday; only Good Friday is a public holiday and not Easter Sunday. (In Singapore, the Monday following a public holiday on a Sunday is a holiday.)

Christmas

Whether you are a Christian or not, Christmas is a great time to celebrate. For the commercial sector, Christmas starts sometime in late October/early November when everyone starts gearing up for sales, especially in the Orchard Road belt and in the shopping malls. By mid-November, almost everyone would be advertising their Christmas promotions and shopping malls would have lined up special treats for the children, usually involving some cartoon or television personality e.g. Pokemon, Justice League, Powerpuff Girls, etc.

By this time, Orchard Road will be decorated with thematic festive bunting and lights and all the major buildings along this stretch would have put up special Christmas décor.

C K Tangs is known traditionally for spiritually-inspired decorations while Goodwood Park Hotel along Scotts Road has come up with some innovative designs as they have lots of space to play with. There is also an annual contest for the best décor among the buildings along Orchard Road. But that isn't the only reason for the time and expense. Even the shopping malls in the heartlands (what the locals call the HDB estates) have realised that sprucing up the façade during this time helps with atmosphere, puts people in a festive mood and makes them want to shop.

But not everything is commercially based. The Boy's Brigade Sharity Box runs through the Christmas period and appeals are made for people to donate gifts to the less fortunate. Different organisations and groups organise events to visit the needy during this period to share the Christmas spirit. One such group is HOG (the Harley Owner's Group) which has an annual Christmas run where a group of them will ride

Even Chinatown Plaza, which is outside of the Orchard Road belt, gets into the act during Christmas and makes the effort to decorate its building for the occasion.

Over the last few years, because of the increasing number of people wanting to attend midnight mass, a number of Catholic churches have an earlier service that starts about 8:00 pm or 9:00 pm. At some churches, the Christmas pageant is also enacted during this earlier Mass. For most, this counts as attending Mass on Christmas day itself. Traditionalists still prefer to attend Mass at midnight though, because they feel the atmosphere is different, more sacred in some sense. For that reason, these Masses are still very crowded.

their bikes to one or more places like hospices and children's or old folks' homes and give out presents.

On the more spiritual side of things, churches (regardless of denominations) will have their own carolling groups and pageants all through the season of Advent, the four weeks leading up to the birth of Jesus Christ. Some churches have Christmas fairs to raise funds for charity, their way of giving to the less fortunate so that the latter are also able to celebrate. A number of church carolling groups will tie up with shopping malls for performances.

The weather may be different, the faces may be different but if you celebrate Christmas, the reminders will certainly be there.

ANNUAL EVENTS

The following are some local and international events that are held annually and anticipated with great enthusiasm. Check them out.

- Great Singapore Sale
  Website: http://www.greatsingaporesale.com.sg/
  Usually held from end May to some time in July every year, this is the time when all retail outlets, regardless of their location, offer great sales. It is a great tourist draw and one capitalised on by the STB.
- The New Paper Big Walk
  Website: http://tnpbigwalk.asia1.com.sg/
  Singaporeans turn up in force for this event. Some come in group, all wearing colour-co-ordinated outfits; some bring their dogs while others bring instruments to make a lot of noise. You might even see a dragon dance troupe taking part. A great way to spend a Sunday morning in May.

- Singapore Food Fest
  Website: http://www.singaporefoodfestival.com/
  How could Singapore not have a food festival? The country is, after all, a food lover's paradise. Held in July every year, this event comprises food trails, culinary workshops and other food related activities.
- World Gourmet Summit
  Website: http://www.worldgourmetsummit.com/
  People actually fly in especially for this event which features master chefs and winemakers from all over the world.
- Singapore Arts Festival
  Website: http://www.singaporeartsfest.com/
  A showcase of performances, exhibitions and events from Singapore and around the world.
- Singapore Fashion Festival
  Website: http://www.singaporefashionfestival.com.sg
  The event the fashion industry looks forward to every year. It includes local, regional and international designers.
- Singapore Film Fest
  Website: http://www.filmfest.org.sg/
  Film buffs await eagerly for this festival every year and you can expect a number of great movies from all over the world and in various languages.
- Terry Fox Run
  Website: http://www.terryfoxsingapore.org/
  Terry Fox was a young Canadian who wanted to run the length of his native land, despite suffering from cancer, to raise funds for cancer research. He lasted 143 days before cancer attacked his lungs and he was forced to stop. His courage lives on every year with this charity run which is usually in September.
- WOMAD
  Website: http://www.womad.org/
  WOMAD (World of Music, Arts and Dance) was the brainchild of Peter Gabriel and the first event was held in England in 1982. Its main aim is to bring the music, arts and dance from different cultures together. The Singapore event has been around since the 1990s and is looked

forward to by many in the community. Check the website for the exact dates of the event.

- Singapore Triathlon
  Website: http://www.singaporetriathlon.com/
  This event was launched in 2003 and has been gaining popularity here. Check the website for the actual dates as this changes from year to year.

- Vertical Marathon
  Website: http://www.swissotelverticalmarathon.com/
  This is a race to the top of South-east Asia's tallest hotel, 73 storeys above ground. Check the website for the exact date.

- Singapore Airshow
  The successor of Asian Aerospace to be launched in 2008 at Changi East. This biennial event is expected to be as good, if not better, than its predecessor with many previous exhibitors already signed up.

THE DIFFERENT TONGUES

'A different language is a different vision of life.'
—Federico Fellini

LANGUAGE IS CULTURE. When one is able to understand the thinking behind the words, behind the construction, behind the sounds, only then can one really begin to comprehend the culture in a deeper sense. In essence, this is why Singapore is understandable, comprehendable and really likeable for so many foreigners. With even a basic knowledge of English, it does not take long for one to get on with daily life. And even more so, for an outsider, it's the English that makes it comfortable and all the mother tongues that make it interesting!

Just the fact that Singapore has four official languages (English, Mandarin, Malay and Tamil) immediately shows to the world how they want to be perceived—multicultural. And by making English the official language of business and essentially, daily life, they have brought the small island nation out of obscurity and onto the world stage. If you think about it, it must have taken pure foresight, gumption and quite a bit of audacity to make English the official language at a time when it was not any of the majority group's first language and in a region where it was not that common place.

But it's clear that Singapore's four official languages are a direct result of the nation's immigration, colonial past and policymakers. From the time the British arrived in 1819 to the time when a steady increase in workers and immigrants from nearby China, Malaysia, India and Indonesia started

English is the lingua franca and the language used for business and administration so it's no surprise that all road signs are only in English.

landing on this small island, Singapore was destined to be a unique country in South-east Asia.

Malay is the national language; Mandarin, the official language of the majority group; Tamil, the language of 60 per cent of the country's Indians and English, the language of business and administration. Practically all Singaporeans are bilingual, speaking their mother tongue and English, as a second language. (For some, especially the younger generation, English is their 'mother tongue' as that is the language most often spoken with family and friends.)

Mother tongues are strongly encouraged as language is an important vehicle for maintaining culture, values and beliefs. And it is because of the government's decision to make English the business language and Mandarin the official language of the Chinese majority that Singapore has been able to compete globally on such a large scale. Through the mastery of English and Mandarin, this small island nation has created a unique and enviable niche and partnerships with neighbouring giants India, China and Australia. Language is Singapore's secret weapon and one that has attributed it a rare advantage in today's marketplace.

Road signs may only be in English but the signboards at MRT stations carry the name of the station in English (above and below), Chinese (above) and Tamil (below). (The name in Malay is the same as that in English.)

For most foreigners arriving in Singapore, the fact that English is the official language for business and administration comes as a welcome bonus. But be prepared, the English spoken by most people is not your typical Queen's English or American English, it has a name all its own and it's unofficially Singapore's fifth and most widely spoken language—Singlish. This is the local version of English which has developed over the country's history and is deeply embedded, used, loved and second-nature to its people. Basically, Singlish is English spoken in a non-grammatical, mispronounced, creatively jointed sequences and spiced with words from Chinese dialects, Malay, Tamil and even some Portuguese. It is the one area where cultures have merged, mixed and created a distinctly Singaporean identity. Going back to the opening quote, the 'culture' behind Singlish is a fascinating study of the people. Yet, despite the strong national identity, the government is not happy with the widespread use of Singlish and finds it detrimental to the country's economy and future. But more on Singlish later.

The Speak Good English Movement was launched in 2000 by then prime minister Goh Chok Tong to encourage Singaporeans to speak proper English. The emphasis of the movement was on good grammatical use and proper sentence structure, not accent, although pronunciation should be correct. The movement is still ongoing and has a different annual focus as well as various activities planned to get everyone in the community involved.

MALAY

Locally known as Bahasa Melayu, Malay is the national language of Singapore. It is also the official language of the neighbouring countries of Malaysia and Brunei, and bears a mutually intelligible similarity to Bahasa Indonesia, the official language of Indonesia. Malay is embedded in Singapore's history and today, it takes pride of place as the country's national language, so it's no surprise that Singapore's national anthem, *Majulah Singapura* ('Onward Singapore') is in Malay.

From the early 19th century and the very beginning of Singapore's bustling trade and port status, Malay was the lingua franca as the Malays were the largest ethnic group.

The Malay that was spoken then was a pidginised version of Malay (also known as Pasar Melayu or Bazaar Malay) since it was the market language of the various ethnic groups. This version of Malay can still be heard in the region, especially among the older generation, although the inter-ethnic language of choice today is definitely English.

Around that time, the British had set up schools but the people who sent their children to English-medium schools were mainly the Europeans, the Eurasians (people of mixed racial ancestry), some of the minorities such as the Jews, some of the Indians and Ceylonese, and also the Peranakans, who had ancestors of long residence in the region. As mentioned before, the Peranakans spoke a variety of Malay called Baba Malay which is heavily influenced by Hokkien Chinese and Bazaar Malay. The fact that all the children and descendants of these first English-speaking Peranakans would have known Malay probably explains why so many of the loan words in Singlish are from Malay.

Due to its cultural and historical background, Malay has borrowed and incorporated many words from Sanskrit and some Indian languages (about 10 per cent), Portuguese, Dutch and certain Chinese dialects. It's relatively simple grammar and undemanding pronunciation (it has a high ratio of vowels to consonants and the vowels are simple and pure vowels) and the fact that it is written in Roman script makes the language sound and look quite 'familiar' from a foreigner's point of view, especially if you speak a Romance or Indian language.

Malay words are commonplace in Singapore for they have influenced Singlish, street names, food, locations, everything in daily life. Here is a list of typically heard and used Malay words:

Welcome	*Selamat datang*
Have a safe journey (used like 'goodbye')	*Selamat jalan* (said by the party staying)
Goodbye	*Selamat tinggal* (said by the party leaving)

Good Morning	Selamat pagi
Good afternoon/ evening	Selamat petang (if at night, use selamat sejahtera)
Greetings (formal)	Selamat sejahtera
Good night	Selamat malam (when ending a meet during the night)
See you again	Jumpa lagi
How are you?/ What's up?	Apa khabar? (literally, 'What news?')
Fine, good	Khabar baik
Thank you	Terima kasih
Yes	Ya
No	Tidak (colloquially tak)
To eat	Makan
Coffee	Kopi
Tea	Teh
Sugar	Gula
Salt	Garam
Milk	Susu
Bread	Roti
Rice	Nasi
Walk	Jalan (common in street names)
Village	Kampung

CHINESE

'Have you had your lunch?' This is a common greeting by taxi drivers, workers and salespeople and it's a direct translation of the popular Mandarin greeting 'Chi guo fan ma?'. Initially, upon hearing this greeting from my taxi driver, I was taken a bit aback and quickly tried to formulate a polite response in order to get out of his proposed lunch date! Thank goodness, it only took a bit to realise that he was only asking, 'How are you?' For the Chinese, if you have some food in your stomach, you cannot be feeling all too badly! Once again, a perfect example of the Chinese people's 'different vision of life' with regards to food.

The dominance of the Chinese and the push to establish Mandarin as the unifying Chinese tongue has been an ongoing movement for the government. With a strong and steady flow of immigrants from every region of mainland China, Chinese dialects have peppered and influenced Singapore's language in a profound way. Realising that the various Chinese dialects could, in the end, be divisive in such a small nation, the government launched the Speak Mandarin Campaign in 1979. The campaign has been successful in its goals to simplify the language environment, understanding and communication among Chinese Singaporeans. Although dialects are still commonly spoken (especially among the older generation), the importance of mastering a strong Mandarin language base for better cultural awareness and understanding is certainly at the forefront of the nation's Chinese but not without some controversy. Many feel that the push to eliminate use of dialects has been a detriment to Chinese culture and clan traditions which are reinforced and passed on through language. Moreover, it has cut off many young Chinese from other South-east Asian Chinese who speak dialects but little Mandarin (i.e. the Chinese from Malaysia or Indonesia). But the government has deemed so important the nation's four official languages that it made it compulsory to study one's mother tongue at school for all Singaporean children.

Speak Mandarin Campaign

Back in the 1970s, the government realised that the due to the various Chinese dialects, the Chinese community was not feeling like a unified group. In an effort to help unify its people, Mandarin was emphasised as the important, unifying Chinese language. Then in 1979, a huge national campaign to 'Speak Mandarin' was thrust into the community with television advertisements, street slogans and radio spots. Today, Mandarin is taught in schools, heard on television and radio, and spoken by a good majority of Chinese Singaporeans. However, the problem is not solved as the older generation is still bound to dialects and the younger generation still struggles with the language of their ancestors.

So what is it about learning and mastering Mandarin that makes it so difficult for so many people? In his book, *Slices of Singapore*, G C Soh gives an insightful look into the intricacies of learning Mandarin. He points out that there is no 'grammar' in the sense that it does not classify the characters ('words') into nouns, verbs, adverbs, adjectives, participles, prepositions and conjunctions. There is neither a past, present or future tense, nor a distinction between singular and plural characters. And characters have no gender, other than 'he' and 'she', which is often not used anyway. The above mentioned is inferred from the context of the phrase, it is not explicit. The examples he notes are that if you want to write about a bird soaring in the air, you write the character for 'fly', whether you want to say fly, flying, flew or flown. The character for 'he' is also used for 'his' and 'him'. If there are ten pigs eating ten pieces of cakes, it is still 'pig eat cake'.

Another interesting fact about the Chinese language is that they verbalise punctuation marks in that these are real Chinese characters, like real words. Consequently, spoken

Chinese is full of *ma*, *mei*, *ne* and *ah*, all which are characters that act as punctuation marks. And this also helps explain the frequent use of *lah* in Singlish. *Lah* is a multi-purpose, verbal punctuation for the comma, full stop and exclamation; although the Malays also use *lah* as a suffix with verbs, thereby further instilling this custom to the majority of the local speakers.

So to learn Chinese is to learn vocabulary words ('characters'). There is no Chinese alphabet with letters and assigned sounds to the letters. (*Hanyu pinyin* doesn't count because that is just the anglicisation of how the word is pronounced.) If you come across a new Chinese character, you cannot 'sound' it out, or decipher it in any way. Someone has to tell you how it should sound. And speaking of sound, there are also four basic tones in Mandarin so one character may be pronounced in four different ways and mean something different. It is pure, heavy-duty memorisation and having a good ear, all the way.

Here are a few popular and useful Mandarin phrases (remember, just because it's spelt the same doesn't mean it has the same tone):

Hello	*Ni hao*
Good bye	*Zai jian*
Thank you	*Xie xie* (pronounced see-yeah see-yeah)
You're welcome	*Bu ke qi*
I'm sorry	*Dui bu qi*
No (don't have)	*Mei you*
No (not so)	*Bu shi*
I don't understand	*Wo ting bu dong*
Do you understand?	*Dong ma?*

Another uniquely Chinese custom that is used daily is their way of showing numbers from five to ten with only one hand. There are some differences in the signage amongst the Chinese but the following gives you an idea of what you may come across:

six	the pinky and thumb are extended, other fingers closed, palm facing the signer
seven	the fingertips are all touching, pointed upwards; or just the fingertips of the thumb and first two fingers
eight	the thumb and index finger make an L, other fingers closed, with the palm facing the observer
nine	the index finger makes a hook, other fingers closed, sometimes with the palm facing the signer
ten	the fist is closed with the palm facing the signer, or the middle finger crosses an extended index finger, facing the observer

And although the hand gestures for the numbers one through five are more common, here is a complete listing:

one	index finger extended
two	index and middle finger are extended
three	the index finger and thumb are closed, last three fingers are extended. Or the thumb and pinky meet in the middle of the palm and the middle three fingers are extended
four	the thumb is held in the palm with the four fingers extended
five	all five digits are extended, but for emphasis (e.g. a shopkeeper signalling that you owe S$ 5) all the fingers are brought together and then extended in rapid motion

TAMIL

Of the small Indian population in Singapore, about 60 per cent speak Tamil as a native language with the remainder speaking a range of Indian languages from Malayalam to Hindi. Tamil is the most widely spoken language of southern India and interestingly, also the most widely spoken Indian language in Malaysia.

Despite its status as an official language, use of Tamil among Tamil Singaporeans is declining in favour of English. Perhaps this can be attributed to its historical context. Tamils came to Singapore and Malaysia to work on rubber and palm oil plantations, thus displacing their usual linguistic context. Two kinds of workers came, the English-educated Sri Lankan Tamils who supervised the workers and the workers from India who were of the lowest socio-economic status. As the plantation industry declined, the labour workers moved into the fields of transportation, maintenance and construction and the more educated people found it easier to advance their life, through their English abilities, into more professional fields.

What has also helped to keep Tamil alive in Singapore is the simple fact that it has served the purpose of being an intra-ethnic language amongst the Indian Muslims, Hindus, Malayalis and Christians. Because Malayalis speak another language from the same linguistic lineage, they have been strong learners and supporters of the language. Additionally, marriage among members of the community obviously helps maintain the language as well as bringing Tamilian-speaking brides from India.

Historically, there was a strong Tamil and Malayali community in and around the naval base at Sembawang, Tanjong Pagar and Serangoon (Little India). Today in Sembawang, the housing has given way to HDB units but in the temples around the area, there is still more Tamil used than in other areas of the island. Even in the hawker centres, Tamil is commonplace.

Although most Tamil speakers are of Indian heritage, several Tamil words have been incorporated into the English language and are used worldwide e.g. anaconda, catamaran, curry, mango, mulligatawny and poppadom.

Here is a short list of some useful Tamil phrases:

Hello	*Vanakkam*
Goodbye	*Poytu varukirehn*
Yes	*Aam*

No	*Il-lay*
Please	*Tayavua saydu*
Thank you	*Nandri*
Excuse me	*Mannikavum*
Sorry	*Mannikavum*
How are you?	*Yeppadi iruk-keeng-geh*

SINGLISH

Singaporean colloquial English is commonly known as Singlish. Love it or hate it, it's instantly recognisable, catchy and so unique in its construction of the English language that you are bound to give in to its charm after an extended stay in Singapore. As mentioned earlier, Singlish is unique to Singapore and a direct result of the country's multi-racial, multilingual background. English is not Singapore's native language, it's many times the person's second or third language and so consequently, it is heavily influenced by the other dominant languages such as Mandarin and Malay.

For a foreigner, Singlish is probably the main reason why the locals often come across as a bit abrupt or coarse. The sentence structure is pared down to the bare minimum, no conditional 'polite' verbs (would you, could you) and consequently, it requires an adjustment to the ear and to the mind! It's definitely not intended to be as harsh as it may sound.

Here are some basics into Singlish's grammatical construction, phonetics and use:

- Most plural or past tense endings are optional in use e.g. "What happen yesterday?" and "Got so many car!".
- Past tense is often shown by adding 'already' or *liao* at the end of the sentence like in the Chinese language e.g. "He threw it *liao*." ('He has already thrown it away.'); "Aiyah, cannot wait anymore must go already." ('Oh dear, I cannot wait any longer and must leave immediately.')
- Very limited use of complex verb groups so grammatical relationships are mainly shown through

word positioning e.g. "The house sell already." ('The house has been sold' or 'I have sold the house').

- The verb 'to be' is used but is most often optional e.g. "She so pretty" and "That one like us".

- Singlish uses about 11 particles, mostly borrowed from Hokkien or Cantonese, to emphasise what is being said. They are used like the phrases, 'you know', or 'you see'. The four most common are *ah* (usually expects agreement e.g. "We go *ah*?"), *lah* (strong assertion e.g. "You take *lah*.") *what* (e.g. usually corrects something e.g. "Like dat what!") and *wah* (normally used on its own) which denotes a sense of amazement or delight (e.g. "Wah! So nice one!".

- The use of *lah* at the end of words for emphasis fits under the same category as those above, yet it deserves a further explanation since it is probably the most widely heard and imitated aspect of Singlish. The Chinese use *lah* as a multi-purpose, verbal punctuation for the comma, as stated earlier. And the Malays use *lah* by appending it to the end of a verb to change it to a command or to soften its tone, especially when usage of the verb may seem impolite. Also, in Malay, *lah* is attached to the verb and never requires a pause or comma in written form but in English, it is usually separated by a comma for clarity. Some examples of its use are "Drink, *lah*!" and "Dun (don't) have *lah*!" (maybe in response to "Do you have some money?". Or used for reassurance, "It's OK *lah*!".

- When the verb 'to be' is used in questions, it is usually correct. However, when other verbs are used to pose a question, the order of the subject and verb is usually not changed e.g. "Go where?"; "Why so stupid?" and "How to fix?".

- The subject is often understood and is to be deduced from the context so misunderstandings or confusion could easily arise e.g. "Finish already" (who, you or I or she?) and "Dun want".

- Borrowing directly from the Chinese construction, phrases are usually led by the topic e.g. "This country, weather very hot *lah*." ('In this country, the weather is very hot.') and "Play soccer he very good also." ('He is very good at playing soccer too.')

- The use of plurality or articles with nouns is optional e.g. "He can play piano." ('He can play the piano.') and "I like to read storybook." ('I like to read storybooks.').
- In addition to the common ways of asking questions, Singlish uses two additional ways. One is to append 'or not' at the end of sentences for yes/no questions. 'Or not' is not used when sentences are already in the negative e.g. "This book you want or not?" ('Do you want this book?') and "Can or not?" ('Is this possible/permissible?'). Secondly, the phrase 'is it' is often appended at the end of yes/no questions. It is used to imply that the speaker is simply confirming what he or she has already stated e.g "They never study, is it?" and "You don't like that, is it?"
- Re-duplication of verbs is very common and strongly reminiscent of the Chinese and Malay construction. Generally speaking, the verbs are repeated two times to indicate that the action goes on for a short period and three times to indicate greater length and continuity e.g.

    "You go tink, tink a little bit then you will get an answer."

    "So what I do was, I sit down and I tink, tink, tink, until I get answer *lor*."

Or the verb may be repeated to give a more vivid description of the activity e.g. "Want to go to Orchard walk walk see see or not?" ('Would you like to go walking and sightseeing on Orchard?')

- Re-duplication of adjectives of one or two syllable lengths can be repeated for intensification e.g. "You go take the small small one."
- The use of 'can' as both a question particle and an answer particle e.g. "Go home lah, can?" ('Just go home now, OK?') or in response to a question "Can I have a biscuit also?", "Can!" or "Cannot!" for the negative. And 'can' can be repeated for greater emphasis or to express

enthusiasm e.g. "Can you show me the drawings tomorrow?" Response, "Can can!" ('No problem!')

A few examples of commonly used Singlish vocabulary (words of various different ethnic origins but that have taken on a new meaning in Singlish) are:

Arrow	pinpoint or pick on e.g. "Why he arrow me to do this?"
Blur	used as an adjective meaning 'confused, ignorant'. e.g. "He so blur, cannot understand the question, cannot give the answer." The superlative of this is 'blur like sotong', making the assumption that squids (*sotong* in Malay) are not too bright.
Chope	to lay claim to, as in reserving hawker centre seats with tissue packs, "Can you *chope* one seat for me?"
Cheem	literally 'deep' in Hokkien; meaning difficult or obscure
Die, die	absolutely, no matter what happens e.g. "Die, die I also must pay my rent by today."
Follow	to come along e.g. "Can I follow?"
Habis	(from Malay) finished, impending doom e.g. "Oh she *habis* man! Her husband catch her having affair."
Sabo	short for sabotage, also meaning to betray or cause failure e.g. "Because he sabo me, now boss mad at me!"
Send	to take somebody somewhere e.g. "I'll send you to school."
Slippers	thongs or flip flops in other countries
Spoil	to be damaged e.g. "This one, spoil."

> **More on Singlish**
>
> If you end up staying in Singapore for an extended period of time, Singlish is definitely the language to know for ease and use in your everyday life. There are some wonderfully entertaining Singlish books and websites that are worth investigating:
>
> - http://www.talkingcock.com
> - *An Essential Guide to Singlish* by Gartbooks

COMMUNICATION OVERALL

Aside from the basic understanding of the different languages, there is the important element of understanding the 'different vision' visible in the communication overall. Asian culture is very different from Western culture as described in Chapters Three and Four, so here are two pointers:

- It is considered polite to show concern for someone's well-being, so try not to be too defensive when questions of weight gain/loss, health overall, paleness/face colouring, -. are commented on.
- What many Westerners consider private is fair game to the Asians (goes back to the concept of harmony and group versus individuals) so you will be asked questions such as 'Where are you going?', 'How old are you?' and 'How much is your rent?'. It's appropriate small talk for Asians because it expresses good will and concern for the other person. For this same reason, they find the Western topics of weather, traffic and shopping too superficial!

NON-VERBAL COMMUNICATION

For anyone who has ever tried to communicate in a foreign language, the importance of becoming versed and knowledgeable in the local non-verbal communication cannot be understated. The importance it plays in communication is often more important than the local language. Here are a few tips:

- Singaporeans often trust the non-verbal message more than the spoken word.
- They rely on facial expression, tone of voice and posture to tell them what someone feels.

- They tend to be subtle, indirect and implicit in their communications.
- They hint at a point rather than make a direct statement, since that might cause the other person to lose face.
- Rather than say 'no', they might say, 'I will try', or 'I'll see what I can do' thus allowing the person making the request and the person turning it down to save face and maintain harmony in their relationship.
- Silence is an important element of communication as is speaking in a low tone, avoiding shouting at all costs.
- Pausing before responding to a question indicates that they have given the question appropriate thought and considered their response carefully. They do not understand the Western ability to respond to a question hastily, and think that this indicates thoughtlessness and rude behaviour.
- They will not say 'I don't understand' or 'I don't have available what you are looking for'. Instead, they will give any other, most likely disjointed response or alternative in order to not 'lose face'. This happens quite often when shopping and asking for sales assistance.
- And the greatest and most universal non-verbal sign is the smile—use it often.

WORK AND BUSINESS

'Business is a matter of being tied into the proper network, which is the result of long-standing personal relationships or the proper introductions.'
—from the country profile on Singapore
from the Kwintessential website
(http://www.kwintessential.co.uk)

CHAPTER 9

ACCORDING TO THE 2000 CENSUS, the population of Singapore has grown by just under one million in the space of ten years (1990–2000). Almost half of this increase has been attributed to non-residents—foreign workers and students as well as other foreigners who have not been granted permanent residence. (These do not include tourists and those passing through Singapore.) This translates to an estimated 9.3 per cent average growth annually and is much higher than the 1.3 per cent average growth in the population of Singapore citizens for the same period. Non-residents and permanent residents (which make up just over 290,000) account for about 26 per cent of the total population.

In 2003, it was estimated that foreigners made up nearly 30 per cent of the workforce in Singapore. This has been fodder for debate as there are some locals who believe that foreigners are taking away jobs that rightfully belong to them. (Isn't this a familiar tune almost everywhere?) On the other hand, others believe that foreign talent has much to offer and they complement the Singapore workforce.

ARE YOU ALLOWED TO WORK?

Whether you are allowed to work in Singapore depends primarily on your status. As a PR, you should have no problems finding a job and some companies prefer their potential employee to be either a citizen or a PR as it saves

Tall skyscrapers characterise the business district in Singapore and these monolithic structures stand side-by-side with older, smaller buildings which have existed since Singapore's history began.

STEP

You can apply for a Short-term Employment Pass (STEP) if you are coming into Singapore to work on a specific project for a maximum period of one month. This pass can only be issued once and cannot be renewed.

them the hassle of having to apply for an employment pass or work permit. If you were hired from outside Singapore or if your parent company from overseas has posted you here, your employment papers should be taken care of by the company. The MOM makes a distinction between what is commonly known as skilled and unskilled/semi-skilled labour—the former requires an employment pass while the latter, a work permit. (*The various types of passes and permits have already by covered in* Chapter Five: Settling In, *page 85.*)

Regardless of whether you are in Singapore on an employment pass or work permit, the law states that you can only do work for the company that hired you. That means no moonlighting or freelance work. Remember that your employer is the one who has applied for the pass or permit for you and they are responsible for you while you are in the country. Should you decide to take on extra work, you do so at your risk and your employer or the MOM can cancel your right to be here at any time. You are, of course, allowed to take on gratis or unpaid work. On the other hand, as an employment pass holder, you are allowed to set up your own business (*see the section* 'Setting Up a Business' *later in this chapter*).

What about those on a dependant's pass? Singapore is very accommodating to spouses in that all that is required to begin a job is a Letter of Consent from the MOM. This is not a difficult procedure and can be done online or in person at the MOM headquarters in Havelock Road.

For those on a student's pass, the situation is a little more complicated. Only if you are a full-time student of a polytechnic or university here are you allowed to work. During term time, you are only allowed to work part-time for a maximum of 16 hours in a week. In addition, you must get permission from your educational institution. You are, however, allowed to work full-time during your vacation period without having to apply for a work permit.

SETTING UP A BUSINESS

Foreigners are welcome to set up their own businesses in Singapore, but as it is with most things in this country, there are a list of guidelines. If you are an employment pass (P and Q1 category) holder and are registering a business in addition to working for your current employer, you will need to inform your employer and obtain a letter from them stating they have no objections to your new venture. If you are a dependant pass holder, you can also set up your own business but once established, you will have to apply to the MOM for a Letter of Consent to work. Setting up a small business is a very popular choice here in Singapore for spouses who may not be looking for full-time work outside the home. Firstly, it is hassle-free and very straightforward to set up the business. Secondly, the market is very receptive to new, innovative products with some well established venues and fairs that are a popular choice for displaying new product ventures.

All You Need to Know About Business in Singapore

EnterpriseOne is the government-linked website run by SPRING (Standards, Productivity and Innovation Board) that gives you all the information you need to get your business started:

http://www.business.gov.sg/

It also contains all the information you need to know before setting up your own business plus articles and resources to ensure a smoother road for your venture.

In addition to EnterpriseOne, another website that you should check out is Accounting and Corporate Regulatory Authority (ACRA) which answers some of the most asked questions about the different types of businesses and companies. The address is:

http://www.acra.gov.sg

Employment pass holders from the S category are not allowed to register businesses in Singapore. Neither are the holders of other passes. The only other exceptions are for PRs and EntrePass holders.

PRs, whether full-fledged or approved-in-principle, need not seek the consent of their employers before registering a local business. EntrePass holders, whose purpose in Singapore is primarily to do business, are naturally allowed to register their business ventures.

Types of Enterprises

Businesses and companies must be registered with the Accounting and Corporate Regulatory Authority (ACRA), the merged body of the now defunct Registry of Companies and Businesses (RCB) and Public Accountants Board (PAB). ACRA makes a distinction between companies and businesses—the latter are not considered legal entities so cannot own or hold properties; nor can they sue or be sued. You need to be at least 21 years of age before you can register a business or company, and cannot be an undischarged bankrupt (*more on this a little later in this chapter*). There are basically four types of enterprises you can register—sole proprietorships, partnerships (both of which are considered businesses), Limited Liability Partnerships (LLP) and companies (both of which are considered companies).

- All you need to register a sole proprietorship is one person or one company that has been incorporated locally. This person or company has full say on how the business is run. This is easy to register but bear in mind that even though others cannot sue a sole proprietor, he or she (or it, if it's a company) is personally liable for any debts or guarantees the business incurs.

- A partnership allows for anything between two and 20 people or companies to set up a venture together. Each person or company has equal rights in the business but may have differing roles in its day-to-day running and decision-making. Normally, this should be decided beforehand and it is recommended that partnership agreements be drawn up to avoid disputes later on. Similar to sole proprietorships, partners in this type of a venture are personally liable.

- Introduced only in April 2005, LLPs are basically partnerships with limited liability, which means that all partners are not personally liable. You can register a LLP or convert an existing business or company into an LLP.

- Incorporating a company is a little more complicated as there are more procedures involved. Unlike businesses, you would need professional help to incorporate and register a company, and self-incorporation is only available for companies where the shareholders, directors and secretaries are Singapore citizens. There are such things as the Memorandum and Articles of Association to be drawn up e.g. how many shares are being issued, who the directors are, etc. Companies can have one or more shareholders as well as one or more directors, and they can be private or public. Private companies can only have a maximum of 50 shareholders (individuals or other companies) and will carry the words 'Pte Ltd' after the company's name.

Government-related Companies

Exempt Private Companies are government companies which have been set up for national interests, and gazetted as such. They can have a maximum of 20 shareholders, all of which must be individuals.

Public companies limited by guarantee are those which conduct non-profit activities for public or national interests.

You can have more than 50 shareholders in a public company and capital may be raised through subscription from the public. In order to offer shares and debentures to the public, a prospectus must be lodged with the Monetary Authority of Singapore (MAS) first. Public companies normally carry the word 'Limited' or 'Berhad' after its name. To find out more about how to incorporate a company, log onto:

http://www.acra.gov.sg/company/
incorporatecompany.html

Converting Your Business Into a Company

If you have problem deciding whether you should incorporate your company right from the start, don't despair. You can always register a business first and incorporate it later. Many locals and expatriates choose this path to give themselves time to build up their ventures slowly. Often, many start out as sole proprietorships or partnerships. Once the business has attained some stability and is set to grow, the owners incorporate it and all assets of the business are converted. Once you're ready to convert, seek professional advice and get them to help you.

Bankruptcy Laws

Once you decide to go into business for yourself, you should be aware of the country's bankruptcy laws. As mentioned before, if you set up a sole proprietorship or partnership, you are personally liable, so if your firm racks up more than S$ 10,000 in debts, your creditors can apply for you to be made bankrupt. Once an application is made, a Statutory Demand will be issued and you will have to pay up within the stipulated time or, if your creditors are agreeable, work a payment schedule with them. If no payment or agreement is reached by the deadline, the petition is filed in the High Court which will set a hearing date. At this stage, you can still contact your creditor and try to work something out. If there is no progress by the hearing date, a bankruptcy order will be issued. When this happens, your full name and identification will be made public in *The Straits Times*, and all other creditors will have to lodge their claims with the Official Assignee who will take over all your assets from then on.

Who is this Official Assignee (OA)? This is a public office under the Insolvency and Public Trustee's Office (IPTO) of the Ministry of Law whose aim is two-fold: to help creditors regain as much of their debts as possible and to help bankrupts obtain a discharge from the state they are in. You will have to surrender all your assets to the OA, all except those considered 'protected' e.g. CPF savings (if you have any), insurance policies considered to be for the benefit of your spouse and

While most people are dismayed at being declared bankrupt, there is one advantage, if you could call it that. When in this situation, other creditors are not allowed to approach you to claim their debts. They must lodge a substantiated claim with the OA. In addition, once you are discharged, these creditors can no longer bother you for payment.

children, limited tools of trade, etc. You will also have to work out a monthly repayment scheme (if you are gainfully employed) with the OA and account to them your income and expenditure every month. The amount you repay and your conduct during your bankruptcy period plays a big part in whether the OA will recommend you for a discharge.

As a bankrupt, you face a number of limitations e.g. you cannot travel overseas without permission from the OA, you are not allowed to operate any other businesses or companies, you can only have one savings account, etc.

So how do you get out of this quagmire? You can obtain an annulment if you are able to offer a full payment of the debt, or if you offer a repayment scheme acceptable by the creditor filing the bankruptcy petition. Otherwise, you can be discharged by the High Court or the OA after a period of three years.

Information on Insolvency

To find out more about bankruptcy laws and procedures, refer the to the IPTO website at:

> http://app.minlaw.gov.sg/ipto/

Click on the section for insolvency to learn more.

Closing the Venture

Your tour of duty in Singapore is coming to an end and you decide you want to close the business you set up. So what do you do? Much would depend on what type of a venture you had set up. If it is a business (i.e. sole proprietorship or partnership), you can just file a notice of cessation or termination online or in person at the ACRA office. If your business is a partnership, all partners must agree to the termination. The actual date your business ceases to exist though will be the date of expiry of your business certificate (business licences have to be renewed annually).

If your company is an LLP, you and your partners can opt to wind the company up but you must be able to pay up all your debts in a 12-month period after the winding-up proceedings have started. For this, it is best to employ professional help. This also applies to other companies wishing to wind up voluntarily. Companies can also apply to ACRA for a striking off particularly if they think their companies will no longer be conducting any business.

Winding Up

In some cases, it may be possible that your business or company is forced to wind up, voluntarily or otherwise. In the case of businesses, this is likely to take the form of a bankruptcy suit as the owners are personally liable. Companies, on the other hand, could either make an agreement with their creditors to wind them up or be forced to wind up by a court order. For more information on this issue, refer to the following:

- Winding up of an LLP
  Website: http://www.acra.gov.sg/llp/closing.html
- Winding up of a private or public company
  Website: http://www.acra.gov.sg/company/endingcompany.html

WORKING LIFE

Whether you are employed, working for yourself or hiring employees, you do need to have some basic knowledge on some common areas and those are highlighted below. It would be good, though, to familiarise yourself with the details and you can find out more at the MOM website at:

http://www.mom.gov.sg/FAQs/

Employment Act

Singapore does have an Employment Act. This covers all employees except:

- those working in managerial, executive or confidential positions
- those in the civil service
- those working in a statutory board
- domestic workers
- seamen
  You can find out more about the Act at the MOM website mentioned in the section above, under the topic 'Labour Relations'.

Employment Contract

This may or may not be in writing but it is recommended that you do have something on paper. This should outline what position the person is employed for, the working hours, renumeration and benefits. Some companies include a confidentiality and exclusivity clause to ensure that company secrets don't get out.

Working Hours

This varies from company to company but the most common is from 9:00 am to 6:00 pm with a one-hour lunch break, giving most a 40-hour week. Some companies have shorter working hours in one day but also a short lunch break while some work shorter hours daily but work for five and a half days a week instead of five. A company's working hours would depend on a number of factors such as whether the company is part of an MNC and where the office is situated. The Employment Act states that full-time employees should not work for more than 44 hours in a week and part-timers, 30 hours per week. This is just a guideline and it is the management's prerogative to decide what this is. Following a government announcement in 2005 that the civil service is moving towards a five-day work week, many private companies have been trying to follow suit.

Those who operate retail outlets may have longer working hours but employees may be compensated with more off days in between the ones they work. In some positions, they are allowed to claim overtime.

Salary and Benefits

Again this varies from company to company and from job to job. While foreign workers are exempt from contributing to the Central Provident Fund (CPF), all Singaporean and PR workers are required to contribute a certain portion of their salary every month to the fund. The employer, too, has to contribute a certain percentage of each employee's salary. You can find out the actual percentage at the CPF website (http://www.cpf.gov.sg/, under general information).

What the company will actually give in addition to the basic salary would depend on what has been stated in the employment contract, which is why the more savvy employees will make sure that everything is documented.

Most companies offer an Annual Wage Supplement (AWS) which is also known as 13th month payment. However, this may not only be one extra month of salary but can be a maximum of three months' worth. In addition, a company may offer a bonus—a one-time 'reward' paid at the end of the year (fiscal or physical)—and a variable payment, another one-time payment either as an incentive or reward for contributions made by the employee.

Companies may offer non-monetary benefits such as medical or dental claims, reimbursement for certain hospitalisation fees, car or computer loans, telecommunication allowance e.g. paying for mobile phone bills or clothing allowance for those who are expected to dress to a certain standard. Some firms may offer recreational benefits like company trips, fitness classes or nature walks.

Holidays and Leave

Public holidays are rest days for all workers and if an employee is required to work on such a day, they will either have to be compensated with another rest day or be paid for that day. If a public holiday falls on a rest day, the company may choose to grant another day off in lieu, pay the employee for that day or add an extra day to their leave. For example, if the company normally works a five-day week and a public holiday falls on a Saturday, the employee will have to be 'compensated' for that day. If a public holiday falls on a Sunday, by law, the following Monday is a holiday as well.

The number of leave days offered in a year varies but almost all allow at least seven days. In most cases, the number of days increase with the years of service with the company. Yearly leave may or may not be brought forward to the next year (most allow a maximum of one year's leave) and would depend on the company's policy, and in some cases, circumstances e.g. if a worker has been tasked with doing a project that doesn't allow for leave to be taken for a long period of time, the management may allow for extra time in the following year for the remaining leave to be consumed.

Other leave normally given are medical or sick leave, maternity leave and the newly introduced childcare leave which allows for a working mother or father to take two days every year if her or his child if under the age of seven.

WORKING WITH THE LOCALS

In all likelihood, you will have locals working with you, either as your subordinates, your peers or your supervisors. What is expected of you depends greatly on what the indsutry and company culture are like as well as on people's perceptions of expatriates. If yours is a branch of a parent company somewhere else in the world, then you would have to follow the corporate policies set down by the head office. If the headquarters is in Singapore and you have been hired for a specific position, then the corporate culture would depend greatly on how Asian or Western the top management is. If it is more of the latter, you are likely to have less problems fitting in. On the other hand,

Like in many offices around the world, cubicles are very common in Singapore and each individual is allowed their own creativity within their own space.

if the company leans towards an Asian style of management, then you might have some idiosyncrasies to get used to such as having an altar in the office or a spot of 'nepotism' here and there.

Take some time to find out what the practice has been before you decide you want to implement changes. There may be 'good' reasons why certain things are done, even if it means just appeasing people's superstitions. Otherwise you're likely not to hear the end of it the next time something doesn't go right e.g. if a deal fails to materialise or profits start to dip.

If you find that you do have to institute changes in order to ensure that processes work better or to increase productivity, try to be sensitive to the cultural aspects that you shouldn't change e.g. not allowing the Muslim staff to take breaks for their prayers or not approving leave for Malaysians to travel home for certain festive occasions.

Asians, especially those who have not been educated overseas, tend to keep their opinions to themselves; or at least among people of their own level. Even if they are not

happy with you, they may not tell it to your face. This could be because they have been taught to respect those in a 'higher' position than they are; or it could be because they do not know how to say things. Keep your ear to the ground, either personally or through a trusted network, and you will soon discover what people are really thinking.

Dress Code

Mainly due to the heat, the dress code in Singapore is fairly informal. However, this can vary depending on which industry you are in and where your offices are located. Take a cue from those at the same leve as you in the company, as well as how management dresses.

And yes, people's perceptions will play a part on how they receive you and the decisions that you make. For those who are against expatriates coming in and taking higher level jobs than locals, whatever you do will be criticised. Don't take this personally. In every organisation, there are bound to be dissenters. Thankfully, they usually make up the minority. If you are a Caucasian, there will be another minority who are likely to put you on a pedestal. But most locals have enough sense to assess you on your own merits. They know you aren't perfect and are willing to adopt a wait-and-see attitude to determine if you are capable.

Singaporeans may maintain some traditional Chinese values but are much more achievement-oriented. Age and position impress. Education also impresses especially degrees earned in Great Britain, Australia or the US.

If you are supervising a team of locals, keep in mind the Asian concept of 'face'. Should you need to reprimand someone, don't do it in front of a group as this will make them 'lose face'. Find an opportune time to call them into your office or pull them aside and speak with them calmly. Raising your voice, using unkind words, pounding the table or gesticulating wildly is also not likely to win you any admirers.

Similarly, you should not openly praise someone over enthusiastically. It's not that Asians don't want the credit for a job well done but most are brought up to be modest about their accomplishments. Moreover, open praise may cause others to be envious and some may get the wrong idea that you are playing favourites. If you do want to credit someone openly, keep it modest. You can always call this person into your office for a more enthusiastic session privately.

DOING BUSINESS
Meetings

Before you turn up for a meeting, it is a good idea to make an appointment before hand, the earlier the better. Two weeks is about the minimum and it is advisable to call the day before just to confirm the time and place. If possible, try to send a list of those who are attending the meeting with you so that your business associates are prepared and if necessary, ask the correct counterparts to attend the meeting as well. When setting up meetings, keep in mind that some companies may be closed during certain times like Chinese New Year, Hari Raya Puasa and Thaipusam.

You may have heard of how notoriously late Singaporeans are when they attend a host of functions such as Chinese wedding dinners. However, for business meetings, they do try to be on time. And you should be too, if you are meeting local business associates, as being late is often seen as a sign of disrespect. Definitely not a good way to start a professional relationship. If you find yourself running late unexpectedly, make it a point to call ahead and let your clients/associates know, giving an estimated time when you will get there. If you don't call, they will consider you rude for keeping them waiting. And not having a phone handy cannot be used as an excuse in Singapore where mobile phones abound and you will be considered odd if you do not have one.

When you are introduced to new business associates, you will be expected to shake hands. An exception would be if you are a gentleman being introduced to a Muslim woman (remember that race is no indicator—a woman who looks Chinese or Indian may be a Muslim). Very traditional Muslim ladies will decline to shake hands with men unless they have some covering over their hand. The easiest way around this would be to let the woman take the lead; if she extends her hand for a shake, take it and return the gesture. Otherwise, a smile and nod will do. Some will also give a slight bow. If you find yourself towering over everyone present, it might be a good idea to bow slightly as well, especially if the people you are being introduced to are older.

A word to the wise—Singaporean handshakes may not be the bone-crushing variety. Most tend to be rather soft or gentle (some border on being limp) but they will hold your hand for a little longer. Some will give your hand a good grip and then let go. Again, take your lead from your counterpart.

Introductions

In Chapter Three: The People of Singapore, you were introduced to the topic of names in the different cultures. In the business arena, this still holds true and a person is likely to be introduced using a title and their first or family name. It is best to keep things formal until you find out how informal you can be. Asians respect the elderly so these will probably be introduced using their title and surname while the younger people in the group are introduced using their title and first names, or just their names alone. In some cases, the older people may not be the most senior in rank so do not make that assumption. When introducing your own team, you might like to use the same method. Speak with your team beforehand on how they'd like to approach this issue so that you know what to do when the time comes.

Business Cards

Business cards (also called name cards) are important and these should be in English. If you are dealing with a traditionally Chinese or Indian company, you might want to consider having your card bilingual on the flipside. When presenting and receiving name cards, make sure you use both hands. If for some reason this is not possible, make sure that you use your right hand. And don't be too hasty in putting the cards away. Take a moment to repeat the name and look at the card. It shows respect. If you are seated at a table, it is advisable to leave the cards on the table throughout the meeting and only put them away at the end of the meeting. Asians consider name cards as an extension of their personae so if you stuff the card into your pocket the moment you receive it, that is a mark of disrespect. You should also refrain from writing on the cards.

Striking a Deal

Now that the formalities are over, what happens next? You may be pleased to know that Singaporeans normally like to get right down to business. There may be instances where some will engage in small talk first, but this is not the norm. If you are faced with this, reciprocate. Don't be impatient or try to rush things along. One important thing to keep in mind is that in Singapore, relationships are very important when closing business deals. The more the other party trusts you, the more they will be willing to do business with you. Like they say, it's not what you know but who you know. The Chinese have a term for this: *guanxi* (which means

Seating Arrangements

In more traditional companies, hierarchy can be seen in the seating arrangements during meetings. The most senior in the group are usually given places of honour, normally furthest into the room. If your team is seated on one side of the table, their counterparts in rank are likely to be seated across from them.

'link' or 'relationship'). You will discover that sometimes, deals are struck more because the decision-maker(s) have something in common with their potential business partner and this could be something as simple as being from the same ethnic or dialect group or even the same alma mater. The more of a personal contact you have with those you do business with, the stronger your relationship and the more likely they will turn their business your way. Be patient, it will bear fruit in time.

While dealing with business clients, keep in mind some of the aspects you have learned about how to deal with your own team: show 'face', be direct but keep your emotions to a minimum, be sincere with your praise and don't overdo it. In business, it is best to keep at least an arm's length from the other person when conversing with him or her, so as not to appear intimidating. Touching (even on the forearm) is also not a good idea unless you know someone very well as this may signal that you are trying to force a more personal relationship than there really is.

Non-verbal language plays a big part when doing business here and you should keep a look out for certain clues. Laughter, which in most cases is meant to signify hilarity, may be used as a mask to cover up nervousness or awkwardness, or even to help gloss over a point your business associates might not want to talk about at that point in time. In many instances, Singaporeans may feel uncomfortable about saying 'no' right to your face, especially if the main decision maker is not present at the meeting. However, so as not to offend you, they may hedge around an issue to throw you off. Watch for actual body language:

If you are a woman, you may face a few more obstacles than your male counterparts. Traditionally, Asian men (and this holds true for Singaporeans as well) expect women to be less aggressive and may resent those who have risen to positions of power within business organisations. If you are a representative of your company, you might have to find some middle ground between being assertive about what your company and you want while at the same time not coming across as being difficult. Also, you do need to show a certain amount of respect to your business counterparts, especially if they are men and this might mean on occasion you should not be so direct with your eye contact. This is something which you will have to use your instincts on as much would depend on the personalities of the people you are dealing with.

sucking in of breath, fidgeting, frequent instances of hesitation, slightly furrowed brows (this could be almost imperceptible) or even moments of silence when they seem to be waiting for you to say something when you are done talking. If you can pick up on these, it will give you a clue as to how well the meeting is actually progressing.

Giving Gifts

In the business world, you need to be careful when you give gifts as this may be construed as bribery. There is a fine line and sometimes it is difficult to know exactly when an appropriate time is. If you are gunning to do business with a company, giving a present before a deal is struck is a definite no-no as you will be seen as trying to buy your way in and whatever respect your potential partners might have had for you will have fallen a few notches. Sometimes, it is just best to wait until the contract is signed and the deal is closed before giving anything. If the company you are dealing with is government-related in some way, you should not even entertain the idea of giving any kind of gift as this can be construed as a bribe and in the wrong circumstances, you may be reported to the police.

If you are friends with someone from the company and would like to get him or her a gift for a social occasion you have been invited to, by all means go ahead. However, if you have yet to close a deal and are not sure if this will be taken the wrong way, make sure you give the present in the open and don't get anything too ostentatious or too expensive. Something to fit the occasion (flowers, chocolates, a bottle of wine if the family can drink) to be given as a token of friendship would be fine. If you really are friends with this person, there will be other occasions to give more presents later once the deal is closed.

For many Chinese companies, giving hampers during certain festive periods (usually Christmas, New Year's and Chinese New Year) is a token of respect suppliers often show to their clients. (Some companies also give moon cakes during the Mid-Autumn Festival.) For example, Company A makes its business off supplying dairy products to its clients of which Company B is one of their largest buyers. When Chinese New Year comes around, Company A makes sure that hampers are sent to all its major clients, Company B included. Company B will not need to reciprocate but may make arrangements for their most valued customers to receive hampers as well. Hampers come in various shapes and sizes and there are companies that deal with this. (Check the *Buying Guide* or the Internet.) For more valued clients, you might like to send a more expensive hamper (it may not necessarily be bigger) and your business partner will be able to tell from the items that come in the basket. If you're not sure what to do, get a Chinese colleague to help you.

Work and Business Etiquette

- Remember the concept of 'face' when dealing with colleagues or business associates.
- Be direct and sincere but don't overdo it.
- Don't be too hasty in instituting changes. Do your homework first and be sensitive to perceptions and expectations.
- Respect the other person's space and keep an arm's length away.
- Touching may be miscontrued so refrain from this.
- When introduced to a Muslim woman, let her take the lead on whether to shake hands.
- Watch for non-verbal cues and body language. This should be seen in conjunction with what is actually said as your business associates (and even your colleagues) may not want to be forthright for a number of reasons.
- Be respectful of other people's business cards.
- Use common sense when exercising your dress sense; observe what others are doing.
- Personal relationships are an important aspect to closing a deal. Take time to cultivate these.

WOMEN IN THE WORKFORCE

In 2004, women made up 45 per cent of the workforce, a 5 per cent increase from ten years before. On the whole, Singaporean women face the same challenges as women in other First World countries. In the 21st century, they are definitely better educated with 29 per cent of them having tertiary education in 2004. This is a 15 per cent increase from 1994. These days, about one in three are corporate managers.

SINGAPORE AT A GLANCE

CHAPTER 10

'Singapura, oh Singapura,
Sunny island set in the sea.
Singapura, oh Singapura,
Pretty flowers bloom for you and me.'
—local children's song popular
in the 1970s and 1980s

Official Name
Republic of Singapore

Capital
Singapore

Flag
Two horizontal bands of equal width, with the red on the top and the white at the bottom. The red stands for brotherhood and equality while the white for purity and virtue. On the left hand side of the red portion is a white crescent moon and, arranged in a circle, five white five-pointed stars. The crescent moon represents a nation on the rise while the five stars stand for democracy, equality, justice, peace and progress

National Anthem
Majulah Singapura (Onward Singapore)

Time
Greenwich Mean Time plus 8 hours (GMT +0800)

Telephone Country Code
65

Land
Island at the tip of the West Malaysian peninsula, separated from the mainland by the Johor Straits

Area
total: 692.7 sq km (267.5 sq miles)
land: 682.7 sq km (263.6 sq miles)
water: 10 sq km (3.9 sq miles)

Highest Point
Bukit Timah (166 m / 544.6 ft)

Climate
Typical hot, humid and rainy tropical weather with two monsoon seasons—north-east from December to March and south-west from June to September

Natural Resources
Deep water ports and fish

Population
4,492,150 (July 2006 est)

Ethnic Groups
2000 census: Chinese (76.8 per cent), Malay (13.9 per cent), Indian (7.9 per cent), other (1.4 per cent)

Religion
2000 census: Buddhist (42.5 per cent), Muslim (14.9 per cent), Taoist (8.5 per cent), Hindu (4 per cent), Roman Catholic (4.8 per cent), other Christian denominations (9.8 per cent), other (0.7 per cent), none (14.8 per cent)

Official Languages
Malay, Mandarin Chinese, Tamil and English. Malay is the national language while English is the lingua franca

Government Structure
Parliamentary republic

Currency
Singapore dollar (SGD or S$)

Gross Domestic Product (GDP)
US$ 132.3 billion (2005 est)

Agricultural Products
Copra (dried coconut meat), eggs, fish, fruit, orchids, poultry, rubber and vegetables

Industries
Chemicals, electronics, entrepôt trade, financial services, life sciences, offshore platform construction, oil drilling equipment, petroleum refining, processed food and beverages, rubber processing, rubber products and ship repair

Exports
Chemicals, consumer goods, electronics, machinery and equipment as well as mineral fuels

Imports
Chemicals, foodstuffs, machinery and equipment as well as mineral fuels

Airports
Total of six, all of which have paved runways. The main international airport is Changi International

FAMOUS PEOPLE
Politics
Lee Kuan Yew
Undoubtedly the most famous Singaporean in the world, Lee is widely acknowledged as the maker of modern Singapore. As a young man, he opposed British colonial rule and was one of the founders of the People's Action Party (PAP). He became the first prime minister of the state of Singapore in 1959, leading the country through a period of limited

self-administration as well as the merger of 1963. When Singapore was expelled from the Federation of Malaysia in 1965, Lee instituted policies, sometimes controversial, that have left their indelible mark on Singapore. In a carefully managed transition, Lee relinquished his post in 1990 to Goh Chok Tong but continued wielding influence as Senior Minister. In 2004, Goh stepped down in favour of Lee's son, Lee Hsien Loong, and Lee occupied a specially created post as Minister Mentor. The ageing statesman is admired and criticised for his leadership marked by pragmatism and autocracy and his championing of 'Asian-style' democracy.

Goh Chok Tong
Goh was a senior civil servant in various ministries before assuming the office of prime minister from 1990–2004. He is considered to have ushered in a more open and consultative style of leadership. Since 2004, he has been Senior Minister of Singapore.

Lee Hsien Loong
Son of Lee Kuan Yew and current prime minister of Singapore after succeeding Goh Chok Tong in August 2004. He is also the finance minister. Lee was a Brigadier-General of the Singapore Armed Forces (SAF) before joining politics.

J B Jeyaratnam
A fiery veteran political activist, Jeyaratnam was the first opposition politician to become a Member of Parliament (MP) in 1981. His political career has, however, been stymied by a series of defamation suits and charges. Disbarred and declared a bankrupt, he has been disqualified from participating in future elections for the time being.

Chiam See Tong
An MP representing the opposition since 1984, Chiam was once from the Singapore Democratic Party (SDP) until his ex-protégée, Chee Soon Juan (see next) ousted him. Together

with other disillusioned members of the SDP, Chiam now heads the Singapore People's Party which is one of the member parties of the Singapore Democratic Alliance (SDA), set up in 2001 in order to gain strength in numbers while fighting in Group Representation Constituencies (GRCs).

Chee Soon Juan

Controversial opposition figure, Chee contested in a number of elections as a member of the Singapore Democratic Party (SDP) with some success. However, his embroilment in lawsuits and a much-publicised hunger strike have divided opinion and his own party.

Diplomatic Corps
Chan Heng Chee

The founding director of the Institute of Policy Studies, Chan is the current ambassador to the United States.

Professor Tommy Koh

Currently the ambassador-at-large with the Ministry of Foreign Affairs, Tommy Koh was Singapore's permanent representative to the United Nations from 1968–1971 and again from 1974–1984. He was also the country's ambassador to the United States from 1984–1990.

Presidents of Singapore

Yusof Ishak (1910–1970)	In office from 1965–1970
Dr Benjamin H Sheares (1907-1981)	In office from 1971–1981
C V Devan Nair (1923-2005)	In office from 1981–1985.
Dr Wee Kim Wee (1915-2005)	In office from 1985–1993. Often known as 'the people's president'.
Ong Teng Cheong (1936–2002)	In office from 1993-1999. First elected president of Singapore
S R Nathan (1924–)	In office since 1999. Was elected to a second term in 2005.

Philanthropists
Tan Tock Seng (1798–1850)
An immigrant from Malacca, Tan Tock Seng made a name for himself with hard work, determination and an entrepreneurial spirit. A successful and prudent businessman who owned many tracts of land in prime areas, Tan donated the initial sum of money to build a hospital which today bears his name. Among his many charitable acts is the effort he made to provide destitute Chinese with a proper burial, a ritual which is important to the Chinese people.

Lee Kong Chian (1893–1967)
A man who made his money on rubber and pineapples and gave generously back to the community, through donations of money and time. In 1958, he set up the Lee Foundation to handle philanthropic work. Since Lee was a firm believer in education, it is not surprising that most of the causes the Foundation supports are in that area. Today, you will see many libraries and educational facilities bearing his name, a tribute to the man who has done so much.

Dr Ee Peng Liang (1913–1994)
Often known as the 'Father of Charity', the late Dr Ee Peng Liang was involved in countless charities and social work organisations, among these the Community Chest, the Scout Association of Singapore, the Rotary Club and Saint Joseph's Home.

Sports
Tan Howe Liang
Singapore's sole medal (silver) at the Olympic Games was won by weightlifter Tan Howe Liang in the 1960 Rome Games. A record-holder and gold medallist even before his Olympics feat, he has since become somewhat of a forgotten hero.

Ang Peng Siong
Champion of the 50-m freestyle, he won the title of 'World's Fastest Swimmer Award' at the 1982 Asian Games in New

Delhi, and held the record for this event at the SEA Games until 1996. To date, he is the only competitor that has made it to the finals of any swim event at the Olympics (1984). Today, Ang runs his own swim school, coaching future hopefuls in the sport he loves best.

Joscelin Yeo

Swimming wonder who splashed her way to winning the most medals for Singapore in the South East Asian (SEA) Games. With 40 gold medals garnered at the 2005 SEA Games, she has broken the record of 1960s golden girl, Pat Chan.

Li Jiawei

The queen of table tennis who is currently (2006) ranked fifth in the world by ITTF (International Table Tennis Federation). Originally born in Beijing, Li now makes her home in Singapore and represents the nation at many international events. At the 2004 Olympics, she was tearful at not being able to garner a medal for Singapore, coming in at fourth place. Li has been voted Sportswoman of the Year five years in a row (2001–2006).

Ronald Susilo

National badminton player who was born in East Java, Indonesia. He was named Sportsman of the Year in 2005 and one of the highlights of his career came when he beat the world number one, Lin Dan of China, in his opening match during the 2004 Olympics in Athens.

Remy Ong

The bright star in bowling these days, Ong won three gold medals at the 2002 Asian Games in Busan, Korea. In 2005, he was ranked sixth by the Asian Bowling Federation (ABF).

Fandi Ahmad

Singapore's Pele, Fandi Ahmad is the country's best-known football player. At 16, he was the youngest player on the national team in 1978. In 1981, he turned professional and has not looked back since. His career has seen him taking football stints with foreign clubs before returning home and passing along what he had learnt through coaching the younger players. Although less in the limelight these days, Fandi is still very active behind the scenes. He is currently married to former South African model, Wendy Jacobs, and they have four children.

Other Sports Personalities of the Past

- Jing Junhong (table tennis)
- Junie Sng (swimming)
- Pat Chan (swimming)
- Grace Young (bowling)
- C Kunalan (athletics)
- Benedict Tan (yachting)
- Zainal Abidin (squash)
- Quah Kim Song (football)
- Samad Allapitchay (football)
- Mark Chay (swimming)
- Saiedah Said (*silat*)
- Asman bin Abdullah (body building)
- Chee Swee Lee (athletics)
- Jojo Sinclair (bodybuilding)

Literary Figures
Catherine Lim
Known for her short stories and novels steeped in local flavour, this understated and prolific writer was reprimanded by Goh Chok Tong, then the prime minister, for two politically critical articles she wrote in 1994. Among her works are *The Bondmaid* (1995), a best-selling novel which was the first to be published outside of Singapore and is to be made into a film.

Philip Jeyaratnam
Son of politician J B Jeyaratnam and a full-time lawyer who writes in his free time. He was named the Young Artist

of the Year in 1993 by Singapore's National Arts Council. Currently, he is gaining prominence as the president of the Law Society.

Kuo Pao Kun (1939-2002)

The founding artistic director of The Theatre Practice, this playwright was a visionary who did much for the artistic scene even though he was once detained under the Internal Security Act and his Singapore citizenship was even taken away from him. In 1997, the French government awarded him with the Chevalier des Arts et des lettres (knighthood of arts and letters).

Edwin Thumboo

Poet and literary critic who was once a lecturer at NUS' English language and literature department. The winner of a number of cultural awards, Thumboo is considered by many as the local poet laureate.

Ho Minfong

The sister of Ho Kwon Ping (see section on business personalities), Ho Minfong began writing while she was studying in the United States and used this as an outlet to overcome her homesickness. Her works focus on life in South-east Asia and are often recommended as good reading material for young adults.

Suchen Christine Lim

The first woman and first Singaporean writer to win the prestigious Singapore Literature Prize (1992), Lim's writing gives her readers a insight to life in Singapore. She has been the writer-in-residence at two international universities.

Dance
Goh Choo San (1948–1987)

Probably the most well-known dancer from Singapore, Goh Choo San was the resident choreographer and artistic director of the Washington Ballet. He is the brother of Goh Soo Khim (see next).

Goh Soo Khim

Co-founder and artistic director of the Singapore Dance Theatre (SDT), Goh Soo Khim has done much to raise the level of dance in Singapore, by being personally involved and through her encouragement of the young. She was a Cultural Medallion winner in 1981.

Santha Bhaskar

Keralese who has contributed greatly to the development of Indian dance in Singapore. A 1991 Cultural Medallion winner, her works have been seen on stage and on television.

Music
Dick Lee

Versatile singer-composer and one of the earliest proponents of Singaporean and pan-Asian music. His album 'The Mad Chinaman' launched his career in the region. He has written songs for top artistes like Sandy Lam and musicals such as 'Beauty World', 'Forbidden City: Portrait of an Empress' and Jacky Cheung's 'Snow.Wolf.Lake'. Lee's numerous talents have led him to be the Associate Artiste Director of the Singapore Repertory Theatre (SRT), creative director of the National Day Parade in 2002, and even a fashion designer.

Stefanie Sun

Petite girl with a big voice, Stefanie Sun is one of the best-selling artistes in the Mandarin pop music scene. She has garnered numerous music awards and her meteoric rise in the region is an inspiration to local musicians.

Taufik

Crowned the first Singapore Idol in 2004, Taufik Bautista is now the spokesperson for the Health Promotion Board's anti-smoking campaign and is an inspiration to many young Singaporeans.

T'ang Quartet

Probably the most well-known classical music group in Singapore, the T'ang Quartet is as much known for its chamber music as the young men who constitute the string quartet. They inject glamour into classical music and have gained a following with their lunchtime concerts and international performances.

Vanessa-Mae

Singapore's answer to Nigel Kennedy, violinist Vanessa-Mae Nicholson moved from a career in classical music to one in pop with her album 'The Violin Player' in 1994. Her electric violin and vampish image have won her admirers, and detractors.

Jeremy Monterio

Another Cultural Medallion winner (2002), Jeremy Monteiro is a much-respected and well-loved singer and jazz pianist who has worked with some of the big names in the music industry e.g. Quincy Jones, Ernie Watts and Natalie Cole. In his illustrious career, he has performed at the Montreux Jazz Festival and also at Caesar's palace in Las Vegas.

Choo Hoey

Founder and musical director (1979–1996) of the Singapore Symphony Orchestra (SSO), Choo Huey has been credited for developing the orchestra and building its repertoire.

Lan Shui

Since taking over the musical directorship from Choo Hoey (see above), Lan Shui—originally from China—has raised the standard of excellence of the SSO even further.

Fashion
Ashley Isham

In 1996, Isham moved to London to pursue his love of fashion and in the space of four years was able to set up his own label. His stylish designs have been featured in Italian *Vogue*, *Marie Claire* and *In Style*. In 2004, he was named the official womenswear designer for BAFTA (British Academy Film Awards). In 2006, he was asked to make a guest appearance on *America's Next Top Model* hosted by Tyra Banks. Isham now has showrooms in London and Paris.

Andrew Gn
Based in Paris, Andrew Gn had worked in the fashion houses of Emanuel Ungaro and House of Balmain before he launched his solo collections which have been well received. His designs are often considered minimalist yet luxurious.

Song and Kelly
Fashion design duo of Wykidd Song and Welsh-born Ann Kelly whose chance meeting in 1993 led to them falling in love and starting a fashion house together. In 1999, the company floundered (as did their relationship) but it has since been given an injection of capital and new lease of life as Song + Kelly21.

Jonathan Seow
A multi-award winner who set up his own label, Woods & Woods, in early 2000. Three years later, he took his collection to Melbourne and in 2005, Seow is one of five designers who have won a place in Who's Next Paris.

The Arts
Tan Swie Hian
A veritable 'Renaissance man', philosopher-artist Tan's body of work includes painting, sculpture, calligraphy and printmaking. He has also penned poetry, essays, criticism, translation and articles for Buddhist publications. In 1978, he was conferred with the title of Chevalier de l'Ordre des Arts et Lettres by France, and awarded the Cultural Medallion by Singapore in 1987. In June 2006, Tan became the first Singaporean to be conferred as an Officer in the National Order of the Legion of Honour, France's highest honour.

Brother Joseph McNally (1923-2002)
Irish-born, Catholic priest Joseph McNally arrived in Singapore in 1946 and began teaching as part of the LaSalle order. Dedicating his life to education and the arts, he founded the

LaSalle-SIA College of the Arts and is a renowned sculptor working with bronze, oak and bogwood.

Ng Eng Teng (1934–2001)

Sculptor and potter who has contributed greatly to the local arts scene especially through his mentoring of future sculptors via the Studio 106 project.

Iskandar Jalil

Master potter who holds a solo exhibition once every five years and participates in many others around the world. In 2004, the artist was in tears after being told that he had to dismantle the kiln in his home—a kiln he had been using for 43 years—as its gas tanks were deemed a fire hazard. Thankfully, engineers from ExxonMobil were able to help him devise a different gas tank that would allow him to continue his artistic work yet comply with fire safety regulations at the same time.

Stage...

Ong Keng Sen

Founder and artistic director of the TheatreWorks performance company, Ong Keng Sen pioneered the docu-performance and uses this to explore the Asian identity in the 21st century and develop cultural exchanges.

Glen Goei

Singapore first started talking about Glen Goei when he won a role opposite Anthony Hopkins in the West End's production of 'M Butterfly' in 1987. More than a decade later, in 1998, Goei released his first film, *Forever Fever*, which was later picked up by Miramax.

Ivan Heng

Founder and artistic director of Wild Rice theatre company, Ivan Heng was the first Chinese graduate of the Royal Scottish Academy of Music and Drama and has been involved in all aspects of theatre, from acting to directing to writing to designing. He has played the role of Song Liling in three different productions of 'M Butterfly' as well as acted opposite Gary Oldman and Bruce Willis in the film, *The Fifth Element*.

Kumar

Singapore's most famous and beloved drag-queen and stand-up comic who performs regularly at the Gold Dust Club in Orchard Road. Kumar also performs in the region and can sometimes be seen in television.

Other Stage Names

Since the talent pool is relatively small, you are likely to hear the same names mentioned, either for stage, film or television. Most of these are primarily actors, although they do dabble in directing or other areas every now and again. Here are some of the most likely:

- Koh Chieng Mun
- Lim Kay Tong
- Lim Kay Siu
- Neo Swee Lin
- Pamela Oei
- Tan Kheng Hua
- Selina Tan
- Emma Yong
- Zhou En-lai
- Beatrice Chia (actor/director)
- Samantha Blackhall-Taylor (director)
- Haresh Sharma (playwright/director)

… and Screen

Zoe Tay

A household name in Singapore, Tay is an enduringly popular Chinese-language television actress. From the time she won a local Star Search contest to her latest real-life role as first-time mother, Zoe is never far from the public eye.

Fann Wong

Another television veteran, model-turned-actress Fann Wong's face can be seen in countless magazines and TV series. She has appeared in *Shanghai Knights* opposite Jackie Chan.

Phua Chu Kang

Loud, brash and sporting a bad perm and trademark yellow rubber boots, Phua Chua Kang (sometimes known as PCK) is a fictional character from a long-running TV sitcom that is portrayed so believably by Gurmit Singh that it's hard to believe he isn't real. This lovable icon, modelled after a construction site foremen has even spawned a musical of the same name, Singapore's most expensive to date.

Gurmit Singh

Alter-ego of Phua Chu Kang, Gurmit Singh is as similar to PCK as chalk is to cheese. For his portrayal of this character, Gurmit has won the Best Comedy Actor award for three years running (1998–2000) at the Asian Television Award. His talents also extend to serious acting and hosting, with the latter role leading him to emcee the National Day Parade for the ast few years.

Adrian Pang

An actor that is popular with both English and Chinese viewers, having acted and hosted in English and Mandarin programmes. Pang had tried to make a living in London theatre but made the decision to move his family back to Singapore in 1991. Since then, he has been making a name for himself on screen as well as in the local theatre scene.

Jack Neo

Originally a Chinese-language TV actor, comedian and host , Jack Neo first became well-known for portraying the female character of Liang Po Po. Since then, he has moved on to producing movies, all of which have been top-grossing films locally and in the region.

Najip Ali

It seems there is nothing this man cannot do: host (in English and Malay), singer, producer, choreographer, director (theatre and in the studio), songwriter; the list goes on and seems to be growing. Najip became a household name in Asia mainly because of his eight-year stint as one of the hosts of *Asia Bagus*. In recent years, he's turned his attention to producing television programmes for the Malay channel as well as the children's channel.

Photography
Russel Wong

Singapore's celebrity photographer can count Jackie Chan, Michelle Yeoh, Naomi Campbell, Claudia Schiffer, Richard Gere and Zhang Ziyi among his subjects. Wong has also photographed covers from Time magazine. In 2005, an exhibition was held at the Singapore Art Museum (SAM) to mark his 25th year in the business. Among the exhibits where his movie set photos from the films, *Crouching Tiger, Hidden Dragon*, *House of Flying Daggers*, as well as *Hero*.

Wee Khim

Photographer to the stars (all the big names in Singapore, including Zoe Tay and Fann Wong) and the choice of many top international companies (Nike, Nokia, Sony) for their advertising campaigns.

Business
Ong Beng Seng and Christina Ong

The husband and wife team behind the very successful public-listed Hotel Properties Limited (HPL) who owns the Hilton and Four Season hotels in Singapore, the Hard Rock Café franchise for Asia, the franchise for designer label such as DKNY, Calvin Klein and Guess.

Jennie Chua

The President and CEO of Raffles International, the holding company that oversees the world famous Raffles Hotel, Jennie

Chua is also the director of many of its other companies. In addition, she sits on a number of boards and councils of associations and companies. Chua is a pioneer in many ways, especially paving the way for women in business. She was named Woman of the Year 1999 by *Her World* magazine, an award that honours women who have been role models to others of the same gender and contributed greatly to society.

Dr Jannie Tay
The woman behind The Hour Glass, building it up from a one-outlet store to a leading retailer of international brands of top-quality timepieces, writing instruments and jewellery. Jannie Tay is also involved in many community and charity projects.

Shabnam Melwani-Reis
The director of Jaygee Enterprises (fashion distributor of such brands as Levi's, Liz Claiborne and Osh Gosh B'Gosh) and co-founder of Soundbuzz, a music portal that allows for legitimate downloading of music and video clips.

Olivia Lum
The brains behind Hyflux, the water treatment that has been tasked with Singapore's NEWater project (creating drinkable water using recycled waste water) in the hope that the country can create its own water supply and be less dependent on outside sources.

Ho Kwon Ping and Claire Chiang
The husband and wife team behind the Banyan Tree Group which own a chain of luxury hotels and resorts around the region.

Sim Wong Hoo
The man behind Creative Techonology. When he first mooted the idea of the Soundblaster, no one took him seriously and his company was refused a spot in the Stock Exchange of

Singapore (SES). Sim decided to list on the New York Stock Exchange instead and made waves, not jut in the industry but around the world. Creative's opening price was about US$ 25 per share. The company is currently going head to head with Apple computers as both are vying for the same market share of mp3 listeners.

Miscellaneous
Dr Woffles Wu
The premier plastic surgeon in Singapore and Asia.

Elizabeth Choy
War heroine from World War II who received the Order of the British Empire in 1946.

Paddy Chew (1960–1999)
Singapore's first AIDS victim who went public with his affliction in 1998.

Reverend Shi Ming Yi
Secretary-general of the Singapore Buddhist Association and abbot of the Foo Hai Ch'an Monastery. Reverend Shi established the Ren Ci Hospital to help all poor and needy patients suffering from chronic illnesses.

Archbishop John Chew
The third archbishop of the Anglican churches in Southeast Asia.

Archbishop Nicholas Chia
Head of the Catholic church in Singapore.

Annabel Chong
Singapore's very own porn star. Annabel Chong is the stage name for Grace Quek, a well-educated Singapore girl who set a world record in 1995 with her ten-hour sex orgy with 80 men. This was subsequently released on film and is one the highest grossing films in the porn industry.

ACRONYMS

Singaporeans love their acronyms and there are so many that even the locals get confused sometimes. The following list is of some of the most commonly used and heard, but it is by no means exhaustive as new ones seem to pop up everyday!

Ministries

ENV	Ministry of the Environment
MCYS	Ministry of Community Development, Youth and Sports
MCIT	Ministry of Communications and Information Technology
MFA	Ministry of Foreign Affairs
MHA	Ministry of Home Affairs
MICA	Ministry of Information, Communications and the Arts
MINDEF	Ministry of Defence
MND	Ministry of National Development
MOE	Ministry of Education
MOF	Ministry of Finance
MOH	Ministry of Health
MOM	Ministry of Manpower
MTI	Ministry of Trade and Industry

Statutory Boards and Government-related Bodies

A*STAR	Agency for Science, Technology and Research
ACRA	Accounting and Corporate Regulatory Authority
AVA	Agri-food and Veterinary Authority
BCA	Building and Construction Authority
BCCS	Board of Commissioners of Currency
BFC	Board of Film Censors
CAAS	Civil Aviation Authority of Singapore
CMC	Community Mediation Centre
CNB	Central Narcotic Bureau
CPF	Central Provident Fund
CRP	Controller of Residential Property

DSTA	Defence, Science and Technology Agency
EDB	Economic Development Board
HDB	Housing and Development Board
HEB	Hindu Endowments Board
HPB	Health Promotion Board
HSA	Health Sciences Authority
ICA	Immigration and Checkpoints Authority
IDA	Infocomm Development Authority
IRAS	Inland Revenue Authority of Singapore
JTC	Jurong Town Council
LTA	Land Transport Authority
MAS	Monetary Authority of Singapore
MPA	Maritime and Port Authority of Singapore
MRTC	Mass Rapid Transit Corporation
MSS	Meteorological Service Singapore
NAC	National Arts Council
NBDCS	National Book Development Council of Singapore
NCSS	National Council of Social Service
NHB	National Heritage Board
NLB	National Library Board
NPB	National Parks Board
NSTB	National Science and Technology Board
OA	Official Assignee
OCS	Officer Cadet School
PA	People's Association
PAB	Public Accountants Board
PMO	Prime Ministers Office
PSA	Port of Singapore Authority
PSC	Public Service Commission
PSD	Public Service Division
PTC	Public Transport Council
PUB	Public Utilities Board
PWB	Public Works Department
RADAC	Renovation and Decoration Advisory Centre
SAF	Singapore Armed Forces
SBA	Singapore Broadcasting Authority

SBS	Singapore Bus Service
SCDF	Singapore Civil Defence Force
SDU	Social Development Unit
SEMAC	Singapore Waste Management Company
SES	Stock Exchange of Singapore
SIMEX	Singapore International Monetary Exchange
SLR	Singapore Land Registry
SP	Singapore Power
SSC	Singapore Sports Council
STB	Singapore Tourism Board
TAS	Telecommunication Authority of Singapore
TDB	Singapore Trade Development Board
URA	Urban Redevelopment Authority
WDA	Workforce Development Agency

Organisations and Other Bodies

ACM	Asian Civilisations Museum
AMP	Association for Muslim Professionals
CDAC	Chinese Development Assistance Council
CDC	Community Development Council
FAS	Football Association of Singapore
MENDAKI	Yayasan MENDAKI (Council for the Development of Singapore Muslim Community)
MUIS	Majlis Ugama Islam Singapura (Islamic Religious Council of Singapore)
NTUC	National Trades Union Congress
SAM	Singapore Art Museum
SDF	Skills Development Fund
SHM	Singapore History Museum
SINDA	Singapore Indian Development Association
SLF	Singapore Labour Foundation
VWO	Voluntary Welfare Organisation

Political Parties

PAP	People's Action Party
SDA	Singapore Democratic Alliance
SDP	Singapore Democratic Party

SPP	Singapore People's Party
WP	Worker's Party

Educational Institutions

CJC	Catholic Junior College
HJC	Hwa Chong Junior College
IPS	Institute of Policy Studies
INSEAD	Institut Européen d'Administration des Affaires (European Institute for Business Administration, now more well-known by its acronym)
ISEAS	Institute of Southeast Asian Studies
ITE	Institute of Technical Education
NAP	Ngee Ann Polytechnic
NJC	National Junior College
NTU	Nanyang Technological University
NUS	National University of Singapore
NUSS	NUS Student's Union
NYP	Nanyang Polytechnic
SILS	Singapore Institute of Labour Studies
SIM	Singapore Institute of Management
SMU	Singapore Management University
SP	Singapore Polytechnic
TJC	Temasek Junior College
TP	Temasek Polytechnic
UniSIM	University of SIM
VJC	Victoria Junior College

Banks

DBS	Development Bank of Singapore
OCBC	Overseas Chinese Banking Corporation
OUB	Overseas Union Bank
POSB	Post Office Savings Bank
UOB	United Overseas Bank

Hospitals

AH	Alexandra Hospital
KK	Kandang Kerbau Women's and Children's Hospital

NUH	National University Hospital
SGH	Singapore General Hospital
TTSH	Tan Tock Seng Hospital

Expressways

AYE	Ayer Rajah Expressway
BKE	Bukit Timah Expressway
CTE	Central Expressway
ECP	East Coast Parkway
KJE	Kranji Expressway
PIE	Pan Island Expressway
SLE	Seletar Expressway
TPE	Tampines Expressway

Miscellaneous

CBD	Central Business District
CISD	Computer Information Systems Department
COE	Certificate of Entitlement
ERP	Electronic Road Pricing
GST	Goods and Services Tax
IU	In-Vehicle Unit
LRT	Light Rail Transit
MRT	Mass Rapid Transit
NDP	National Day Parade
PR	Permanent Resident
PSI	Pollution Safety Index
PVP	Professional Visit Pass
SAM	Self- Service Automated Machine
SIA	Singapore International Airlines
WITS	Work Improvement Team

CULTURE QUIZ

SITUATION 1

You're invited to a co-workers home for a Christmas open house. You arrive dressed in your holiday sparkle with a small hostess gift. Much to your surprise, everyone is outside on the lawn, barefooted and completely casual and relaxed. Your reaction is to:

A Make an excuse and leave as soon as possible for you are not dressed to take the heat outside.

B Ask the hostess if she has something you can change into so you can be more comfortable and enjoy the rest of the evening.

C Make a joke of your situation and step into the house as much as possible so you can cool off a bit with the air-conditioning.

Comments

C is the best reply, as it shows some the ability to laugh at oneself and doesn't offend or make the hostess uncomfortable. Life in Singapore is generally quite casual because of the tropical weather. If the family has a nice garden area, you can be sure that it will be used for entertaining so learn to either ask in advance if the party will be outdoors or simply dress in cottons and light materials (for men, a jacket is almost never required). Additionally, the custom of removing shoes before entering a home also tends to invite casualness. The hostess gift is common practice and even bringing something (chocolates or small toy) for the young children is quite common and acceptable. It is also customary in Singapore and most of Asia to not open gifts immediately (so as to not appear greedy). Also, for holidays and special celebrations such as Chinese New Year, Hari Raya and Deepavali, don't be surprised if you also leave with a small gift from the hostess for either yourself or your children.

SITUATION 2

It's Hari Raya Puasa or the end of the Muslim fasting month and you have been invited to a friends home for the typical open house. You've just had lunch and figure you will stop by for just a few minutes to say hi and wish everyone *Selamat Hari Raya*. The home is full of friends and family and you immediately are shown the way to the vast and luscious buffet—it all looks and smells delicious but you couldn't eat another bite. What do you do?

A Say it all looks delicious, thank you, but I just had lunch and simply cannot eat another bite. Take a glass of water and sit down to chat with someone.

B Take a plate and small sample of the beef rendang and jackfruit curry, your favourites.

C After trying to avoid the food, you finally have to accept the small plate of food that has been consistently presented to you by the hostess. You eat it and suffer stomach discomfort quietly and privately, later.

Comments

B is the best response. It's not taken well if you totally refuse to accept any food in these circumstances. Sample as much as you can manage without getting ill; after all, it's delicious home cooking that you won't find every day. Food is a matter of pride in Singapore. The faster you learn its place and importance in the people's heart, the easier it will be in the long run! Celebrations such as Hari Raya, Chinese New Year and Deepavali serve as a showcase for a family's culinary skills. If at all possible, when you know you will be attending one of these celebrations, plan accordingly and arrive with a bit of an appetite. On the other hand, don't be ravenous and eat an unsightly amount! The custom is to taste everything in small amounts since the typical Malay will usually visit several homes in one day, thereby having more than a full share by day end. The more compliments you give and the more you enjoy the food, the better you will be in your hostess' eyes. Be generous and sincere. Refusing food flat out is not appropriate. Take and taste whatever you can and next time, go to the open house first, then lunch!

SITUATION 3

You are in a large department store and need assistance in finding a particular item. The first saleslady you approach says, "Just wait a while," and motions for you to sit. After just a few minutes, she returns and leads you down the aisle to another item, not exactly what you wanted. You:

Ⓐ Say, "Never mind, thank you" and walk around until you do happen to find what you are looking for in another section.

Ⓑ Say "Thank you" and storm off, thinking what a waste of time!

Ⓒ Say "Thank you", keep explaining what it is you want, and summon the manager to help.

Comments

Through experience and perseverance, I would say reply **Ⓐ** is the best approach. Of course, communication is the major problem but having that service-oriented mentality is not that easy to come by. Take things in stride and don't be put off by the popular expression, 'just wait a while' (or sometimes 'wait, ah'). Coming from the West, this phrase implies that it will take a long time and just sit back and relax. The reality is that it usually only takes a minute or two. And using the 'never mind' in your response is actually speaking local Singlish; it is not rude but the equivalent of 'its okay'. That's the good news; but don't expect to have your hand held as you are shown precisely what you are looking for. Learn to enjoy the 'hunt' and ask around as much as necessary. Chances are you will find your item where and when you least expect it.

SITUATION 4

It's your child's birthday and you have organised a barbecue and pool party at your apartment complex. Wouldn't it be fun for the kids to set up a sprinkler on the lawn so they could continue to play? You approach the management office and get a clear 'no' after taking it one step up the hierarchy ladder.

Ⓐ This isn't the first disagreement you have had with your condo's management office; you decide to move out.

Ⓑ You do it anyway but the security guards approach you during the party and ask you to remove it. You oblige.

Ⓒ Well, at least you tried! Rules are rules and they are for the best although you certainly do not agree with many of them.

Comments

This situation may seem a little silly but it's here to illustrate the point that Singaporeans have many rules and the overwhelming majority of people do not question them or test them. This can become especially frustrating at times if you come from a more 'creative thinking' country but rules and abiding by them are the norm. The best response is **Ⓒ**. You are being sensitive to their way of doing things but have at least tried to bring in some new thinking! Not to discourage you from trying, because you may be surprised and get your way. Purposely breaking the rules will only cause more problems so do as the locals do and be respectful of authorities and the rules.

SITUATION 5

You are at the grocery store with your family in tow and while waiting in line to pay, an elderly lady is smiling at your young daughter and son. She is speaking to them in her local language with a few words of English. She then pulls out two sweets from her purse and offers them to the children. You:

Ⓐ Say "No, thank you. The children do not eat sweets." and refuse to accept them.

Ⓑ Make sure the children respond with a 'thank you, Auntie' and allow them to enjoy the treats.

⊙ Say "thank you, they will have them after lunch" and keep them in your purse for later.

Comments

The best reply is **❸** since you are responding with the same good will that was intended by the Auntie. Refusing to accept the sweets would be taken as an insult by a local person, since there is no harm intended. Here, children are prized and given much attention—they will be played with by the waiters, chased around by the shop attendants and given sweets everywhere. Not only do the locals love children but foreign children are of even more interest! Expect to receive all kinds of comments, questions and observations; some may be surprisingly blunt and forward but the comments are always well-intentioned and just plain curious.

SITUATION 6

A local friend has taken you out to a Chinese seafood restaurant for dinner. Among the dishes ordered are deep-fried tiger prawns with oats and the national favourite, chilli crabs. The prawns come complete with the heads and shells while the crabs are chopped into pieces but the pincers look like they are mostly in tact. You are also given a bowl of rice, a side plate, spoon and chopsticks, which you are not very adept with. Your friend puts a large prawn, a crab pincer and small portions of other dishes onto your side plate and urges you to eat, indicating that you should try the chilli sauce from the crab dish on your rice. What do you do?

❶ Use the chopsticks as best you can to tackle the rice and food on the side plate. However, you refuse to eat the prawn and crab, not being able to handle them with the chopsticks.

❷ Ask for another plate and a set of fork and spoon, then transfer the rice onto the plate. You put a little bit of sauce onto your rice and then use your fingers to tackle the prawn and crab.

Ⓒ You gamely attack the prawn and crab with your hands and, since it is more convenient, use your fingers to take handfuls of rice from the bowl the to eat with the other dishes.

Comments

While there is really no hard and fast rules when it comes to eating in a Chinese restaurant, there are certain things to keep in mind. While your friend will appreciate your efforts to use chopsticks, he or she may not be so happy to see that you have left the choicest part of the meal behind. Prawns (the tiger ones in particular) and crabs are normally some of the most expensive items on the menu so you should make the effort to try them. In a seafood restaurant, you are within your limits to use your hands if you order dishes where the food comes with shells, so go ahead and get them dirty. Chances are, everyone else at the table will be doing the same. If you really don't like the head of the prawn, you can peel that off and leave it to one side. And no, you're not expected to eat the prawn shell, although you're welcome to try if you're game. If the prawns have been deep-fried, they may actually be rather tasty. If you have problems getting to the meat in the crab pincer, ask for help. The restaurant will either provide a nutcracker or a small hammer for you to crack the shell. You will then be able to remove the meat.

Using your fingers in this situation is fine; using them to eat everything might not be wrong but it would certainly raise a number of eyebrows, especially if you are taking rice from the bowl. If you are hesitant about dirtying the chopsticks and spoons with your hands after they have been handling your food, don't be. This is part of eating out at a seafood place and you will soon notice your friend alternating between using his or her hands and the cutlery. By the way, these days, there is nothing wrong with asking for Western crockery and cutlery especially if you haven't quite mastered the art of using chopsticks and do not want to embarrass yourself. You may be comforted to know that many of the younger Singaporean Chinese will do this to as most do not use chopsticks at home. So, yes, **Ⓑ** is the best choice.

SITUATION 7

The Mid-Autumn Festival is a week away and one of your suppliers has kindly presented three boxes of moon cakes to be shared among your staff, something they do every year. The boxes were given through one of your staff, someone who they deal with on a regular basis, who leaves it in the common area for everyone in the office. By the time you find out about it, the staff has already finished one box.

Ⓐ Leave it be as the gift was a token of good will from your supplier and join your staff for a piece of moon cake. The next time you meet a representative from the supplier's company, you say a word of thanks.

Ⓑ Kick up a fuss as the boxes should have been presented to you. Besides, how do you know this was not a bribe?

Ⓒ Speak to the employee the boxes were given to and ask why it was given, whether they expect anything in return and what the supplier hopes to achieve.

Comments

It would be very easy to blow this whole situation out of proportion. The best response is **Ⓐ** as token gifts such as these are fairly common and the supplier is probably someone who has been doing business with your company for quite a while. Unless you have good reason to doubt their intentions, just take it for what is it: a token of good will. This means that if you question your staff too much about it (**Ⓒ**), he or she may feel that something is amiss. The person may not say anything to your face but will definitely speak to his or her colleagues about it. This person may start to question whether he or she did something wrong by accepting the gift or if he or she is being penalised in some way. This person may also tell the supplier what happened and that might create problems where there was none. Kicking up a fuss (**Ⓑ**) would be melodramatic on your part. There may be a number of reasons why the present was not given directly to you. One could be that the gift is meant to be shared by the entire team of people the supplier does business with and is a token from one company to another, not from one top management to another. Another reason could be that the person delivering the gift may think it inappropriate to hand the gift to you as he or she is not of the same business status. You can rest assured that if it was something important, it would have been someone of the same business status as you who would have delivered the gift. If that happens, especially if it is out of the blue, then you might like to think about whether there was some ulterior motive.

SITUATION 8

You and the family decide to have dinner at the *cze cha* stall close to where you live. This is your first time at this stall, even though you have dined at other *cze cha* outlets before and know what to order. While waiting for the food to be served, your youngest child decides that he wants some *roti prata* from the neighbouring self-serve Indian Muslim stall so you order two. The *cze cha* stall finally serves your dishes and you are dismayed that there are no serving spoons. What do you do?

Ⓐ Immediately ask for serving spoons from the *cze cha* stall, even though they may give you annoyed looks.

Ⓑ Walk over to the Indian Muslim stall and take some spoons from them.

Ⓒ Decide that if the locals have lived so long dipping their cutlery into the communal dish that there can't be anything wrong. You grin, bear it and use your individual cutlery to get portions of food for yourself.

Comments

There is nothing really wrong with **Ⓒ** as Chinese Singaporeans do not really have a habit of using serving spoons. This is changing, but very slowly. Most *cze cha* will provide serving spoons but there may be a few who either forget or just don't bother. Feel free to ask them for extra spoons. Just develop a thick skin and ignore their annoyed looks. **Ⓑ** is a definite no-no. Even when eating the *prata*, it is best you use your hands (which is allowed) or the Indian stall's own cutlery. As most *cze cha* stalls serve pork, it is not right to use that stall's cutlery as it will come into contact with the plate which is meant to serve *halal* food. While most stall owners in this position are not that particular, other Muslims may be around and may not be too happy with this. If you don't want to keep changing cutlery or if you want to eat the prata with other dishes from the *cze cha* stall, the best thing to do is transfer the *prata* onto a plate from the *cze cha*, and returning the '*halal*' plate straightaway. That way you don't get mixed up.

DO'S AND DON'TS

DO'S

- Remember that the concept of group, harmony and mutual security are more important than that of the individual.
- Always be respectful of elders, treating them with utmost respect and courtesy.
- Compliment freely on children and family; Singaporeans love it.
- Eating together is a common form of socialising, so don't pass up too many invitations of sharing a coffee or lunch if you want to make friends.
- Be discreet and indirect (for instance, never in front of other people) when showing disapproval as too much confrontation could cause a person to 'lose face', the worst insult that could happen.
- Be prepared to queue up for most things, especially at a food stall or taxi stand. People will be offended if you jump in front of them or do not stand in line at all.
- Address an older woman as 'Auntie' or an older man 'Uncle'. This is an informal form of addressing someone who is middle-aged or older and is the acceptable form for children to address adults in general.
- Be aware of the different eating habits and customs. If inviting a mixed group to your home or dining out make sure the selection is large enough to please everyone. Vegetables and fish are considered common ground.
- Remember to remove shoes before entering a private residence and especially temples and mosques.
- When taking food from a communal dish, use serving spoons. Ask for extra spoons if no serving spoons have been provided.
- Make an effort to eat as the locals do by using your hands or chopsticks as appropriate.
- An additional 10 per cent service charge is commonly placed on bills; if the service was exceptional, it is acceptable to leave a few dollars more, discreetly on the table, never openly.

DON'TS

- Don't rely heavily on the spoken word. Trust non-verbal messages more (tone of voice, eye contact, silence, posture, giggling tends to imply nervousness).

- Don't extend your hand immediately to greet a more traditional Malay or Indian woman. Wait to see if they do so first, or a simply smile, nod or '*salaam*' (bowing the head, for the Malay) is usually sufficient.

- Don't use your left hand for most social interactions and gift-giving. It is taboo to use your left hand to handle food that you put in your mouth. Although the Chinese do not have a problem with this, it is good practice to stick to only eating with your right hand while in Asia.

- Don't expect people to open the gifts immediately. The custom is to set it aside and open it later in private.

- Don't point your feet at anyone. Feet are considered unclean and the sole of one's shoe should never be pointed towards someone when sitting.

- Don't point fingers at anyone. Learn to point with your knuckle or turn your hand palm face up and fold in your thumb.

- Don't touch a person's or child's head. The head is considered sacred.

- Don't stand too close to people when conversing. Spatial distances vary among cultures and genders. Usually standing at one arm's length is acceptable.

- Avoid discussing religion or politics. Don't criticise the government or speak badly about the different races and religions.

- Don't debate, correct or disagree with an older person or superior in public. You will not only lose their respect but also that of anyone who witnessed the confrontation. This applies even if you are the boss in a company of Singaporeans.

- When using a serving spoon, don't let it touch anything on your individual plate.

- Don't use cutlery from a *halal* stall to pick up food on non-*halal* food.
- Don't stick chopsticks straight up in a bowl of rice as this is reminiscent of Chinese funeral rites. It is also impolite to transfer food from one pair of chopsticks to another.
- Don't serve other people unless you are certain of their dietary customs and rituals.
- Don't immediately address people by what you would think is acceptable. It is best to ask either directly what they would prefer to be called or ask a colleague.
- Do not show anger or emotions or raise your voice. Remain disciplined and in control.
- Avoid public displays of affection.

GLOSSARY

While it is entirely possible to survive in Singapore without learning to speak any of the local languages or dialects, some may like to know a few words that will help them get by. This list is by no means exhaustive but contains some of the more common words and phrases. The Mandarin words are given in Hanyu Pinyin while Malay and Tamil are standard English transliterations. For a start, you might like to ask a local friend or colleague to help you out with the pronunciations.

USEFUL WORDS AND PHRASES

English	Malay	Mandarin	Tamil
Hello	Hello	—	*Vanakkam*
How are you?	*Apa khabar?*	*Ni hao ma?*	*Nalamaa? Eppadi irukkireenga?*
Fine, thanks	*Baik, terima kasih*	*Hao, xiaxia*	*Nalam, nalla irukkiren*
OK	OK	*Hao*	*Parava illai*
Good morning	*Selamat pagi*	*Zao, ni hao* ('Morning, you are fine?')	*Vanakkam*
Good afternoon	*Selamat petang* (if at night, use *selamat sejahtera*)	Not a usual Chinese greeting. They would just say, '*Ni hao*'.	*Vanakkam*
Good evening	*Selamat petang*	As above. Use *Ni hao*	*Vanakkam*
Good night	*Selamat malam*	*Wan an*	*Vanakkam*

English	Malay	Mandarin	Tamil
Good bye	*Selamat tinggal*	*Zai jian*	*Poi varuga* or *poi varugiren* †
See you later/ again	*Jumpa lagi*	*Dai hui-er jian*	*Piragu paarppom* or *piragu ungalai paarkkiren* †
Take care	—	*Bao zhong*	*Kavanama* or *paarthuk-kollunga* †
Yes	*Ya*	*Shi*	*Aama*
No	*Tidak*	*Bu she*	*Illai*
Maybe	*Mungkin*	*Ke nen*	*Irukkalaam*
Please	*Tolong*	*Qing*	*Thayavu seithu* or *anbu koornthu*
Thank you	*Terima kasih*	*Xia xia*	*Nandri*
Thank you very much	*Terima kasih banyak banyak*	*Duo xia*	*romba nandri* or *mikka nandri*
Sorry	*Maaf*	*Duei bu qi*	*Varunthugiren*
How much is that?	*Berapa harganya*	*Na duo shao qian?*	*Ithu evvaalavu?*
I	*Aku*	*Wo*	*Naan*
Me	*Saya*	*Wo*	*Ennai, enakku*
My	*Saya*	*Wo de*	*Ennudaia*
You	*Engkau* (formal)/ *awak* (informal)	*Ni/ ning* (respectful term, usually for someone older)	*Nee/ neengal* (subject); *unnai/ ungalai* (object)

† When more than one word appears this is because the form will vary according to the speaker's relationship to the person spoken to.

English	Malay	Mandarin	Tamil
Your	*Engkau* (formal)/ *awak* (informal)	*Ni de/ ning de*	*Unnudaia* or *ungaludaia* †
Yours	*Engkau* (formal)/ *awak* (informal)	*Ni de/ ning de*	*Unnudaiathu* or *ungaludaiathu* †
He	*Dia*	*Ta* *	*Avan* or *avar* †
Him	*Dia*	*Ta*	*Avanai/ avarai* or *avanukku/ avarukku* †
His	*Dia punya*	*Ta de*	*Avanudaia* or *avarudaia* †
She	*Dia*	*Ta* *	*Aval* or *avar* †
Her	*Dia*	*Ta*	*Avaludaia/ avalukku/ avalai* †
Hers	*Dia punya*	*Ta de*	*Avaludaiathu/ avarudaiatau* †
It	—	*Ta* *	*Athu*
Its	—	*Ta de*	*Athanudaia*
We	*Kita*	*Wo men*	*Naam* (including 'you'); *naangal* (excluding 'you')
Us	*Kami*	*Wo men*	*Namakku; engalukku*
Our	*Kami*	*Wo men de*	*Nammudaia, engaludaia*

* While the pronunciation and tone is the same for these three words, the Chinese character is different.

English	Malay	Mandarin	Tamil
They	*Mereka*	*Ta men*	*Avargal, avaigal*
Them	*Mereka*	*Ta men*	*Avargalukku/ avargalai* (humans); *avaigalukku/ avaigalai* (non-humans)
Theirs	*Mereka punya*	*Ta men de*	*Avargaludaiathu (vai)* (humans); *avaigaludaiathu (vai)* (non-humans)
Man	*Lelaki*	*Nan*	*Manithar* or *manithar* † *aan* (male)
Woman	*Wanita*	*Nu*	*Maathu/ pen*
Boy	*Lekiki*	*Nan hai*	*Paiyan, siruvan*
Girl	*Perempuan*	*Nu hai*	*Pen/ sirumi*
Husband	*Suami*	*Zhang fu/ lao kong*	*Kanavar*
Wife	*Isteri*	*Lao puo*	*Manaivi*
Delicious	*Sedap*	*Hao chi*	*Nalla suvai*
Good	*Bagus*	*Hao*	*Nalla*
Bad	*Tidak bagus*	*Bu hao/ Huai*	*Ketta*
Beautiful	*Cantik*	*Mei*	*Azhagaana*

† When more than one word appears this is because the form will vary according to the speaker's relationship to the person spoken to.

English	Malay	Mandarin	Tamil
Interesting	*Menarik*	*You qu*	*Inimaiana, suvaiyaana* (used with respect to art, dance, food)
Strange	*Ganjil/ aneh*	*Qi guai*	*Puthia, pazhakkap-padaatha*
Big	*Besar*	*Da*	*Periya*
Small	*Kecil*	*Xiao*	*Siriya*
How much?	*Berapa harga?*	*Duo shao?*	*Evvalavu*
Cheap	*Murah*	*Pian yi*	*Malivu*
Expensive	*Mahal*	*Gui*	*Vilai uyarntha*
Early	*Awal*	*Zao*	*Seekkiram*
Late	*Lambat*	*Che*	*Thaamatham*
Fast	*Laju*	*Kuai*	*Vegam*
Slow	*Perlahan*	*Man*	*Medhuva*
Very	*Sangat*	*Hen*	*Migavum* (*romba* also colloquial)
Where is...?	*Mana...?*	*... jai na li?*	*Enge?*
Left	*Kiri*	*Zuo*	*Idathu*
Right	*Kanan*	*You*	*Valathu*
Not far (from here)	*Tidak jauh*	*Bu yuan*	*Romba thooram illai*
Post office	*Pejabat pos*	*You zhen ju*	*Anjal nilayam*
Police post/ station	*Balai polis*	*Jing cha ju*	*Kaaval nilayam*
Fire station	*Balai bomba*	*Huo che zhan*	*Thee anaippu nilayam*
MRT station	*Stesen MRT*	*Di tie zhan*	*MRT nilayam*

English	Malay	Mandarin	Tamil
Bus	Bas	Ba shi	Bus or perunthu
Taxi	Teksi	De shi	Taxi or vaadagai kaar
Shop	Kedai	Dian	Kadai
Bakery/cakery	Kedai roti/kedai kek	Gao bing dian	Roti thayarikum idam
Wet market	Pasar basah	Ba sha	Santhai
Supermarket	Pasaraya	Chao ji shi chang	Perangaadi or supermarket
Bookshop	Kedai buku	Shu dian	Puthagakkadai
Library	Perpustakaan	Tu shu guan	Nool nilayam
Bank	Bank	Yin hang	Vangi
Doctor	Doktor	Yi shen	Maruthuvar or doctor
Clinic	Klinik	Zhen suo	Clinic
Pharmacy	Kedai ubat	Yao fang	Marunthagam or marunthu kadai
Toilet	Tandas	Ce suo	Kazhivarai or toilet
Help (emergency)	Pertolongan cemas	Jiu ming!	Udhavi
Help (assistance)	Tolong/bantu	Bang mang	Udhavi
Can you speak English?	Awak boleh berbahasa Inggeris?	Ni huai jiang ying yu ma?	Ungalukku aangilam pesa theriyuma?
No chilli	Tidak manu chili	Bu yao la jiao	Uraippu vendaam

English	Malay	Mandarin	Tamil
I'm vegetarian	—	*Wo shi chi su de* or *Who shi su shi zhe*	*Naan saivam*

NUMBERS

English	Malay	Mandarin	Tamil
One	*Satu*	*Yi*	*Ondru*
Two	*Dua*	*Er*	*Irandu*
Three	*Tiga*	*San*	*Moondru*
Four	*Empat*	*Si*	*Naanku*
Five	*Lima*	*Wu*	*Ainthu*
Six	*Enam*	*Liu*	*Aaru*
Seven	*Tujuh*	*Qi*	*Ezhu*
Eight	*Lapan*	*Ba*	*Ettu*
Nine	*Sembilan*	*Jiu*	*Onpathu*
Ten	*Sepuloh*	*Shi*	*Pathu*
Eleven	*Sebelas*	*Shi-yi*	*Pathinondru*
Twelve	*Dua belas*	*Shi-er*	*Pannirandu*
Thirteen	*Tiga belas*	*Shi-san*	*Pathinmoondru*
Fourteen	*Empat belas*	*Shi-si*	*Pathinaanku*
Fifteen	*Limas belas*	*Shi-wu*	*Pathinainthu*
Sixteen	*Enam belas*	*Shi-liu*	*Pathinaaru*
Seventeen	*Tujuh belas*	*Shi-qi*	*Pathinezhu*
Eighteen	*Lapan belas*	*Shi-ba*	*Pathinettu*
Nineteen	*Sembilan belas*	*Shi-jiu*	*Pathonpathu*
Twenty	*Dua puloh*	*Er-shi*	*Irupathu*
Thirty	*Tiga puloh*	*San-shi*	*Muppaathu*
Forty	*Empat puloh*	*Si-shi*	*Naarpathu*
Fifty	*Lima puloh*	*Wu-shi*	*Aimbathu*
Sixty	*Enam puloh*	*Liu-shi*	*Arupathu*

English	Malay	Mandarin	Tamil
Seventy	Tujuh puloh	Qi-shi	Ezhupathu
Eighty	Lapan puloh	Ba-shi	Enbathu
Ninety	Sembilan puloh	Jiu-shi	Thonnooru
One hundred	Satu ratus	Yi-bai	Nooru
Two hundred	Dua ratus	Liang-bai	Irunooru
Three hundred	Tiga ratus	San-bai	Munnooru
One thousand	Satu ribu	Yi-qian	Aayiram
Ten thousand	Sepuloh ribu	Wan	pathayiram
One hundred thousand	Satu rauts ribu	Shi-wan	Latcham
One million	Satu juta	Bai-wan	Pathu latcham
One billion	Satu billion	Wan-yi	Nooru kodi

DAYS OF THE WEEK

English	Malay	Mandarin	Tamil
Monday	Isnin	Xing qi yi/ li bai yi	Thingal
Tuesday	Selasa	Xing qi er/ li bai er	Sevvai
Wednesday	Rabu	Xing qi san/ li bai san	Puthan
Thursday	Khamis	Xing qi si/ li bai si	Viyaazhan
Friday	Jumaat	Xing qi wu/ li bai wu	Velli

English	Malay	Mandarin	Tamil
Saturday	*Sabtu*	*Xing qi liu/ li bai liu*	*Sani*
Sunday	*Ahad*	*Xing qi tian/ li bai tian*	*Gnayiru*

MONTHS OF THE YEAR

The months of the year are the same in Tamil as they are in English.

English	Malay	Mandarin
January	*Januari*	*Yi yue*
February	*Februari*	*Er yue*
March	*March*	*San yue*
April	*April*	*Si yue*
May	*Mei*	*Wu yue*
June	*Jun*	*Liu yue*
July	*Julai*	*Qi yue*
August	*Ogos*	*Ba yue*
September	*September*	*Jiu yue*
October	*Oktober*	*Shi yue*
November	*November*	*Shi-yi yue*
December	*Desember*	*Shi-er yue*

358

RESOURCE GUIDE

Numbers that begin with '6' are landlines while those which begin with '8' or '9' are mobile numbers. 1-800 numbers are toll-free. When calling within Singapore, you need not include the country code of 65.

EMERGENCY NUMBERS

Police	999 (toll-free)
Emergencies/Ambulance/Fire	995 (toll-free)
Non-emergency ambulance	1777
Police Hotline	(65) 6225-0000
Traffic Police	(65) 6547-0000
Pet Ambulance and Transport	(65) 6552-2222
AAS Emergency Road Service	(65) 6748-9911
Local call enquiry	100
International operator	104

USEFUL WEBSITES

- ExpatChoice Relocation Guide
  Website: http://www.expatchoice.com/relocation_guide/useful_resources/useful_numbers.htm
- Uniquely Singapore
  Website: http://www.visitsingapore.com
  An excellent website that should answer many questions that a tourist will have about Singapore.
- Singapore Infomap
  Website: http://www.sg
  A very thorough website that will give you information on just about anything you need to know about living in Singapore, including details and links for business, education, hotels and entertainment.
- Singapore Expats
  Website: http://www.singaporeexpats.com
  A relocation and housing portal for expatriates in Singapore, with a large range of topics and tips.
- Expat Singapore
  Website: http://www.expatsingapore.com

Another good website that will guide expatriates on settling in Singapore.

- Enter Singapore
  Website: http://www.entersingapore.info
  Yet another good website with lots of useful information for the new person in Singapore.
- Can.com.sg
  Website: http://www.can.com.sg
  A website for locals and expatriates with an extremely helpful listing of places in Singapore, complete with maps on how to get there.
* Singapore Government Information
  Website: http://www.gov.sg
  The official Singapore government website.
- Singapore Government Directory interactive (SGDi)
  Website: http://app.sgdi.gov.sg
  A Singapore government directory interactive website, with links to the different ministries, organs of states, statutory boards and educational institutions and others.
- Singapore Tourism Board
  Tourism Court, 1 Orchard Spring Lane
  Tel: (65) 6736-6622
  Website: http://www.stb.gov.sg

EMBASSIES

- Ministry of Foreign Affairs Singapore
  Website: http://www.mfa.gov.sg/internet
  Click 'Foreign Missions Accredited to Singapore' and choose the country accordingly.

HEALTH CARE

- Ministry of Health
  College of Medicine Building, 16 College Road
  Tel: (65) 6325-9220
  Website: http://www.moh.gov.sg
- Singapore Medicine
  Website: http://www.singaporemedicine.com
  Provides you with information on the medical and health facilities available in Singapore.

- National Healthcare Group
  Tel: (65) 6471-8900
  Website: http://www.nhg.com.sg/
- Singhealth
  11 Third Hospital Avenue, #07-00 SNEC Building
  Tel: (65) 6225-0488; fax: (65) 6557-2138
  Email: www.singhealth.com.sg
  Website: http://www.singhealth.com.sg/

Hospitals

The following are some of the more well-known hospitals in Singapore. A full listing can be found at:
    http://www.moh.gov.sg/corp/est/hospitals/index.do

Public Hospitals

- Singapore General Hospital
  Outram Road
  Tel: (65) 6222-3322
  Website: http://www.sgh.com.sg
- National University Hospital
  5 Lower Kent Ridge Road
  Tel: (65) 6779-5555
  Website: http://www.nuh.com.sg
- Tan Tock Seng Hospital
  11 Jalan Tan Tock Seng
  Tel : (65) 6256-6011
  Website: http://www.ttsh.com.sg/asp/index.asp
- Changi General Hospital
  2 Simei Street 3
  Tel: (65) 6788-8833
  Website: http://www.cgh.com.sg
- K K Women's and Children's Hospital
  100 Bukit Timah Road
  Tel: (65) 6293-4044
  Website: http://www.kkh.com.sg
- Alexandra Hospital
  378 Alexandra Road
  Tel: (65) 6472-2000
  Website: http://www.alexhosp.com.sg

- Ang Mo Kio Community Hospital
  17 Ang Mo Kio Ave 9
  Tel: (65) 6453-8033
  Website: http://www.amkh.com.sg

Private Hospitals
- Mount Elizabeth Hospital
  3 Mount Elizabeth
  Tel : (65) 6737-2666
  Website: http://www.mountelizabeth.com.sg
- East Shore Hospital
  321 Joo Chiat Place
  Tel: (65) 6344-7588; 24-hour Information Service Hotline:
  (65) 6340-8688
  Website: http://www.eastshore.com.sg
- Gleneagles Hospital
  6A Napier Road
  Tel: (65) 6473-7222
  Website: http://www.ghl.parkway.com.sg
- Mount Alvernia Hospital
  820 Thomson Road
  Tel: (65) 6347-6688
  Website: http://www.mtalvernia-hospital.org
- Raffles Hospital
  585 North Bridge Road
  Tel: (65) 6311-1111
  Website: http://www.raffleshospital.com

Clinics and Medical Centres
Polyclinics are government-owned medical centres that provide general and specialist services. These are conveniently located in all the housing estates and you can get a full listing at:

http://polyclinic.singhealth.com.sg

A full list of clinics (general and specialist) and dental surgeries around the island can be obtained at:

http://www.moh.gov.sg/corp/est/clinics/index.do

ACCOMMODATION
Housing
- IT Realtor
  Website: http://www.itrealtor.com/
- Housing and Development Board
  HDB Hub, 480 Lorong 6 Toa Payoh
  Tel: (65) 6490-1111
  Website: http://www.hdb.gov.sg
  Linked website: http://hsg.ecitizen.gov.sg

Utilities
- Public Utilities Board (PUB)
  111 Somerset Road #15-01
  Tel: (65) 6235-8888
  Website: http://www.pub.gov.sg
- Power Supply
  111 Somerset Road, #10-01 Singapore Power Building
  Tel: (65) 6823-8888; fax: (65) 6823-8188
  Email: corpcomms@singaporepower.com.
  Website: http://www.singaporepower.com.sg/

Public Utility Repair Numbers	
Electricity	1800-778-6666
Gas	1800-298-8711
Water	1800-284-6600

- SembCorp Environmental Management
  Tel: 1800-278-6135
  Website: http://www.gowaste.com.sg
- Colex Holdings
  Tel: (65) 6268-7711; fax: (65) 6264-1219
  Email: wastemgt@colex.com.sg
  Website: http://www.colex.com.sg/
- FME Onyx
  Website: http://www.fmeonyx.com/

TRANSPORTATION

- Land Transport Authority
  1 Hampshire Road
  Tel: 1800-2255-582
  Website: http://www.lta.gov.sg
- Streetdirectory.com
  Website: http://sg.streetdirectory.com
  The online directory that will show you how to get to any place in Singapore.
- SMRT
  Tel: 1800-336-8900
  Website: http://www.smrt.com.sg
  SMRT is a major corporation than provides train, bus and taxi services. Search the specific service for the information you want. (TIBS is part of SMRT).
- SBS Transit
  Tel: 1800-225-5663
  Website: http://www.sbstransit.com.sg
  The leading bus operator in Singapore and also the operator of the North-East Line (NEL) of the MRT.

Taxis

- CityCab
  Tel: (65) 6552-2222
  Website: http://www.citycab.com.sg/index.htm
- Comfort Transportation/Yellow-Top Cab
  Tel: (65) 6552-1111
  Website: http://www.comfort-transportation.com.sg
- SMRT/TIBS
  Tel: (65) 6555-8888
  Website: http://www.smrttaxis.com.sg
- Premier Taxis
  Tel: (65) 6363-6888
  Website: http://www.premiertaxi.com

TELECOMMUNICATIONS

- Singtel
  Mobile lines   tel: 1626
  Residential/commercial lines   tel: 1609

Internet services   tel: 1610
Website: http://www.singtel.com
- M1
Mobile services   tel: 1627
Enterprise services   tel: 1622
Website: http://www.m1.com.sg
- Starhub
Tel: 1633
Website: http://www.starhub.com

MONEY MATTERS
- Ministry of Finance
100 High Street, #10-01 The Treasury
Tel: 1800-226-0806
Website: http://app.mof.gov.sg
- Monetary Authority of Singapore
10 Shenton Way, MAS Building
Tel: (65) 6225-5577
Website: http://www.mas.gov.sg

Banks
- Development Bank of Singapore (DBS)
6 Shenton Way, DBS Building Tower One
Tel: (65) 6878-8888
Website: http://www.dbs.com/sg
- POSB
Banking (in Singapore)   Tel: 1800-111-1111
Banking (from overseas)   Tel: (65) 6327-2265
Credit cards (in Singapore)   Tel: 1800-835-1234
Credit cards (from overseas)   Tel: (65) 6835-1234
Website: http://www.dbs.com/posb/
- United Overseas Bank (UOB)
80 Raffles Place, UOB Plaza
Tel: (65) 6533-9898
Website: http://www.uob.com.sg
- Citibank Singapore
3 Temasek Avenue #12-00, Centennial Tower
Tel: (65) 6225-5221
Website: http://www.citibank.com.sg

- Hongkong and Shanghai Bank Corporation Ltd (HSBC)
  21 Collyer Quay #14-01, HSBC Building
  Tel: (65) 6472-2669
  Website: http://www.hsbc.com.sg
- Overseas-Chinese Banking Corporation Ltd (OCBC)
  65 Chulia Street #29-00, OCBC Centre
  Tel: (65) 6535-7222
  Website: http://www.ocbc.com.sg
- Standard Chartered Bank
  6 Battery Road, 3rd Floor Priority Banking Centre
  Tel: (65) 6530-3238
  Website: http://www.standardchartered.com.sg

Taxes

- Inland Revenue Authority of Singapore
  55 Newton Road Revenue House
  Tel: (65) 6356-8233
  Website: http://www.iras.gov.sg

EDUCATION

- Ministry of Education
  1 North Buona Vista Drive
  Tel: (65) 6872-2220
  Website: http://www.moe.gov.sg

For a list of junior colleges, polytechnics, secondary and primary schools in Singapore, go to:

http://app.sgdi.gov.sg/index.asp

Click 'Schools' or 'Junior Colleges' under the 'Others' category. You can also go to:

http://www.moe.gov.sg/schdiv/sis/

to find out more about the schools and generate comparative lists of schools based on specified parameters.

Institutes of Higher Learning

- National University of Singapore (NUS)
  21 Lower Kent Ridge Road
  Tel: (65) 6516-6666
  Website: http://www.nus.edu.sg

- Nanyang Technological University (NTU)
  Nanyang Avenue
  Tel: (65) 6791-1744
  Website: http://www.ntu.edu.sg
- Singapore Management University (SMU)
  81 Victoria Street
  Tel: (65) 6828-0100
  Website: http://www.smu.edu.sg
- SIM University (UniSIM)
  461 Clementi Road
  Tel: (65) 6248-9777
  Website: http://www.unisim.edu.sg
- National Institute of Education (NIE)
  Nanyang Technological University, 1 Nanyang Walk
  Tel: (65) 6790-3888
  Website: http://www.nie.edu.sg

International Schools

Singapore Education (http://www.singaporeedu.gov.sg/htm/index.htm) is a very good website for people intending to study in Singapore. It provides you with information on the local and international academic institutions available and explains the Singapore education system in detail. It also gives you useful tips on living and studying in Singapore, including transportation, telecommunications, accommodation etc. Contact Singapore also has a full list of international schools in Singapore. Check out the website at:

> http://www.contactsingapore.org.sg/
> moving_schooling_international.shtml

- Singapore American School
  40 Woodlands Street 41
  Tel: (65) 6363-3403
  Website: http://www.sas.edu.sg
- Australian International School
  1 Lorong Chuan
  Tel: (65) 6883-5155
  Website: http://www.ais.com.sg
- Canadian International School (Singapore)
  5 Toh Tuck Road

Tel: (65) 6467-1732
Website: http://www.cis.edu.sg
- Chatsworth International School
  37 Emerald Hill Road
  Tel: (65) 6737-5955
  Website: http://www.chatsworth-international.com
- Eton House International School
  51 Broadrick Road
  Tel: (65) 6346-6922
  Website: http://www.etonhouse.com.sg/
- ISS International School
  21 Preston Road
  Tel: (65) 6475-4188
  Website: http://www.iss.edu.sg
- Lycee Francais De Singapour
  3000 Ang Mo Kio Ave 3
  Tel: (65) 6488-1160
  Website: http://www.lyceefrancais.edu.sg
- Tanglin Trust School
  95 Portsdown Road
  Tel: (65) 6778-0771
  Website: http://www.tts.edu.sg
- Overseas Family School
  25 Paterson Road
  Tel: (65) 6738-0211
  Website: http://www.ofs.edu.sg
- United World College of South East Asia
  1207 Dover Road
  Tel: (65) 6775-5344
  Website: http://www.uwcsea.edu.sg
- The Japanese School (Secondary)
  201 West Coast Road
  Tel: (65) 6779-7355
  Website: http://www.sjs.edu.sg/English/e_index.html
- Global Indian International School
  1 Mei Chin Road
  Tel: (65) 6479-1511
  Website: http://www.giissingapore.org

Private Schools

Look up the MOE website (http://www.moe.gov.sg/privatesch/) for a list of private schools in Singapore.

PLACES OF WORSHIP
Christian Churches

There are many Christian churches in Singapore and you can consult the *Yellow Pages* or Street Directory for a more comprehensive listing. Here, we list the main church of various denominations.

- Saint Andrew's Cathedral Church
  11 Saint Andrew's Road
  Tel: (65) 6337-6104
  Website: http://www.livingstreams.org.sg
- Wesley Methodist Church
  5 Fort Canning Road
  Tel: (65) 6336-1433
  Website: http://www.wesleymc.org
- Lutheran Church of Our Redeemer
  30 Duke's Road
  Tel: (65) 6466-4500, 6466-4559
  Website: http://www.lutheran.org.sg/
- Orchard Road Presbyterian Church
  3 Orchard Road
  Tel: (65) 6337-6681
  Website: http://www.orpc.org.sg/
- Calvary Baptist Church
  48 Wan Tho Avenue
  Tel: (65) 6289-3900
  Website: http://www.calvary.org.sg/
- Covenant Evangelical Free Church
  10 Jelapang Rd
  Tel: (65) 6892-6811
  Website: http://www.cefc.org.sg/
- Emmanuel Assembly of God
  165 Upper East Coast Road
  Tel: (65) 6445-5566
  Website: http://www.emmanuel.org.sg/

Chijmes Hall is a converted chapel which has been restored to retain much of its old architecture and charm.

- Cathedral of the Good Shepherd
  'A' Queen Street
  Tel: (65) 6337-2036
  For a complete list of Catholic churches in Singapore, see the official website for the Catholic church in Singapore:
  http://www.catholic.org.sg/

Chinese/Buddhist Temples

- Kong Meng San Phor Kark See Temple
  88 Bright Hill Road
  Tel: (65) 6453-4046, 6458-4454
- Tan Si Chong Su Temple
  15 Magazine Road
  Tel: (65) 6533-2880
- Thian Hock Keng
  158 Telok Ayer Street
  Tel: (65) 6423 461
- Lian Shan Shuang Lin Temple
  184E Jalan Toa Payoh
  Tel: (65) 6259-6924
- Sakaya Muni Buddha Gaya Temple
  366 Race Course Road
  Tel: (65) 6294-0714

Mosques

For complete list of mosques in Singapore, see:
http://cmsweb.mosque.org.sg

- Masjid Sultan
  3 Muscat Street
  Tel: (65) 6293-4405
  Website: http://www.mosque.org.sg/sultan/
- Masjid Abdul Gaffoor
  41 Dunlop Street
  Tel: (65) 6295-4209
- Masjid Hajjah Fatimah
  4001 Beach Road
  Tel: (65) 6297-2774

- Masjid Jamae Chulia
  218 South Bridge Road
  Tel: (65) 6221-4165

Hindu Temples
For complete list of Hindu temples in Singapore, see:
http://www.heb.gov.sg/

- Sri Mariamman Temple
  244 South Bridge Road
  Tel: (65) 6223-4064
- Sri Thendayuthapani Temple (Chettiar Temple)
  15 Tank Road
  Tel: (65) 6737-9393
- Sri Senpaga Vinayagar Temple
  27 Ceylon Road
  Tel: (65) 6345-3783

Others
- Maghain Aboth Synagogue
  24/26 Waterloo Street
  Tel: (65) 6337-2189
- Armenian Church
  60 Hill Street
  Tel: (65) 6334-0141
- Central Sikh Temple
  2 Towner Road
  Tel: (65) 6299-3855

ENTERTAINMENT AND LEISURE
Performance Centres
- The Esplanade: Theatres on the Bay
  1 Esplanade Drive
  Tel: (65) 6828-8222
  Website: http://www.esplanade.com
  Dubbed 'the Durian' by locals, the Esplanade is one of
  Singapore's most exciting performance arts venues, featuring
  music, theatre, dance and visual arts performances.
- Singapore Indoor Stadium
  2 Stadium Walk

Tel: (65) 6344-2660; fax: (65) 6344-5903
Website: http://www.sis.gov.sg/

- Kallang Theatre
  1 Stadium Walk
  Tel: (65) 6345-8488; fax: (65) 6344-2340
- University Cultural Centre
  c/o Centre of the Arts, NUS, 10 Kent Ridge Crescent
  Tel: (65) 6874-1224; fax: (65) 6874-1002
- Victoria Concert Hall
  11 Empress Place, Victorial Memorial Hall
  Tel: (65) 6338-1230; fax: (65) 6336-6382
- Victoria Theatre
  9 Empress Place
  Tel: (65) 6338-8283; fax: (65) 6339-5440
- The Substation
  45 Armenian Street
  Tel: (65) 6337-7535
  Website: http://www.substation.org
  Singapore's first independent contemporary arts centre.
- DBS Auditorium
  6 Shenton Way, DBS Building, Tower 1, 3rd Floor
  Tel: (65) 6224-9633; fax: (65) 6224-1920
- Jubilee Hall
  Raffles Hotel, 1 Beach Road
  Tel: (65) 6331-1732; fax: (65) 6337-0778

SISTIC

This is the largest ticketing service and handles a majority of the events staged in Singapore. It sells tickets to events ranging from pop concerts, musicals, theatre, family entertainment to sports.
Address: 2 Stadium Walk, #01-08 Singapore Indoor Stadium
Tel: (65) 6319-3299
Website: http://www.sistic.com.sg

Cinemas

- Golden Village
  Ticket hotline: 1900-912-1234
  Website: http://www.gv.com.sg

Provides information on movie show times, information, and online cinema ticket sales for all Golden Village cinemas in Singapore.

- Shaw Organisation
  Ticket Hotline: 6738-0555
  Website: http://www.shaw.com.sg
  A similar website featuring online cinema ticket sales for all Shaw cinemas.
- Eng Wah
  Ticket Hotline: 6836-9074
  Website: http://www.ewcinemas.com.sg
- Cathay Orgnisation
  Tel: 6235-1155
  Website: http://tickets.cathay.com.sg

Museums

- National Museum of Singapore
  93 Stamford Road
  Tel : (65) 6332-5642
  Website: http://www.nationalmuseum.sg
- Singapore Art Museum
  71 Bras Basah Road
  Tel : (65) 6332-3222
  Website: http://www.nhb.gov.sg/SAM
- Asian Civilisations Museum
  1 Empress Place
  Tel: (65) 6332-7798
  39 Armenian Street
  Tel: (65) 6332-3015
  Website: http://www.nhb.gov.sg/ACM

Library

- National Library Board
  100 Victoria Street
  Tel: (65) 6332-3133
  Website: http://www.nlb.gov.sg
  You can also access this website to find the library nearest to you.

Bookstores

- Times the Bookshop
  Website: http://www.timesone.com.sg
- Borders
  Tel: (65) 6235-7146
- Kinokuniya
  Website: http://www.kinokuniya.com.sg
- MPH Bookstores
  Website: http://www.mph.com.sg
- Select Books
  Website: http://www.selectbooks.com.sg/
- Popular Bookstores
  Website: http://www.popular.com.sg

CLUBS

- The American Club
  10 Claymore Hill
  Tel: (65) 6737-3411
  Website: http://www.amclub.org.sg
- The British Club
  73 Bukit Tinggi Road
  Tel: (65) 6467-4311
  Website: http://www.britishclub.org.sg
- The Hollandse Club (Dutch Club)
  22 Camden Park (off Adam Road)
  Tel: (65) 6464-5225
  Website: http://www.hollandseclub.org.sg
- The Swiss Club
  36 Swiss Club Road
  Tel: (65) 6466-3233
  Website: http://www.swissclub.org.sg
- The German Club (Deutsches Haus)
  61A Toh Tuck Road
  Tel: (65) 6467-8802
  Website: http://www.germanclub.org.sg
- The Tanglin Club
  5 Stevens Road
  Tel: (65) 67376011
  Website: http://www.tanglinclub.org.sg

- Singapore Polo Club
  80 Mount Pleasant Road
  Tel: (65) 6854-3999
  Website: http://www.singaporepoloclub.org
- Singapore Cricket Club
  A Connaught Drive
  Tel: (65) 6338-9271
  Website: http://www.scc.org.sg
- Singapore Recreation Club
  B Connaught Drive
  Tel: (65) 6338-9367
  Website: http://www.src.org.sg
- The Pines
  30 Stevens Road
  Tel: (65) 6735-2288
  Website: http://www.thepines.com.sg

FURTHER READING

GENERAL

Singapore in a Nutshell: Nuggets. Arlene Bastion. New York, NY and Singapore: Prentice Hall, 2005 (3rd edition).

Singapore Yearbook 2006. Ministry of Information, Communication and the Arts. Singapore: MICA, 2006.
- A compilation of facts and data about Singapore, with historical background and information about politics, the economy and the people.

The Singapore Story: Memoirs of Lee Kuan Yew (Vol.1) and *From Third World to First: the Singapore Story, 1965–2000: Memoirs of Lee Kuan Yew* (Vol. 2). Lee Kuan Yew. Singapore: Marshall Cavendish Editions, 2006.
- For an insight into the mind of the man who created modern Singapore and an understanding of the underpinnings of Singaporean society.

Singapore A–Z: A Pictorial Overview. Benjamin Yap. Singapore: Marshall Cavendish Editions, 2006.
- Photographs presenting famous landmarks and landscapes of Singapore in alphabetical order.

PRACTICAL GUIDES

Handbook for Expatriates Working and Living in Singapore. Goh Kheng Chuan. Singapore: Rank Books, 2005.

Fasten Your Seat Belts: Welcome to Singapore. Lee Gek Ling. Singapore: McGraw Hill Education (Asia), 2005.

Living in Singapore. A Reference Guide. Ed. Joy L Stevenson. Singapore: American Association of Singapore, 2005 (9th edition).
- With chapters on local customs, housing, transportation, health, consular services etc., this up-to-date guide is indispensable for those settling in.

Who's Who in Singapore. Ed. Low Tar Kiang. Singapore: Who's Who Pub, 2006.
- The title says it all: 1,200 updated entries on prominent individuals in all fields.

Education Guide 2005/6. Singapore: Times Business Information for the Singapore Tourism Board, 2006.
- A handy compendium of educational institutes and courses available in Singapore, as well as procedures for studying here. Updated yearly

Shopsmart Singapore: The Unbiased Guide for Those Who Love (and Hate) to Shop. Singapore: C Licence, 2004.
- Detective work by reporters has yielded the low-down on retail and wholesale suppliers for almost everything. Includes maps and regular website updates.

HISTORY AND POLITICS
A History of Singapore, 1819–1988. C M Turnbull. Singapore: Oxford University Press, 1991.
- A classic academic text.

Singapore: A Pictorial History 1819–2000. Gretchen Liu. Singapore: Archipelago Press in association with the National Heritage Board, 1999.
- A history of Singapore as told through numerous photographs gathered from the archives.

The Syonan Years: Singapore under Japanese rule, 1942–1945. Lee Geok Boi. Singapore: National Archives of Singapore and Epigram, 2005.
- A very well researched and documented book presenting every aspect of life during the Japanese Occupation.

Pastimes: A Social History of Singapore. Ed. Chan Kwok Bun and Tong Chee Kiong. Singapore: Times Editions, 2003.
- A journey through Singapore's social history, told through beautiful archival photographs and meticulously researched essays.

Singapore's Foreign Policy: Coping with Vulnerability. Michael Leifer. London, UK and New York, NY: Routledge, 2000.
- A brilliant and widely circulated analysis of Singapore's stance and position in the region by a lauded intellectual.

A Citizen's Guide to Government and Politics in Singapore. Raj Vasil. Singapore: Talisman Publishing Pte Ltd, 2004.
- Find out how Singapore is governed with this succinct book that introduces readers to the institutions and processes of governance.

The Eagle in the Lion City: America, Americans and Singapore. Jim Baker. Singapore: Landmark Books, 2005.
- An American expatriate's account of two centuries of interaction between the United States and Singapore that goes beyond mere economic ties.

SOCIETY

Notes from an Even Smaller Island. Neil Humphreys. Singapore: Marshall Cavendish Editions, 2006.

Social Change and the Chinese in Singapore. Lim Keak Cheng. Singapore: Singapore University Press, 1985.

Portraits of Places: History, Community and Identity in Singapore. Ed. Brenda S Yeoh and Lily Kong. Singapore: Times Editions, 1995.
- Essays by geographers, sociologists and other professionals reveal the true identity and deeper roots of places of Singapore.

Singapore: Wealth, Power and the Culture of Control. Carl A Trocki. London, UK and New York, NY: Routledge, 2006.
- The author discusses the transformation of Singapore into an economic powerhouse and examines the question of control in one of the world's most prosperous societies.

The Singapore Dilemma: The Political and Educational Marginality of the Malay Community. Lily Zubaidah Rahim.

Kuala Lumpur, Malaysia and Oxford, UK: Oxford University Press, 1998.
- A groundbreaking book on the Malay community of post-1959 Singapore: their identity, political development and education.

A Life Less Ordinary. Wong Kim Hoh. Singapore: Marshall Cavendish Editions, 2005.
- The collected columns of a veteran journalist give a peek into the under side of life in Singapore through the stories of unconventional individuals.

A Slice of Singapore: People. Portraits. Places. Hermie van Laar. Singapore: Marshall Cavendish Editions, 2006.
- Quirky, humourous photographs of oft-neglected places and people of Singapore let you see life as lived by the locals.

BUSINESS AND ECONOMY

Multinationals and the Growth of the Singapore Economy. Croom Helm Growth Economics of South-east Asia series. Hafiz Mirza. London, UK: Palgrave Macmillan, 1986.

Doing Business in Singapore: An Information Guide. Singapore: Price Waterhouse, 1996.

Singapore Government Directory. Singapore: Times Business Information Pte Ltd, 2005.
- Provides all the names and numbers you need to navigate your way through the myriad government bodies.

Handbook for Businessmen. Goh Tianwah. Singapore: Rank Books, 2005.
- For locals and foreigners doing business in Singapore: directories, lists and guidance on procedures.

CULTURE AND COMMUNICATION

Communication and Culture: A Guide for Practice. Cynthia Gallois and Victor Callan. Chichester, England and New York, NY: John Wiley and Sons, 1997.

The Art of Crossing Cultures. Craig Storti. Boston, MA: Nicholas Brealey Publishing/Intercultural Press, 2001 (2nd edition).

The Simple Guide to Customs and Etiquette in Singapore. Audrey Perera. Kent, England: Global Books Ltd, 1996.

Slices of Singapore. G C Soh. Singapore: Soh Gim Chuan. 2003.

Cultures of the World: Singapore. *Cultures of the World* series. Lesley Layton and Pang Guek Cheng. Tarrytown, NY: Benchmark Books/Marshall Cavendish, 2002; Singapore: Times Books International, 2001 (2nd edition).

Gateway to Indian Culture. Chitra Soundar. Singapore: Asiapac Books, 2003.

Gateway to Malay Culture. Asiapac Editorial. Singapore: Asiapac Books, 2003.

Gateway to Chinese Culture. Geraldine Chay and Y N Han. Singapore: Asiapac Books, 2003.

Gateway to Eurasian Culture. Asiapac Editorial. Singapore: Asiapac Books, 2003.

An Essential Guide to Singlish. Singapore: Gartbooks, 2003.

The Coxford Singlish Dictionary. Colin Goh. Singapore: Angsana Books, 2002.
- This comprehensive and entertaining dictionary of commonly used words and phrases will help you decipher Singlish, the brand of colloquial English spoken by locals.

LITERATURE AND THE ARTS

A Fortune-teller Told Me. Tiziano Terzani. New York, NY: Three Rivers Press, 2002 (reprint)
- A good read of a journalist's travel in the region wth an excellent chapter on Singapore.

The Lands of Charm and Cruelty. Stan Sesser. London, UK: Picador, 1994.
- Another journalist's perceptions and views on the region, with a chapter on Singapore and its often overlooked side.

A Teenage Textbook or *The Melting of the Ice Cream Girl*. Adrian Tan. Singapore: Hotspot Books, 1988.
- Set in a fictitious junior college, this rib-tickling novel will introduce you to the mores and lingo of Singaporean youth.

Raffles Place Ragtime. Philip Jeyaratnam. Singapore: Times Books International, 1988.
- A convincing portrayal of Singapore in its financial heyday of the 1980s and the preoccupations of its yuppie class.

Little Ironies: Stories of Singapore. Catherine Lim. Singapore: Heinemann Educational Books, 1978.
- Vignettes of life in Singapore told with a masterly touch by Singapore's most well known writer.

Notes Across the Years: Anecdotes from a Musical Life. Paul Abisheganaden. Singapore: Unipress, 2005.
- This accomplished musician who has always been at the forefront of the musical scene tells his story and that of the local music scene from the 1930s till today.

Latent Images: Film in Singapore. Jan and Yvonne Uhde. Singapore: Oxford University Press, 2000. (2003 version in CD-ROM.)
- Currently the only book that provides an overview of Singapore cinema from its beginnings: the films, directors, studios, operators and media policies.

Theatre and the Politics of Culture in Contemporary Singapore. William Peterson. Middletown, CT: Wesleyan University Press, 2001.
- A study of theatre in Singapore in its social context, with analyses of plays, government policies and issues.

Touches: 10 Years of the Singapore Dance Theatre. Ed. Ng Siew Eng. Singapore: Singapore Dance Theatre, 1998.

- A commemorative volume to celebrate the founding of Singapore's premier dance group.

HERITAGE

Discover Singapore On Foot. Dominique Grêlé and Lydie Raimbault. Singapore: Select Publishing, 2004.

A Walking Tour Singapore. G Byrne Bracken. Singapore: Marshall Cavendish Editions, 2004.

- Contains 11 planned walks with detailed itineraries, maps and delightful illustrations.

Singapore's 100 Historic Places. National Heritage Board. Singapore: Editions Didier Millet, 2004.

- For a better appreciation of the historical and cultural legacy of Singapore, this slim guide unveils the stories behind the buildings and sites you come across.

The Religious Monuments of Singapore: Faiths of our Forefathers. Lee Geok Boi. Singapore: Landmark Books, 2002.

- Photographs accompanied by maps, plans and anecdotes flesh out well-known and lesser-known religious monuments.

Singapore: City of Gardens. William Warren. Hong Kong: Periplus Editions, 2000.

- View the pockets of green in this city from the sprawling Botanic Gardens, landscaped gardens to tree-lined roads, in this beautifully photographed book.

Black and White: the Singapore House, 1898–1941. Julian Davison. Singapore: Talisman Publishing Pte Ltd, 2006.

- History and photographs showing the evolution of the distinctive but fast-disappearing black-and-white colonial bungalows in Singapore.

FOOD

Not Just a Good Food Guide: Singapore. Naleeza Ebrahim and Yaw Yan Yee. Singapore: Marshall Cavendish Editions, 2006.

- Don't know *laksa* from *rojak*? Or how to order your tea just the way you like it? This very useful guide explains local delights and lists places where you can find them.

Makasutra Singapore Food Guide. K S Seetoh. Singapore: Makansutra Pte Ltd, 2005.

- Singaporeans have been known to turn up at food spots armed with this guide to sniff out the best of local street food.

The Best of Singapore Cooking. Leong Yee Soo. Singapore: Times Books International, 2001.

- A veritable institution in the Singaporean food scene, Mrs Leong provides invaluable and time-tested recipes passed down through generations. Part of a six-volume series.

The New Mrs Lee's Cookbook Vol 1. Nonya Cuisine & The New Mrs Lee's Cookbook Vol 2. Straits Heritage Cuisine. Lee Chin Koon. Singapore: Times Editions–Marshall Cavendish Cuisine, 2004.

- To recreate classic Peranakan dishes that are a highlight of Singaporean cuisine, many have turned to the authentic yet simplified recipes of this doyen of Straits Chinese cooking.

ABOUT THE AUTHOR

Looking back, one could say that Marión Bravo-Bhasin has been preparing all her life to write a book on cultural exchange. Originally from Chile, Marión's family moved to the United States when she was a young girl. After college, she joined the Peace Corps as a Math and English teacher, and taught in Benin, West Africa for two years. The 'culture shock' training and cross-cultural experience she received left her knowing that an international path was the direction she wanted to take. After teaching in Africa, she enrolled at Thunderbird University (currently known as the Garvin School of International Management) and received a Masters degree in International Management. While at Thunderbird, Marión met her future husband Sanjay, who is originally from India.

After seven years in New York City, where she worked in public relations, advertising and international marketing for *Time* magazine, the family was transferred to Singapore through Sanjay's work. Life overseas has presented many new and creative opportunities that Marión is fully enjoying. As a freelance writer, Marión has put pen to paper for a number of magazines in Singapore and the region. Most recently, she completed writing *The Global Table*, a book on international celebrations and creative table settings. She is currently working on another interior book.

INDEX

A

accommodation 100–111
  condominiums 104–105
  furnishings and appliances 119
  HDB flats 102–103
  housing tips 106–109
  landed homes 105–106
  maintenance and renovations 110–111
  moving in 111
  renting or buying 109–110
  serviced apartments 101–102
  utilities 111–113
arts and culture 227–236
  art and sculpture 227–228
  dance 230–231
  film 231–232
  literary arts 235–236
  music 229–230
  opera 233–234
  theatre and drama 231

C

children 125–131
  child care centres 126
  education 126–128
Chinese customs 66–73
  birthdays 68–69
  funerals 71–73
  gifts 67–68
  pregnancy 66–67
  weddings 69–71
clubs and groups 119, 205–206

D

domestic help 122–125

E

ethnic races
  Chinese 32–39
  Eurasians 49–50
  Indians 44–49
  Malays 39–44
  Peranakans 50–51
etiquette 62–65

F

festivals and celebrations 236–270
  annual events 270–272
  Buddhist festivals 257–258
  Chinese celebrations 241–257
  Christian celebrations 267–270
  Hindu celebrations 263–267
  Muslim celebrations 258–263
  school celebrations 240–241
  secular celebrations 237–240
financial matters 131–132
  banks 131
  cheques 132
  credit cards 132–133
  opening an account 131–132
  taxes 133–136
food and entertaining 171–203
  coffee shops 186–188
  delis and coffee places 191
  desserts and drinks 177–178
  drinking water 195
  eating etiquette 180–182
  entertaining etiquette 201–203
  fast food 190–191
  food courts 188–189
  hawker centres 183–186
  hidden charges 192
  international food 171
  kosher food 200
  meats and seafood 174–175
  popular dishes 178–179
  restaurants 189–190
  shopping 196–201
  signs 193–195
  staples 172–174
  taxes 192
  tipping 192
  vegetables and fruits 175–176
  vegetarian food 177
  wines, beer and alcohol 195–196
formalities 85–96
  cancellation 89–90
  employment passes 86–89
  EntrePass 90–91

general visit visas 86
student passes 92–93
visitor passes 93–96
work passes 89
work permits 90

G
geography 13–16
Goh, Chok Tong
28, 277, 317, 321
government 27–28

H
health care 136–142
alternative medicine
141–142
ambulance and emergency
(A&E) 139
having a baby 137–138
health tips 141
hospitals 136
insurance 142
polyclinics 136
Traditional Chinese Medicine
(TCM) 139–140
history 16–26
British colonial days 17–22
early independence 25–26
Japanese Occupation 22–23
pre-colonisation 16–17
pre-independence 23–25

I
Indian customs 79–83
funerals 82
Hinduism 79–80
other Hindu rituals 82–83
pregnancy and births 80
weddings 80–82

L
language and communication
274–290
Chinese 279–283
English 9, 274, 275, 277
Malay 277–279
mother tongue 274, 275, 280
non-verbal 289–290
Singlish 10, 285–289
Tamil 283–285

Lee, Hsien Loong 6, 28, 317
Lee, Kuan Yew 4, 6, 7, 9, 24, 28, 59,
316–317, 317

M
Malay customs 74–79
funerals 77–79
pregnancy and births 74–75
weddings 75–77
moving 96–100
what to bring from home
120–122

N
National Service 65

P
PAP *See* People's Action Party
People's Action Party (PAP)
24, 25, 27, 28, 52, 316, 334
places of interest
Botanic Gardens 210
Bukit Timah Nature Reserve
212–213
Chinese Gardens 213
ethnic enclaves 214
HSBC TreeTop Walk 210
Japanese Gardens 213
Jurong BirdPark 209
MacRitchie Reservoir 213
Mandai Orchid Garden 209
Pulau Ubin 216
Sentosa 215
Singapore Science Centre
216–217
Sungei Buloh Wetland Reserve
212
war history sites 216
zoo and Night Safari 207–208

S
safety and security 166–169
offences and punishments 168
Sheares, Benjamin H 49, 318
shopping 155–166
ethnic enclaves 162–166
for food 196–201
for leisure 156
places to shop 156–162
Singaporean identity 51–55

society and culture 58–62
  face and respect 58–59
  group dependence 58
  hierarchy 59–60
  high context culture 61
  monochronic time culture 60–61
sporting activities 218–223
  Asian sports 222
  extreme sports 223
  keeping fit 222
  land sports 220–221
  water sports 219–220

T

telecommunications and media 113–117
  Internet services 115
  local school system 128–130
  postal services 115–116
  publications 117–119
  telephony services 113–114
  television, cable and radio 117
things to do
  duck and hippo Tours 217
  G-Max 217
  heritage trail 217
transportation 142–154
  buses 148–150
  driver's licence 144–145
  driving rules 145–147

Electronic Road Pricing (ERP) 54, 143, 144, 146, 154, 336
MRT (Mass Rapid Transit) 150–152
owning a car 143–144
shuttles 154
taxis 152–154

W

work and business 292–312
  bankruptcy laws 298–299
  business cards 307–308
  closing the venture 299–300
  converting your business 297–298
  employment contract 301
  giving gifts 310–311
  holidays and leave 302–303
  introductions 307
  meetings 306–307
  salary and benefits 301–302
  setting up 295–297
  striking a deal 308–310
  types of enterprises 296–297
  women 312
  working hours 301
  working with the locals 303–306

Y

Yusof, Ishak 39, 318

388

Titles in the CULTURE**SHOCK**! series:

Argentina	Hawaii	Pakistan
Australia	Hong Kong	Paris
Austria	Hungary	Philippines
Bahrain	India	Portugal
Barcelona	Indonesia	San Francisco
Beijing	Iran	Saudi Arabia
Belgium	Ireland	Scotland
Bolivia	Israel	Sri Lanka
Borneo	Italy	Shanghai
Brazil	Jakarta	Singapore
Britain	Japan	South Africa
Cambodia	Korea	Spain
Canada	Laos	Sweden
Chicago	London	Switzerland
Chile	Malaysia	Syria
China	Mauritius	Taiwan
Costa Rica	Mexico	Thailand
Cuba	Morocco	Tokyo
Czech Republic	Moscow	Turkey
Denmark	Munich	Ukraine
Ecuador	Myanmar	United Arab
Egypt	Nepal	Emirates
Finland	Netherlands	USA
France	New York	Vancouver
Germany	New Zealand	Venezuela
Greece	Norway	Vietnam

For more information about any of these titles, please contact any of our Marshall Cavendish offices around the world (listed on page ii) or visit our website at:

www.marshallcavendish.com/genref